THE LIVE WEB: BUILDING EVENT-BASED CONNECTIONS IN THE CLOUD

DR. PHILLIP J. WINDLEY, PH.D.

Course Technology PTR

A part of Cengage Learning

COURSE TECHNOLOGY
CENGAGE Learning®

Australia • Brazil • Japan • Korea • Mexico • Singapore • Spain • United Kingdom • United States

COURSE TECHNOLOGY
CENGAGE Learning®

The Live Web: Building Event-Based Connections in the Cloud
Dr. Phillip J. Windley, Ph.D.

Publisher and General Manager, Course Technology PTR: Stacy L. Hiquet

Associate Director of Marketing: Sarah Panella

Manager of Editorial Services: Heather Talbot

Marketing Manager: Mark Hughes

Acquisitions Editor: Heather Hurley

Project Editor: Kate Shoup

Technical Reviewer: Randy Bohn

Copy Editor: Kate Shoup

Interior Layout Tech: MPS Limited, a Macmillan Company

Cover Designer: Mike Tanamachi

Indexer: Valerie Haynes Perry

Proofreader: Megan Belanger

For product information and technology assistance, contact us at
Cengage Learning Customer & Sales Support, 1-800-354-9706

For permission to use material from this text or product,
submit all requests online at **www.cengage.com/permissions**

Further permissions questions can be emailed to
permissionrequest@cengage.com

All trademarks are the property of their respective owners.

All images © Cengage Learning unless otherwise noted.

Figure 3.2 reprinted with permission from Best Buy

Figure 7.1 courtesy of PrintActivities.com

Figure 9.3 reprinted under Creative Commons License (CC-SA-BY)

Library of Congress Control Number: 2011936048

ISBN-13: 978-1-133-68668-2

ISBN-10: 1-133-68668-0

Course Technology, a part of Cengage Learning
20 Channel Center Street
Boston, MA 02210
USA

Cengage Learning is a leading provider of customized learning solutions with office locations around the globe, including Singapore, the United Kingdom, Australia, Mexico, Brazil, and Japan. Locate your local office at: **international.cengage.com/region**

Cengage Learning products are represented in Canada by Nelson Education, Ltd.

For your lifelong learning solutions, visit **courseptr.com**

Visit our corporate website at **cengage.com**

Printed in the United States of America
1 2 3 4 5 6 7 13 12 11

To Lynne

Foreword

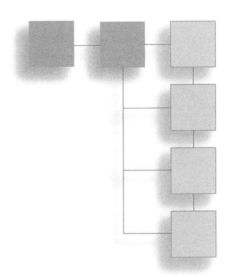

I remember exactly when my mind was blown by the words "Live Web." It was in late spring of 2003, and I was getting into my car in a parking lot in Santa Barbara, talking on a cell phone to my son Allen. At the time, Allen had a small startup devoted to getting answers to questions in close to real time—kind of like what Quora finally succeeded at becoming many years later.

Back then, the Web wasn't about real time. The closest we had to it was RSS—Really Simple Syndication—which was Dave Winer's format for notifying the world when something is published, and the first search engines to follow RSS were months away from getting traction. (Only one, Icerocket, is still in that business today.) Google and its competitors were years away from paying any attention.

That's because the Web we had then was a static one. Consider the vocabulary: We had "sites" with "locations" at "domains" that we "built" like real-estate projects, for users to "visit" and "browse." Web site developers might be "designers" or "architects," but the process of producing wasn't much different from contracting in the physical world. That's why it was common to see "under construction" art as a placeholder at sites that were still being built.

Google and other search engines were moving fast if they "crawled" and "indexed" the whole Web every few days. The assumption was that, even if sites on the Web often changed, most sites were static enough for search purposes.

As Allen explained it to me, this static stuff was a primitive stage for the Web. The next stage would be what he called the "World Live Web." By "live," he meant two things. One was that it was living, current, and changing as fast as life itself. The other was that, as with life, most of it would happen outside the walls of the Web's static real-estate holders.

In an instant I could see he was right. I could also see that we had all been seduced by the Web's dramatic successes to continue thinking inside the box we first built in 1995, when cookies allowed sites like Amazon and eBay to keep track of visitors and customers. That box was called "client-server." It was actually an old design that had been around for a long time. The label "client-server" was chosen, as I recall, because "slave-master" didn't sound so nice. But slaves are what we became.

On the static Web, we had all the rights that site owners would give us. Aside from that, we were free to surf, but not to interact as free agents and equals to the sites and their owners. This wasn't because they wanted to enslave us, but because client-server was designed to divide work between slaves and masters. And that's where we've been stuck ever since.

I realized immediately, when Allen told me about the Live Web, that it couldn't work on the slave-master model any more than a free market could work in the manorial feudal system. Individuals had to be free agents. So did every other participant, whether big or small. As Allen pointed out, the static Web would continue to persist, but the Live Web would grow outside and around it, much as the free market grew outside the city-states of Renaissance Europe.

So I began to write about the Live Web, and how it was inevitable, eventually. I got involved with companies that had Live Web ambitions, such as Technorati, one of the earliest RSS search engines. But I didn't see the Live Web showing up for real until I got hip to what Phil Windley and his team were doing with KRL at Kynetx. Here were two things—a language and a rules engine—that allowed anyone to easily program *actions* triggered by *events*, outside the boundaries of any of the static Web's billion silos.

By then, in 2009, many of those silos in a way had turned inside out, so the core competencies were exposed through APIs, or application programming interfaces. When you see a Google map on your Yelp search, that's supplied by the Google API. Same when you click on a Facebook button to log into a non-Facebook Web site. Or when you click on a button to post to Twitter, Facebook, or some other site. KRL lets you program what could be done between multiple APIs.

Yet Phil and Kynetx were thinking farther downstream than that. They wanted APIs to be fully live, interactive, and conversational. So they developed the Evented API spec for full Live Web interactivity. Where that will be, or where KRL and Kynetx will be, by the time you read this, are all up in the air—as are everything in The Future. But what we can see now, clearly, is how the Live Web will work.

It will be networked, diverse, and full of interactive activity by free agents large and small. Big companies will still build skyscrapers, but they won't own or run the whole city, and they'll be glad they don't have to. The Live Web will look much more like modern civilization, with free markets thriving all over the place rather than ones contained in corporate or governmental walled gardens and silos.

When this happens, I am convinced, we will look back on what Phil and his team at Kynetx got rolling as no less important than what Tim Berners-Lee started with the World Wide Web back at the turn of the '90s. And I say that with full respect to Sir Tim.

The big difference is that, while Tim did not intend for the World Wide Web to become a World Wide Shopping Mall of customer-enslaving silos, Phil *does* intend the World Live Web to be an open and thriving free marketplace, with all the good effects that free markets tend to have. Time will tell whether I'm right or wrong, but the ambition matters no less. We've accepted slavery for too long. Any light that leads us toward freedom is a good light. And the brightest is the one shining across the pages ahead.

Doc Searls

Cambridge, MA

ACKNOWLEDGMENTS

I owe a great debt to many people who have supported and guided me as I developed the concepts in this book and committed them to paper.

My biggest thank you goes to my wife Lynne. I'm not sure she knew what she signed up for when we got married. Twenty-eight years of adventure later, she willingly entertains my wild dreams. Each of my children is an inspiration and comfort, but I thank my son Bradford specifically for countless hours reviewing and editing the original manuscript.

I also owe a great debt to my business partner Steve Fulling. He has supported my research projects and writing far beyond the call of duty. I'm sure there have been times he wished he'd gotten into a business without so grand a vision as redoing the entire Web. Steve has been a great support and unflinching ally.

Doc Searls and Craig Burton have been my friends and advisors as well as dedicated cheerleaders for the ideas in this book. Doc and his son Allen came up with the name "Live Web" and graciously allowed me to apply it to my ideas. Doc also developed important thinking around commerce on the Live Web, particularly the notions of vendor-relationship management (VRM) and fourth-party transactions discussed in Chapter 13. Craig helped with lexicon, consistency, and continuity.

Kristen Knight, Dave McNamee, and Sam Curren provided me with critical insights and inspiration in the development of the concepts in the book. Many of the best explanations owe their existence to discussions I had with them.

Mark Horstmeier worked hard to make an honest man out of me. He implemented my specifications for temporal and aggregate event expressions. He also corrected most of the bugs that the examples in this book illuminated in the underlying code.

Every language writer needs people to use the language and find its rough edges. Ed Orcutt has written more KRL than anyone else. Often, he took ideas that were only vague outlines of how something could be done and turned them into a production quality system.

Kate Shoup, my editor, has been a joy to work with and has made my writing look better than it is.

Wade Billings kept everything running.

CREDITS

Sheila Anderson of www.PrintActivities.com kindly granted permission to use the dot-to-dot puzzle in Chapter 7.

Randall Bohn did the technical editing and built the sprinkler controller in Chapter 9.

Sam Curren wrote the calendar module code from Chapter 8, the sprinkler controller code in Chapter 9, and the evented API specification in Appendix F.

Danny Debate of Frameaction Media came up with the concept for the cover.

Mike Farmer wrote the code for the email endpoint and Ruby gem in Chapter 9.

Mike Grace developed the Exampley.com Web site that we use for examples throughout the book. Mike is also a prolific KRL developer who pushed the envelope and made it a better language.

Jessie Morris wrote the Node.js IRC endpoint and example rules and the Arduino endpoint and examples from Chapter 9. He also wrote the Android library for the Android endpoint in Chapter 10.

Steve Nay wrote the class wiki code used in Chapters 8 and 10.

Alex Olsen wrote code for the module demo from Chapter 8 and KEA Objective C library for the iPhone endpoint in Chapter 10.

Ed Orcutt contributed the explicit event examples, including the rule set controller example, in Chapter 11 and the initial version of the blogging example in Chapter 12.

ABOUT THE AUTHOR

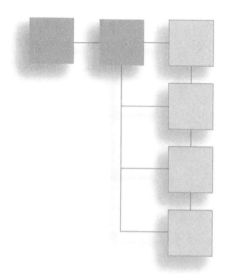

Phillip J. Windley, Ph.D. is the Founder and Chief Technology Officer (CTO) of Kynetx, an early-stage company providing an application platform for creating social products and services. As CTO, Dr. Windley directs the company's product strategy and is responsible for product architecture, implementation, and operations.

Dr. Windley is a frequent author and speaker on event-driven systems, digital identity, Web architectures, Web services, and programming language design. He writes the popular Technometria blog, which contains numerous articles in these areas and others. Dr. Windley is the author of the book *Digital Identity*, published by O'Reilly Media in 2005. Dr. Windley is also an Adjunct Professor of Computer Science at Brigham Young University and Executive Producer of IT Conversations, a popular network of technology podcasts.

Prior to joining BYU, Dr. Windley served from 2001 to 2002 as the Chief Information Officer (CIO) for the state of Utah, serving on Governor Mike Leavitt's Cabinet and as a member of his senior staff. In this capacity, he was responsible for effective use of all IT resources in the state and advised the governor on technology issues. During his tenure, many national groups repeatedly recognized the state for its excellence in the areas of IT and eGovernment.

Prior to his appointment as CIO, Dr. Windley served as Vice President for Product Development and Operations at Excite@Home, managing a large, interdisciplinary team of product managers, engineers, and technicians developing and operating large-scale Internet and e-commerce products. Dr. Windley served for two years as Chief Technology Officer (CTO) of iMall, Inc., an early leader in electronic commerce, and was part of the team that sold iMall to Excite@Home for $450 million.

Windley received his Ph.D. in Computer Science from the University of California, Davis, in 1990. Prior to doing graduate studies, Windley worked for four years as a nuclear metallurgist and a member of the technical staff at the Division of Naval Reactors in Washington, D.C. His duties included overseeing nuclear-core and plant-material testing in the advanced test reactor.

CONTENTS

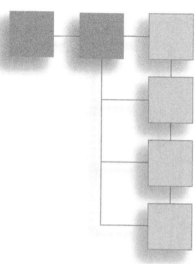

INTRODUCTION

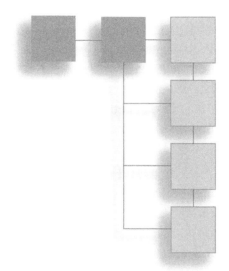

For many years, pundits have foreseen a world in which everything will be connected to the Internet. We're getting there. We now have Wi-Fi–enabled refrigerators, thermostats, and bathroom scales. But what happens after things are online? Will they merely connect to the Internet or will they connect to each other?

Connecting everything we use—products and services—to each other is a powerful idea. An idea that is bigger than mobile and social. Mobile's big because everyone is connected all the time. Social is big because we're connected to each other. Connecting us to everything around us is the next step.

Connecting our things to each other and setting them to work on our behalf is transformative. Imagine a world in which your phone automatically mutes the ringer when you start watching a movie. Imagine a world in which your alarm clock sets itself based on your schedule and other information like the weather, the traffic, and your past behavior. Imagine a world in which the mundane parts of business travel or scheduling an appointment with a new doctor are automatically taken care of according to your preferences. That world is the Live Web.

The Live Web: Building Event-Based Connections in the Cloud is a book about specific concepts, architectures, and technologies you can use to build Live Web experiences. This book is not easy; it requires that you think about Web programming from a brand new perspective. That's hard for any of us. I have no business asking that of you unless there is a big payoff. There is: I believe the ideas and techniques in this book will help you build brand new types of Web experiences unlike those you can create using traditional Web technologies or languages like PHP or Rails. Don't let this intimidate you. While this book asks a lot, the ideas are familiar and their application is engaging and fun.

The premise of this book is simple, but profound: The Web of the future—the Live Web—will link our lives in ways we can hardly imagine…and you can start building that Web today. While the request-response programming model we've been using has led to incredible applications and services, we can do more with a new model that complements—rather than replaces—the thinking that has led us so far. That new model is based on events.

Whereas today's Web sites are about users interacting with relatively static pools of data, the cloud is giving us a brand new kind of data: data that is flowing, moving, and real-time. Data that links sites and services together. The cloud is about way more than just APIs to data and services—as important as that is. At its best, the cloud creates real-time interactions enabled by streams of data. The problem is that this kind of data doesn't look like a request. Consequently using the tried and tested tools we've used to build Web services won't take us where we need to go. Event-based interactions are the perfect model for taming these rivers of dynamic data and creating applications that make the most effective use of them.

Event-based applications are more loosely coupled than those built using a request-response model. I cannot overstate the case for loose coupling. As we move to a world in which more and more applications must coordinate their actions on our behalf, there is simply no way that we can pre-plan and orchestrate all the required interactions between them. Using systems that are supportive of and are architected for loosely coupled applications will play an important role in enabling the cloud-based future we envision.

This may seem a little overwhelming, but I have a secret weapon to help you out: a new programming language. I know what you're thinking, "Wait, I've got to think differently about the Web and learn a new language too!?!" But in fact, I think the language helps, rather than hurts.

Tools shape how we think and work. I learned long ago that the best way to think differently about a problem is to create a nomenclature that describes and illuminates the new domain. In this book, you'll use a language called the Kinetic Rules Language (KRL) to channel your thinking for this new model. KRL will lead you into the world of event-based programming on the Web.

KRL is a rule-based language that is custom built for the domain of event-based applications that operate on real-time data in the cloud. KRL was designed from the ground up with events and the cloud in mind. KRL provides a number of familiar touch-points for users already accustomed to Web programming and JavaScript, but provides a framework for making the most of an evented Web. While KRL is open and runs on an open source rules engine, you can get started with it right away using a cloud-based service.

While the ideas and techniques in this book can be implemented in any language, there is significant value in using a purpose-built language to guide our thinking. Remember, the ultimate value you will gain from this book isn't learning any specific programming language, but in forcing your thinking down a new road—one in which events, rather than requests, reign supreme.

ROADMAP

This book can be divided into two parts.

Chapters 1–5 introduce the concepts and architectures necessary for building the Live Web.

- Chapter 1, "The Live Web," introduces the ideas and concepts around the Live Web.

- Chapter 2, "Events on the Live Web," introduces events.

- Chapter 3, "Event Expressions: Filtering the Event Stream," explains an expression language for formally describing event scenarios.

- Chapter 4, "Telling Stories on the Live Web," describes the role of identity and context.

- Chapter 5, "Architecting the Live Web," gives the architecture of a system for building Live Web applications.

These chapters, along with much of Chapters 13–15, should be accessible to non-programmers with a technical bent.

Chapters 6–14 introduce specific techniques for building Live Web applications using KRL and the Kinetic Rules Engine.

- Chapter 6, "Live Web Rules," introduces KRL.

- Chapter 7, "Creating Contextual Web Experiences," shows how KRL can be used to link Web services and Web sites together.

- Chapter 8, "Using the Cloud," talks about using cloud-based APIs and services in KRL applications.

- Chapter 9, "Events Around the Live Web," moves beyond the Web to build systems that incorporate events from other domains like email and IRC.

- Chapter 10, "Mobile and the Live Web," builds Live Web applications that include voice and SMS. This chapter also introduces mobile apps that raise events.

- Chapter 11, "Building Event Networks," explains event abstract, an important concept for building sophisticated applications that use multiple rule sets.

- Chapter 12, "Advanced KRL Programming," introduces the idea of cooperating groups of rule sets.

- Chapter 13, "Business on the Live Web," shows how Live Web apps will affect commerce.

- Chapter 14, "Designing Event Systems," describes the design of a set of Live Web applications for automating a complex healthcare scenario.

- Chapter 15, "Building the Live Web," describes trends affecting the Live Web.

KEEPING UP

The Live Web is a topic that is new enough that it's constantly growing and changing. I write about the Live Web, event processing, and identity on my blog at http://www.windley.com. Tune in there to keep up with my latest thoughts.

CHAPTER 1

THE LIVE WEB

The Web is an amazing place. In less than two decades, it has completely transformed commerce, banking, travel, media, and even social interactions. Entire industries have been created, and others destroyed—and many that are left have been changed to the point that they are nearly unrecognizable. No one, of course, could have predicted this in 1993. From static Web pages, through simple forms, to today's beautiful, interactive Web sites, the evolution of the Web has been dramatic.

Of late, some of the most compelling parts of the Web aren't even sites at all, but services like Twitter and Foursquare. Certainly, these services *have* Web sites, but the site isn't the only—or even the primary—means of interacting with users. Developments like these are the vanguard of a completely new way to use the Web. In fact, some quip that with social networking, the Web has finally achieved its purpose in being: connecting people rather than simply connecting machines.

Even with all the mind-boggling changes that have happened in the last 15 years, I believe the biggest changes are yet to come. The pace of change is accelerating. The World Wide Web is still growing. As you look around, you will find the seeds of technology that, if nurtured, will make the Web useful in ways you can barely imagine.

The Web of the future will link together the devices you use, your online personas, and even things you don't think of as being "on the Web" now, like your car and your house. Acting as a cooperative, loosely coupled mesh, the future Web will work to achieve results important to you in context and at the right time. The current world of Web sites and services is inadequate for building this future Web—what's being called the *Live Web*.

The current Web certainly won't go away; it's too valuable. But the Live Web will be built along side of it. This book will examine the concepts and techniques that will take the Web forward into a purpose-based future, discuss gaps and ways to fill them, and introduce architectures and systems for building tomorrow's Live Web applications *now*.

BAD NEWS FROM YOUR RADIOLOGIST

To glimpse the potential of the Live Web, imagine you've just received bad news from your radiologist: Your recent MRI reveals you have two ruptured disks. That means you'll need to do the following:

1. Choose a good orthopedic surgeon who is nearby and who works with your insurance provider.

2. Schedule appointments with the surgeon you select for an initial consultation and follow-up visits.

3. Arrange to transfer your medical-history information to the new doctor.

4. Make payments for services.

Today, you must approach this task in an ad hoc, out-of-context way. Sure, there are online resources to make it easier, but you must still organize, contextualize, and orchestrate the individual tasks yourself to complete the overall objective.

Instead, imagine the following scenario:

1. An email arrives from the patient-management system used by your radiologist, telling you the results of your MRI.

2. An application that you control processes the email, extracts relevant tasks, and places them on your to-do list.

3. When you're ready to complete the first task, picking a surgeon, an application designed to help select service providers is engaged to display surgeons who meet criteria you have established (e.g., they must be nearby and within your insurance plan), as well as those who meet the criteria set by the radiologist (e.g., practice type). You use the selector application to review and choose a surgeon.

4. Your calendar begins the task of scheduling an appointment, giving you a selection of times that are free on both your calendar and the surgeon's.

5. You pick an appointment time and receive confirmation from the doctor's office that your appointment has been scheduled.

6. The surgeon's office sends a request for medical history. An application that manages your personal data gives you the opportunity to authorize the data transfer and to select what information will be sent.

You can easily imagine other scenarios, like moving or business travel, that present just as much opportunity for the products and services people use every day to cooperate and automatically accomplish many necessary but mundane tasks.

Right now, having even this small set of tasks completed automatically seems like science fiction to most people, but you'll see examples of all the services necessary for this scenario throughout the book. I'll weave them all together in Chapter 14, "Designing Event Systems." Creating an architecture that is flexible enough to carry out these tasks without being purpose-built and brittle isn't impossible, but it does require some new thinking. You'll see that although you do need to make a few simplifying assumptions, nothing about the applications one might build for this prototype is outside the bounds of what can be done today, using tools and techniques that are available right now.

THE LIVE WEB

The Live Web is a recognition that time matters online. The term *live* was applied to search early on to describe search results that included recent, rather than simply relevant, results. Real-time search results have recently gained significant traction with Google, Twitter, Facebook, and others providing the ability to search the most recent tweets or status updates. But I'm convinced that the Live Web goes well beyond search—as important as that is—to inform a completely new way to viewing online interactions. The Live Web doesn't replace the old static Web, but will grow and exist in symbiosis with it.

The Live Web isn't just about speed and timeliness; it's about context. On the static Web, each site comes with its own context. As you move from site to site, the context changes. The only continuity is what you can maintain in your head. On the Live Web, you bring your context with you; applications weave the sites, data, and services from the static Web into a single, purpose-based, living tapestry. The service becomes personal, not in some superficial "Hello, Phil Windley!" way, but with respect to what I'm interested in right now—my context.

The Live Web uses endpoints to represent me in a particular context. Endpoints maintain the continuity of context as I move from place to place. Events at those endpoints can trigger rules on my behalf. Rules can be written by anybody and executed by engines that can be located anywhere. The Live Web connects to the static

Web, but is not a subset of the static Web. Nor is it subject to the limitations of the client-server model.

In the static Web, the default state is one in which all sites are independent and all visitors are dependent on them, leading to its classic silo-like nature. Each Web service people use is unaffiliated with the others, and they rarely connect to each other in any meaningful way. This is a function of the old client-server model; individual users have no independent HTML status. One symptom of this is boilerplate agreements in which the dominant party (the site owner) can say or change what they please, while the submissive party (the visitor) has to submit completely. In contrast, on the Live Web, the default state for endpoints is independence. Choices about dependence start there. Endpoints work on behalf of individuals. When individual users can bring their own context to an engagement, interaction is richer and has greater possibilities. On the Live Web, many more things can be done, and much more wealth can be created, than on the old static Web alone.

While the old world of individual sites and services won't go away—after all, you need their infrastructure—the Live Web will live alongside them, making them richer and more useful to everyone.

THE EVOLUTION OF THE WEB

Since the World Wide Web was introduced the world in 1993, it has undergone many significant changes. Table 1.1 summarizes the evolution of the Web from the standpoint of several important characteristics, including the following:

- How identity information is managed
- How data is represented
- Who controls the data
- What essential services are offered

Document Web

The "document-based Web" was the very first Web, where people put up Web sites that were really nothing more than their company brochures reformatted in HTML. Identity was non-existent, leading to the famous *New Yorker* cartoon with the caption "On the Internet, no one knows you're a dog." Any data that made its way out of brochures and into HTML wasn't structured in a way that made it useful. The site owner controlled the data, such as it was, and the primary service was returning a document for rendering by the user's browser.

Table 1.1   The Evolution of the Web

	Identity	Data	Control	Services
Document Web	You're a dog*	Stuck in structured documents	Site owner	Document return
Web 1.0	Cookies and siloed credential	Unstructured documents and proprietary database with dynamic queries	Site owner	Document return and siloed CRUD**
Web 2.0	Cookies and shared credential via OAuth	Structured documents, proprietary databases and APIs with dynamic queries	Site, app owners, or users	Document return, siloed CRUD, apps, and API response
Live Web	Personal data under the control of the user	Semantic documents, proprietary databases and APIs, public/private data streams, static and dynamic queries	Data originator (usually users) with granular control	Document return, CRUD, apps, API response, semantic mapping, and event handling

*See the next section.
**CRUD is an acronym for the primary database operations: create, retrieve, update, and delete.

Web 1.0

We didn't call it Web 1.0 at the time, but the document-based Web quickly gave way to one based on primitive forms and pages with a few dynamic features. Web sites were still primarily collections of static pages with a sprinkling of dynamically generated content. Querying the site's database was the primary means of interaction. Logins, supported by cookie-backed sessions, first began to appear so that a site could be "customized." The site owner still controlled the data, although the concept of privacy was becoming an issue. The primary service was still document returns, but some site-specific database operations began to appear.

Web 2.0

Web 2.0 was the era of the interactive Web application. Although the underlying basis of the Web hadn't changed, developers were creating increasingly sophisticated Web applications rather than mere Web sites. Rather than being based on home-grown login systems, identity was beginning to be established through the use of cross-site credentials over protocols like OAuth. API calls returned structured data.

Users might use a Web browser or a purpose-built client (e.g., a mobile phone app) to access Web 2.0 applications. With the emergence of more sophisticated identity regimens, users began to be put in charge of their own data and how it is shared.

Note

> API originally stood for "Application Programming Interface" and applied to services provided by operating systems to applications, but hardly anyone thinks of that anymore. The acronym has more generally come to apply to any interface to programs, data, or services that a program can use to interact with them.

Live Web

I've placed each of the previous eras in the evolution of the Web in what I call the "static" Web. Some might bristle at the term, since the rate of evolution and the levels of interactivity seem anything but static. But all these eras have something in common: They are based on Web servers that hold relatively static collections of documents or data. When users interact, they query, add, or update this data. In contrast, the Live Web is characterized by dynamic streams of data, tied closely to the user's identity and typically under their control. This data comes in a variety of forms. The static Web is still there, under the Live Web. Data is accessible programmatically and in real time.

THE CLOUD AND PROGRAMMATIC ACCESS TO DATA

More and more companies are putting the data and services that drive their Web sites online using an API. The result of this move has been called the *cloud*. There are good reasons cloud-based data and services are gaining traction: Cloud-based services are more accessible, more convenient, and cheaper than equivalent services delivered using more traditional means.

As I write this in late 2011, programmableweb.com, a directory of online APIs, lists more than 4,000 APIs in its index. That's up from 3,000 just six months ago. The list includes APIs for searching, financial services, blogging, ad networks, dating, email, government, security shopping, and so on. Some are free and others charge money. Some are personalized (like my Twitter friend feed) and others are general information (like the Google news feed). APIs are the unit of programming on the Web— similar to libraries in traditional applications.

The move to APIs and the programmatic access to data that they represent is nothing short of a tectonic shift in how the Web works, realigning the forces that drive the Web and making new applications possible. As with most shifts, the move to

APIs seems sudden, but it's been building for years as developers struggled to create programs that mashed up information and services from multiple Web sites.

At first glance, you may wonder why companies would be willing to give programmatic access to their data through APIs. Further analysis shows that there's a good business reason for it. Consider the diagram (adapted from Dion Hinchcliffe[1]) in Figure 1.1.

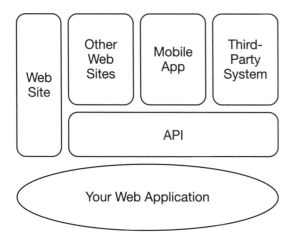

Figure 1.1
APIs give your Web application reach beyond your Web site.

More and more traffic to Web applications is coming through the API because APIs let other programs use your Web application. This extends your online reach significantly. Sam Ramji said, "For successful companies, 80% of traffic will be coming from beyond the browser."[2] Giving your Web application an API enables other applications to carry your service to their users.

APIs are one way to get other smart people to help you build your product and service into something people find valuable. Rather than "Build it and they will come," APIs are a way to have others "Come and help build it." As the creator of a Web application, you can never come up with all the interesting ways people may find for using it. Providing an API enables them to extend your application in ways that meet their needs and, in the process, do the same thing for others. Later, you will see how concepts like Web hooks extend this idea even further.

Indirect models will enable the market for Web applications to scale well beyond what is possible with just a Web site. The hoopla over cloud computing isn't really about Amazon, Rackspace, and the infrastructure plays you've heard about. What makes cloud computing interesting is the move to the API by thousands of companies. This wealth of APIs is a significant change in how the online world operates and portends the changes that will comprise the real-time Web.

THE REAL-TIME WEB

But mere APIs aren't enough. To see why, imagine two scenarios:

- Your teenage daughter is out with friends. Her curfew is midnight, but it's 12:20 a.m., and you haven't heard a word. You're worried, imagining an accident on the freeway or worse. You're calling her cell, her friends, and trying to keep calm.

- Your daughter is again out with friends, but this time, a few minutes before midnight, you get a call that goes something like, "Hi, Mom. I'm going to be 15 minutes late…the movie ran long."

One scenario is filled with hassle and anxiety, the other with convenience and tranquility. There's no doubt which scenario you'd rather be in. And yet, online, you're rarely in a situation where a service anticipates your needs and meets them without prodding on your part. The location metaphor of the static Web puts in the mode of "seek and find" or "go and get."

When an API merely responds to requests, it's like a program that only accepts input but can never send its output to another application unless it's asked first. Such APIs are unidirectional. Readers familiar with the Web and the underlying client-server model will recognize the roots of unidirectional APIs in the foundational technologies of the Web.

In the early days of the Web, all that mattered were domain names and Web pages—brochure-ware, I called it. Later, the name Web 2.0 embodied the idea of interactive Web sites where users could actually do something beyond filling out simple forms. The earliest interactive Web services were ecommerce tools in the late 1990s. The idea of interactive Web sites eventually extended to all kinds of services from finance to document editing.

Interactive Web services have several problems. First, they tend to be silos that interact with other sites and services in only the most rudimentary ways. If the service doesn't do everything the user wants, there's almost never a way to combine two services to solve a unique problem. Second, and more problematically, they are built on a request-response model that requires the user to initiate each interaction. In contrast, some Web applications are beginning to push information to users—something that is not only more convenient for users, but creates data streams that other tools can use. We call the set of technologies and practices that enable users to receive information as soon as it is published by its authors the real-time Web.[3]

You don't have go any further than the Facebook, Twitter, or Foursquare apps on your iPhone to see the real-time Web in action. These services aren't just interactive Web sites; they create streams of data about the people you follow. The stream of tweets from my friends is available to me in a variety of places without me needing to visit any particular Web site. The real-time Web won't replace the interactive Web—we'll always need Web sites—but the real-time Web will augment it in important ways.

TURNING THE WEB INSIDE OUT

The Live Web is a radical shift in how people use the Internet. Rather than simply viewing static pages or even interacting with a Web site, the Live Web uses dynamic streams of information to present contextual, relevant experiences to users. These dynamic streams of information include diverse data flows from Twitter streams and Facebook news to RSS feeds of product recalls. Many of these data streams are enabled and supported by APIs because programmatic access to the data is critical to its reuse in various guises.

Information reuse is a major premise of the Live Web because much of the information available is not nearly as interesting by itself as it is in combination with other data streams. Further, this reuse is often highly personal because what you want from the information stream and how you want it mixed with other data is different from what I want.

Making streams real-time skews application design to favor interrupts over polling. Protocols like PubSubHubbub and services like push.ly are created with the explicit purpose of giving polling-based technologies like RSS an interrupt-driven facade.

Dynamic Queries, Static Data

By the mid 1990s, the Web had developed enough that people were starting to build form-based, data-driven Web sites. MySQL was on the rise, but connecting to databases and building Web pages from the results was still a complex programming task. Out of this environment, PHP emerged as the tool of choice for building interactive Web sites. Later, Ruby on Rails took this model to the extreme and became the *de facto* standard for building interactive Web applications.

As shown in Figure 1.2, the modern Web is founded on an architecture where a Web browser makes a request of a Web server and gets a response that it renders and shows to the user.

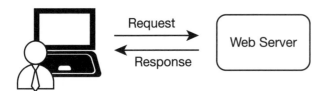

Figure 1.2
Web browsers and servers.

For interactive, data-driven Web applications, you can expand the Web server box to reveal an architecture that has become the norm for modern Web applications. This architecture, shown in Figure 1.3, variously called an n-tier or model-view-controller (MVC) architecture, is at the heart of all well-designed interactive Web applications. The architecture exhibits good performance while providing good separation of concerns to ease the program construction and maintenance efforts.

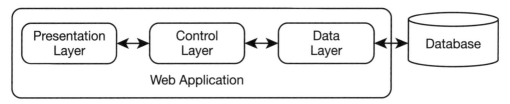

Figure 1.3
Data-driven Web application architecture.

One of the hallmarks of this architecture is the database. The Web application is written to create and modify entries in the database. The Web application is driven through queries against the database. PHP, Ruby on Rails, and other Web application languages are designed to make the task of managing the data and dynamically constructing queries against it as easy as possible. You can characterize this pattern as dynamic queries against static data, or DQSD.

Dynamic Data, Static Queries

The Live Web demands the dual of the DQSD model. In the Live Web, the data is dynamic. You view it as streams or rivers of information flowing past you, rather than as a pool of data that you collect and control. Making use of these information flows requires that you recognize patterns in the flows as well as patterns between flows. Here are some examples:

■ Tell me when someone mentions my company on Twitter.

■ Tell me when someone checks into the same place I am.

- Tell me when one of my Facebook friends posts an update on his or her blog.

- Tell me when someone calls my customer-service line after visiting the customer-service page on my company's Web site.

These simple patterns represent static queries against the dynamic information streams. You can characterize this pattern as dynamic data against static queries, or DDSQ. In the DDSQ model, a data source produces a stream of data that is continually changing. The query is run against that stream; only items passing the query are processed further (see Figure 1.4).

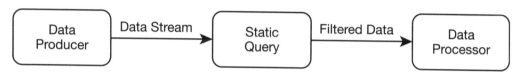

Figure 1.4
Data producers stream data and queries are run against these streams.

The DDSQ model doesn't replace, but rather complements, the DQSD model. After all, the data streams start somewhere, and most of those starting points are pools of data managed through traditional DQSD Web applications.

There are several well-known examples of this concept:

- **Stock alerts.** These trigger buy and sell orders when certain events occur. The triggers continuously monitor the stream of data about stocks you care about.

- **Google alerts.** When you create a Google alert, you're giving Google a standing, static query that it continuously runs over the stream of new stuff it sees. When there's match, you get an email.

- **Twitter searches.** Once you've done the search, Twitter continues to apply it to the stream of tweets, looking for matches.

For each of these examples, static queries are established once and changed infrequently. These static queries run continuously against streams of dynamic data.

The aforementioned sample queries all started with "Tell me...," but you can do much more than merely notify people of certain patterns. You can create compelling, sophisticated applications that programmatically react to patterns in dynamic information streams.

The request-response model of a typical Web site puts the focus on the server and location for a simple reason: To make the request, the client has to know where to go. Forgetting about location and moving to streams of events frees you from server silos. Going a step further and envisioning these streams of events as being individualized for a given person or entity enables you to concentrate on the user's context and purpose.

Putting static queries over dynamic data streams to work for the individual will require better abstractions for modeling these streams of data and writing programs that work against them in context. Modeling them as events gives you a way to watch for scenarios that matter to the user. Without an event-like abstraction, this is hard and expensive to pull off.

EVENTS

An *event* is a formal notification of an occurrence of interest. A given event happens at a particular time, contains information about what happened, and might contain parameters to further distinguish the event.

Events are a natural way to think about online interactions. When someone sends a tweet, updates his or her Facebook page, or checks into a location on Foursquare, this generates an event. Further, events are a natural way to pull physical systems into the online world. Consider, for example, a point-of-sale system that could generate events when a product is rung up, a sale is totaled, or payment is tendered.

Viewing updates on the real-time Web as events gives you a model for classifying and processing them. For example, a tweet can be seen as a Twitter event that occurs at a given time and has required parameters like message and user with optional parameters such as client used.

Each event is a member of a certain event type that defines certain required and optional parameters through an event schema. While a Twitter event has a required parameter representing the message of the tweet, a Foursquare event might have a required location parameter with an optional message parameter. But an event model goes beyond the darlings of the real-time Web like Twitter, Facebook, and Foursquare to encompass other online activities. Updates in an Atom or RSS feed, for example, can be thought of as events—especially when viewed through the lens of protocol extensions like PubSubHubbub.

The Evented Web

If you crack open a book on complex event processing, you'll find descriptions of enterprise-class systems built on message-oriented middleware busses. (See Appendix B, "Resources," for a list of books and articles on event processing.) With the Live Web, events are moved out of the enterprise and onto the Web, giving you a powerful tool for working with real-time data and creating contextual, Live Web applications.

Events contrast with the client-server model used by many Web applications in being message-oriented and asynchronous. An event is a signal that something has happened, whereas a request is a signal that the requestor wants something to happen. When one system raises an event, it does so by sending some kind of message and doesn't necessarily wait for responses before continuing.

Enterprise event systems use special message busses for transport based on expensive middleware, but that's not realistic on the Web. Consequently, if events are to be used online, they need to be built on top of the protocol of the Web, HTTP. Fortunately, that work has already begun. The following sections discuss some of these developments and their importance to building the evented Web. The following chapters introduce a system for using events to build applications for the Live Web.

Please, Interrupt Me

As you've already seen, extensions to common protocols, such as PubSubHubbub for RSS and Atom, can turn a formerly request-response–style protocol into one that makes calls to subscribers when relevant updates are posted. That means the task of determining when a feed has changed can be done with interrupts rather than polling.

PubSubHubbub works using a server, called a *hub*, running software that implements the PubSubHubbub protocol. When a publisher changes its feed, it pings the hub. The hub signals its subscribers using an HTTP callback URL they've provided. They can then retrieve the changed feed in the usual manner. RSS and Atom feeds can signal that they support PubSubHubbub by putting a link tag with the rel attribute set to hub and an href attribute pointing to the hub.

Web Hooks

As useful as PubSubHubbub is, it only works for Atom or RSS feeds. The embedded pattern of using URLs to define the interface that one system should use to call another when an event of interest happens—like a new item being placed in a feed—is called a *Web hook*.

Web hooks are HTTP callbacks.[4] The listener or subscriber gives the publisher a URL. When the publisher wishes to signal the subscriber, it makes an HTTP post to the URL. Web hook–enabled Web applications can be extended by the system responding to the Web hook call.

For an example of how Web hooks work and the problem they solve, consider the Twilio API. Twilio is a cloud-based telephony service. Twilio applications can answer and make phone calls as well as send and receive SMS messages. Twilio issues phone numbers on its service. When someone calls that number, Twilio has to do something. This is where Web hooks come in. Twilio developers have to be able to tell Twilio what to do when it receives a call. Obviously, the more flexible and configurable Twilio is in responding to calls, the more valuable it will be to developers and end users alike. Twilio could have just let developers configure actions via a menu, but menu-based systems can't provide as much flexibility as developers would like. The kind of flexibility Twilio wanted demands the ability to script the system.

Rather than deploying a scripting language on its system that developers use to create applications, Twilio uses Web hooks. When developers configure a phone number, they supply a URL that Twilio will call using an HTTP POST. As a result of the call, Twilio expects to receive instructions (in Twilio's XML command language) about what to do next. Those instructions usually include another Web hook to call when Twilio is finished and has received a response from the caller.

In this way, developers control Twilio using programs they create on their own Web server rather than Twilio's. Without Web hooks, Twilio would be either much less powerful or much more complex. With Web hooks, it's simple, easy, and powerful. Web hooks show how the evented Web can be created on top of HTTP using a simple pattern. This pattern is critical to building the Live Web.

Note

You'll look at Twilio in detail and use it to build some Live Web applications in Chapter 10, "Mobile and the Live Web."

THIS IS GETTING PERSONAL

The Live Web is intensely personal. If you imagine the scenario outlined at the beginning of the chapter, about scheduling an appointment with a doctor, you can readily see that much of the data—including the events—must be kept private. This is why I characterized identity on the Live Web as "personal data under the control of the user" in Table 1.1.

Moreover, your events and my events are different and must be separable. So even for things you might not mind sharing, the system has to know what's yours and what's mine. For both of these reasons, identity is at the foundation of the Live Web—not something that can be tacked on afterward.

Consequently, it's useful to think of each participant on the Live Web as having a personal event network rather than envisioning one giant event network signaling everyone's events. Technically, of course, you won't actually construct a special, physical network for each participant, but the architecture will be such that each participant *does* have a virtual network of events that is all his or her own.

A personal event network needs more than events; it needs programs to respond to and process them. Each person will use a collection of apps that he or she has chosen to mediate his or her interactions on the Live Web. In large part, your experience on the Live Web will be personalized by the collection of apps you have chosen to activate on your event network.

BUILDING THE LIVE WEB

The static and interactive versions of the Web use a model that places servers in the center of the interaction and make people mere appendages to the server through the use of what end up being second-class clients. The Live Web doesn't displace this model, but envisions a Web that works for and in behalf of people and what matters to them. The Live Web will prove to be more valuable to everyone and more profitable for companies that adapt to it than what has gone before.

Building the Live Web will require a new model that enables developers to conceptualize people using the Web to work for them. Events provide a mental abstraction for describing the Live Web and building applications that make it real. Context enables events to be correlated in meaningful ways. The Live Web will be built upon contextually correlated events. As developers begin to use events in parallel with the interactive Web development techniques they have already mastered, they will build new, exciting applications.

This book presents a new architecture and language for a Web-based event-processing network that is already being used to create applications for the Live Web. The architecture, called the Kinetic Event Processing Network, is supported by an open-source event processing system and an open specification for how events can be raised on the Web. Together, they allow for the building of contextually aware event processors and handlers that easily take user context into account. (See Appendix C, "Getting Started with KRL," for information about using the hosted service or downloading and installing your own node.)

The next chapters explore events and event expressions in more detail, as well as the role that context and data play in creating Live Web experiences. Then, following a chapter about the architecture of the Kinetic Event Processing Network, you will start to build Live Web applications. You'll finish up by exploring where all of this leads and what it means to business.

The Live Web links together all your devices and all the information that matters to you into a cooperating, loosely coupled mesh that works to achieve your purpose. The tools, techniques, and models necessary to build the Live Web are available now. Let's get started.

ENDNOTES

1. Hinchcliffe, Dion. (2008). Open APIs Reach New High Water Mark as the Web Evolves. *ZDNet.* http://www.zdnet.com/blog/hinchcliffe/open-apis-reach-new-high-water-mark-as-the-web-evolves/215.
2. Ramji, Sam. (2010). Darwin's Finches, 20th Century Business, and APIs. http://www.slideshare.net/samramji/darwins-finches-20th-century-business-and-apis.
3. Wikipedia. Real-Time Web. *Wikipedia.* http://en.wikipedia.org/wiki/Real-time_web.
4. Lindsay, Jeff. WebHooks. *Webhooks.* http://wiki.webhooks.org/w/page/13385124/FrontPage.

CHAPTER 2

EVENTS ON THE LIVE WEB

Events play a central role in the Live Web. Unlike other interaction models that have prevailed on the static Web, such as request-response and remote procedure call (RPC), events allow extreme loose coupling for applications. Modeling Live Web interactions with events makes programming sophisticated applications simpler and more flexible.

Before I dive into the details of events, I want to explore, by means of an example, the difference between event processing and the traditional remote procedure call interactions that are so prevalent on the Web. In a May 2001 *Scientific American* article entitled "The Semantic Web," Tim Berners-Lee, James Hendler, and Ora Lassila relate the following scenario:

> The entertainment system was belting out the Beatles' "We Can Work It Out" when the phone rang. When Pete answered, his phone turned the sound down by sending a message to all the other local devices that had a volume control. His sister, Lucy, was on the line from the doctor's office....

I was immediately enamored with this vision of the Semantic Web, but I was confused by the tight coupling between components that it presented. (The topic of how evented systems reduce unnecessary coupling and the attendant advantages will be taken up in Chapter 4, "Telling Stories on the Live Web.") When the phone sends a "turn sound down" command to local devices with volume controls, it has to know which devices are in the vicinity that have volume controls and explicitly script them. Discovery of this kind of information is difficult and computationally expensive (hence the need for the Semantic Web). Knowing what commands to send to which device entails significant complexity.

Suppose however, the scenario read instead:

> The entertainment system was belting out the Beatles' "We Can Work It Out" when the phone rang. When Pete answered, his phone broadcast a message to all local devices indicating it had received a call. His stereo responded by turning down the volume. His sister, Lucy, was on the line from the doctor's office….

In the second scenario, the phone doesn't have to know anything about other local devices. The phone need only indicate that it has received a call. Each device can interpret that message however it sees fit or ignore it altogether. For example, if Pete had been watching a movie on his DVR instead, it could have paused the program.

When individual devices are loosely coupled, the complexity of the overall system is reduced significantly. The phone software is much simpler and the infrastructure to pass messages between devices is much less complex than an infrastructure that supports semantic discovery of capabilities. Events—the messages about things that have happened—are the key to enabling simple, loosely coupled scenarios.

EVENTS

Events are part of everyday life. You experience events all the time. Some events are expected and some are not. Some events are good and others are unpleasant. Phones ring. Emails arrive. Milk is spilt. Cars crash. Babies are born. Each of these is a life event that must be handled.

Events have long been used to order business processes. Consider, for example, a paper-form process for issuing an insurance policy, as might have existed before computers were widespread. The arrival of a form in an inbox represented an event that indicated the processor was to start work. When an insurance agent was finished with the task, the agent sent it on, the message and its location moving the process forward in an event-driven way.

Events are nothing new in computer systems, either. Events, in various forms, have been used in operating systems, graphical user interface design, message-oriented middleware, service-oriented architectures, database triggers, and even the more mundane SMS and email messages.

An event is the notification of a detectable condition in a computer system. I will define the detectable condition as a state change. As shown in Figure 2.1, there are three required parts of event detection and notification:[1]

■ A change of state occurs.

■ A process notices the state change.

■ The process sends a notification of the state change.

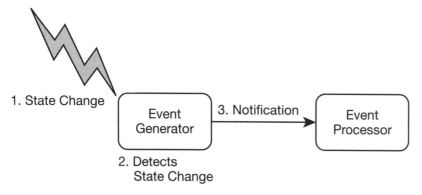

Figure 2.1
Event detection and notification.

The word *event* is used in several different ways. In common usage, event signifies the actual happening. The word *event* is also used to refer to the notification. Of course, the notification isn't the event, but is rather a representation of the event. Where it is not confusing, I will, for convenience, speak of the notification as the event even though it's really merely a representation. Event generators are said to "raise events" as shorthand for "send notifications that a state change occurred." The processor "listens for" or "handles" events.

Event Semantics

Notifications are data transfers, not transfers of execution control. This is one of the hallmarks of evented systems and distinguishes them from others. Interrogatory-style systems use a request-response mode of interaction: "Will you do this?" Imperative-style systems use an RPC mode of interaction: "Do this!" In contrast, event interactions are declarative, stating only that a specific state change occurred: "This happened."

Because they are declarative, event notifications impose the semantics of what an event means on the processor rather than a generator. This is called *semantic encapsulation*. The event generator doesn't know how a given processor will interpret the event. What's more, an event processor is not required to take any action whatsoever. Each processor is free to interpret the event independently of other processors and generators in the system according to its context and particular purpose.

Semantic encapsulation is one of the features of evented systems that leads to looser coupling of system components compared with other styles of interaction. New processors can be added to the event system and old ones go away without any change to the generator or other components in the system.

Another way to view the declarative style of interactions found in event systems is through the lens of component binding. In computer science, the term *late binding* indicates that the meaning of a name is resolved at runtime. Late binding usually includes the concept of dynamic loading because one of the key reasons for resolving a name late is to be flexible in what the name means, resolving to one component one time and another component the next depending on context. Most of the languages that have gained favor over the last decade, such as Python and Ruby, are late-binding languages.

Events allow for late binding of components. In contrast, request-response and RPC interaction modes are bound early and, almost always, statically. Early, static binding allows for a kind of simplicity in the first stages of design, but early decisions are also more likely to be wrong. On top of this, early binding increases the coupling between system components, making the overall system less flexible and more difficult to change. Thus, early binding means that you're more likely to have made the wrong choice and thus need to change it. At the same time, early binding makes that change more difficult and costly.

As described in Chapter 1, "The Live Web," the Web is going real-time. But the more dynamic the Internet gets, the more data there is floating around. And the more you mash up things to create just what you need, the more important late binding becomes—in life, in a programming language, and in Web technology. Events are an interaction model that supports putting off binding decisions as long as possible, making the resulting system more flexible in a world of dynamic information flows.

Event Detection

Detecting events depends on observing a state change. Plenty of things happen in computer systems that are never noticed because the state change isn't visible. Sometimes this occurs because the system wasn't instrumented; making the state change visible is a simple matter. For example, detecting the change in value of a variable inside a system is easy—probably only a matter of a few lines of code. In other cases, the state change might be difficult to detect without additional instrumentation. The arrival of an email to an inbox can be directly observed only if a special software component is installed on the system and watching the email inbox. In still other cases, the state change isn't something that can be detected directly and must be inferred from other events. Inferred events are the aggregation of other directly or indirectly observed events. For example, the `meeting_can_start()` event might be inferred from the individual events indicating that all participants have arrived.

Inferred events are defined by situations. A situation defines the conditions under which an inferred event happens. In the `meeting_can_start()` example, the situation might require that all participants have arrived, or perhaps it specifies that n unique participants have arrived out of the total expected (a quorum). As you'll see in Chapter 12, "Building Event Networks," you can create rules that give inferred events names, making them explicit and reusable.

Event Properties

An event is atomic—it either happens completely or not at all. Events in the real world can be long-lived affairs like a wedding. For our purposes, however, events signal a change of state. Thus, events are also instantaneous. A wedding is not an event as I've defined it, but is an activity that is defined by a number of events such as start, vows, ring exchange, cake cutting, and so on.

Events have several important aspects:[2]

- **Significance.** An event signifies a change of state in a particular domain. Because we want to avoid associating an event with a long-lived activity, talking about state changes is more precise.

- **Salience.** An event may or may not be of interest to a particular event handler. Obviously, there are too many state changes in even a single activity to pay attention to all of them. Salience is a property shared by events that are relevant to a particular event handler.

- **Structure.** Every event has important attributes that define the event. Some attributes are required, like the timestamp of the event. Others are optional. Attributes are an important part of context. Many events are raised on behalf of a particular entity.

- **Relativity.** Events can be related to each other in several ways, including time, causality, and aggregation. Aggregation is a means of abstracting events by combining several events into one. You can also relate events to each other based on the attributes they have in common, such as domain, entity, and so on. The relativity of an event is not usually encoded in the event's structure, but is computed when needed.

Event Schema

As noted, events have a particular structure. Event systems are more flexible if generators and processors can communicate events without having to be aware of specific requirements or structure. Events have a type. In addition, most events also have two other attributes:

- A timestamp indicating when the event notification was created

- A globally unique identifier (GUID) that serves as a unique identifier for the event

Beyond that, the attributes that are included in the event are open-format. Event generators pick the type and attributes of the event when they send notification that it has occurred.

The next chapter discusses a formal language for describing event patterns. In this chapter, we will use the following simple format for describing events:

```
for_sale(product, price)
```

This describes an event with type `for_sale` that includes the attributes `product` and `price`. Note that there is no mention of the timestamp or GUID attributes, because in informal discussion, they are almost always uninteresting. When describing a specific event, with specific parameters, you use the preceding format with values given for the attributes:

```
for_sale(product: "iPhone 4", price: "$299")
```

EVENT PROCESSING

When you know an event has occurred, you can react to it in appropriate ways. You answer the phone, read the email, or clean up the milk. Some reactions to events are simple. For example, when the phone rings, you answer it. Some events require responses that are more complicated. For example, when you wake up late, you may have to reschedule your entire morning.

Event-driven architectures employ event notifications to disseminate information between distributed components in the architecture and to drive the execution of processes that will achieve the ultimate aim of the system.

In general, event-processing networks have three primary components, as shown in Figure 2.2:

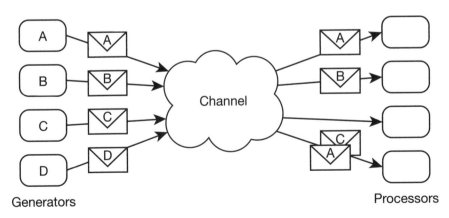

Generators   Processors

Figure 2.2
Event processing network components.

- **Event generator.** The generator is responsible for noticing that the event has taken place and producing the notification (the system's representation of the event). In Figure 2.2, each generator is generating a single event.

- **Event channel.** The channel is the messaging system used to transmit the event notification from the generator to systems performing downstream processing. In Figure 2.2, the channel is shown as a cloud to emphasize that there is no direct connection between generators and processors.

- **Event processor.** The processor listens for and handles relevant events. Processors are also sometimes called event listeners, or handlers. The processor sees the stream of events, filters it for events of interest, and reacts to those events. Processing includes manipulating the event itself, connecting to outside systems for additional context to interpret the event, and taking action. The action might include logging the event for analysis or generating additional events. In Figure 2.2, event A is handled by two processors, event B is handled by another, event C is handled by the one of the same handlers that is also handling event A, and event D is ignored.

Note

Many authors describe event architectures with more components than the three described here, but this breakdown is sufficient for our needs.

The goal of event-driven architectures is to process information in near real-time by reacting to the publication of that information when it happens. Event-driven architectures lower the latency of information propagation while promoting loose coupling between components compared with sequential workflows programmed in traditional models.

Event-processing systems have several important fundamental aspects:[3]

- **Push-based messaging pattern.** As discussed in Chapter 1, the traditional messaging pattern on the Web has been request-response—what one might call a "pull" messaging pattern because the client pulls information from the server by sending a request. In contrast, in event systems, event generators push events into the system when they occur.

- **Autonomous messages.** Events are signaled by notifications that are independent of other events. (This doesn't mean event processors might not correlate an individual event with other event processors as part of the processing, merely that event producers have no dependency on the overall system in determining whether to produce a particular event.) Because of semantic encapsulation, events are not dependent on the generator for their meaning, and each processor is free to interpret the event independently of others. An event contains information about the state transition it represents and any associated attributes. An event generator sends the event notification whenever it detects a salient state transition.

■ **Higher decoupling.** Compared with other system-architecture styles, event-processing systems exhibit higher decoupling along several important axes. I've discussed several of these already, and I will summarize them here:

■ Because event notifications do not contain processing instructions, destination information, and other details about how an event should be processed, the schema of the event is simple and flexible, requiring less coordination between event generator and event processor.

■ Event generators do not necessarily need to know which processors are interested in the event. The event generator sends notification of the event to the event channel, not to a specific processor.

■ Unlike RPC-style interactions, event notifications do not include specific processing instructions. For example, if my phone receives a call, it can raise the `inbound_call()` event and the stereo system can interpret that as "turn down the volume." In an RPC-style architecture, my phone would send the `turn_down_volume()` instruction to the stereo instead.

■ System components can be added or removed with less coordination in the overall system. Other components that want to respond in their own way to an `inbound_call()` event can join the network without the event generator or any existing event handlers being affected. Similarly, components can be removed without the event generator and other event handlers being updated.

■ **Receiver-driven flow control.** After an event generator sends an event notification, its role in determining what happens to that event is over. Downstream event processors can ignore the event, handle it as appropriate for their domain, or propagate it to other processors. A single event can induce multiple downstream activities as it and its effects propagate through the event-processing network.

■ **Near real-time propagation.** Event-processing systems work in real-time. This is in contrast with batch-oriented, fixed-schedule architectures. Events propagate through the network of event processors soon after they happen and can further affect how those processors will interpret and react to future events from the same or different event generators. Event-processing networks thus allow a more natural way to design and create real-time information systems. As more and more information online gains a real-time component, event processing becomes increasingly important.

These important aspects of event-processing systems lead to architectures that are potentially more flexible, agile, and scalable than more tightly coupled request-response designs.

EVENTS ON THE LIVE WEB

Events are a natural way to order and script online interactions—especially those that cross devices and domains. The following examples show how event processing can be used to create new Live Web applications that achieve the user's purpose.

Example 1: Device Automation

A person has a number of devices or appliances that raise events specific to that type of device. These devices are all known to a set of Live Web applications that the person has configured to match her preferences. Suppose the person receives a phone call on her cell phone. This raises an `inbound_call()` event. One of the applications the user has installed sees the `inbound_call()` event and, in response, pauses the DVR and raises the lights. Directives are sent to those devices to affect that behavior. When the person hangs up the phone, another event, `call_disconnected()`, is raised, and the DVR and lights return to their previous state.

By automating the interaction of the various devices the person owns and uses, the Live Web delivers a richer and more integrated experience. Just as most people barely remember the days when they got up off the couch to change the TV channel, in the future, people will just accept this kind of device cooperation as the way things ought to be.

Example 2: Social Network Monitor

A person participates in a number of social networks and activates a Live Web application to help him monitor the stream of updates from each of those networks. He installs an application that connects to each of the social networks using standard authorization technologies. As updates come through on each social network, the service treats those updates as events and processes them according to the person's desires, identifying the kinds of updates that are important to the person. The monitoring application provides notifications through whatever channels are configured. For example, important messages, such as someone changing jobs or entering the hospital, can be sent via SMS, while less urgent messages can be sent in a digest email.

While Facebook, Twitter, and other social networks are trying to be the one-stop shop for social interactions, the use of ancillary services is exploding. It's happening faster than anyone could hope to integrate it onto a single platform. The Live Web promises to integrate online social services in ways that are individualized to your specific needs and desires. Loose coupling ensures that these integrations can happen without up-front coordination. Don't like how something works? There's an app for that.

Example 3: Kid Tracker

A parent wants to keep up on the activities of her teenager and better track the child's academic performance. The parent activates a Live Web application that will aggregate events from different systems and provide alerts based on rules defined by the parent. This includes an app on the teenager's cell phone that receives spatiotemporal limits from the application and generates events that are transmitted back to the application if the child violates any of those limits. It also includes a Web service that monitors the school's online grading and attendance system and generates events when key data elements change (such as attendance, tardiness, or grading data). The application automatically sends directives to the child's cell phone to limit usage based on behavioral thresholds.

The Live Web will encourage the individualized interaction of devices and services for specific purposes. Many parents already love the ability to connect with their children regardless of where they are. The Live Web will allow this electronic tether to be customized to meet each family's specific needs and parenting style.

Example 4: Personal RFP Service

Suppose an event-driven marketplace exists where consumers raise events to the marketplace by indicating their interest in buying a certain product in a specific geography for a given price (`request_for_quote(product,location, price)`). Merchants or other individuals create Live Web applications that listen for `request_for_quote()` events and respond with appropriate offers, themselves events. As this marketplace matures, consumers could assign a price to every item they own, and the event-driven marketplace will match buyers and sellers automatically. In this case, consumers indicate they are willing to part with an item by lowering the price to market levels, generating an event, of course.[4]

Events are a natural way to express activities in a marketplace. Moreover, commerce demands good user-controlled identity. Consequently, the Live Web will create new opportunities in ecommerce that will far exceed the ecommerce activities of the static Web. While static Web-based ecommerce has tended to mirror the siloed retail commerce of the physical world, ecommerce on the Live Web will enable consumers to use techniques like RFPs. These have previously been the exclusive domain of big enterprises that could afford the overhead of issuing, managing, and responding to RFPs and similar channels. You will build a simple request-for-quotes application in Chapter 13, "Business on the Live Web."

Example 5: Live Customer Contact Management

A company implements a Live Web application that includes software agents for monitoring all of the different contact channels available to customers, such as Twitter, Facebook, email, phone, and SMS. Suppose a customer tweets about the company. The Twitter agent recognizes the tweet and generates an event. The application processes the event and uses an external API to match the customer to internal CRM records. The application then determines the most appropriate channel for responding to the customer based on lifetime value, social influence, and previous contact with the company through other channels. The Live Web will enable companies to establish and service more personalized relationships with customers by automating many of the interactions. Such systems will allow companies to have meaningful relationships with customers at scale.

Example 6: Home Maintenance

Appliances are instrumented with agents that monitor their performance and status. When the status of an appliance changes, the agent raises an event that is processed by Live Web applications activated by the homeowner. For example, suppose the pilot light in the furnace is extinguished. The furnace's agent raises an event. The application handling these events determines whether the homeowner is at or near their home through a cell phone location API. If he or she is, the homeowner is sent a message to relight the pilot light. If not, the application might decide to shut off gas to the home or alert a home maintenance service. The Live Web will give unprecedented insight in to the status and performance of your environment and, at the same time, automate many of the mundane activities associated with living in them. You'll be safer and more comfortable.

Example 7: Groupon Annotation

Groupon and similar services represent an opportunity for people to realize significant savings on goods and services. A person could gain even more value from these services if the available deals were correlated with the person's behavior. Suppose a person installs a Groupon deal-management application that operates in his Web browser and in his mobile phone. Agents monitor the deal services and actively notify the user when deals are offered that meet the person's criteria. Additionally, the service watches for events such as Web searches or location changes that correspond to available deals. It then notifies the person of these through the most convenient channel.

Many new services on the static Web offer significant value, but unlocking that value requires too much attention from harried people. Live Web applications can relieve that burden by filtering the information and making relevant information available on the right channel at the right time.

Example 8: Location-Enabled Merchant Offers

Services such as Foursquare provide an interesting game for people, as well as a platform for commercial offers. Suppose a service, similar to Foursquare, is configured that allows people to opt in by installing apps onto their mobile devices. This service might alert me that the book I placed on my Amazon wish list this morning is available at the Borders next door to the coffee shop I'm sitting at. Unlike the location services of the static Web, Live Web location-based applications enable both users and merchants to configure the application to respond to location-based events to provide value back to users.

Example 9: Home Inventory

A homeowner has activated a Live Web application that allows her to apply tags containing a two-dimensional bar code (e.g., a QR code) to items in her home. After the item is uniquely identified, the homeowner quickly associates relevant information with each tag. For example, she might apply a tag to the bins in her garage and store information about what's in them. A home-storage application might then help the homeowner locate things stored in tagged bins. A homeowner's insurance app might automatically adjust coverage to accommodate new purchases, or a lending application might keep track of who has borrowed what.

The Live Web doesn't just link devices with built-in computers, but almost anything that can be given a unique identity. Attaching digital information to physical things and allowing them to participate in an evented Web enables disconnected devices to participate in the Internet of Things.[5] These entities are full participants on the Live Web when other devices raise events on their behalf.

Example 10: Personal Relationship Management

A user has installed a Live Web application that helps him manage communications. When the user receives a phone call, his phone raises the `inbound_call()` event. The application processes the event and pops up information in the user's Web browser that enables the user to learn more about the caller by linking to his social network profiles, tweet streams, recent email messages, and other contextual information. Fancy "who's calling" features have been available on high-end CRM systems, but have required enterprise-scale IT budgets and the ability to perform custom integrations between these software systems and the company's PBX. On the Live Web, everyone can be recontextualized to people with whom they interact quickly, cheaply, and with little effort.

LIVE WEB APPLICATIONS

As the examples in the previous section show, the Live Web promises to enrich our lives by reducing the complexity of our interactions with the many automated systems that surround us. The Live Web will encompass diverse areas of our lives—even non-computerized objects.

Building Live Web applications like the ones described will not only require events, but also the ability to recognize and respond to complex event scenarios. That will be the subject of the next chapter.

ENDNOTES

1. Faison, Ted. (2006). *Event-Based Programming: Taking Events to the Limit*, Section 2-1. APress.
2. Luckham, David. (2002). *The Power of Events*, Chapter 5. Addison Wesley.
3. Chou, David. (2008). Using Events in Highly Distributed Architectures. *MSDN Architecture Journal.* http://msdn.microsoft.com/en-us/library/dd129913.aspx.
4. David Siegel originally proposed this scenario.
5. For a more complete description of the Internet of Things, see http://en.wikipedia.org/wiki/Internet_of_Things.

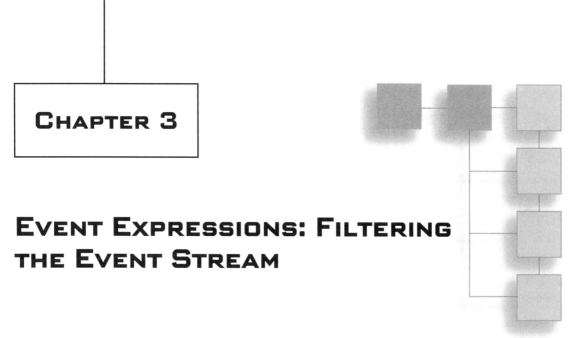

CHAPTER 3

EVENT EXPRESSIONS: FILTERING THE EVENT STREAM

As discussed in Chapter 1, "The Live Web," the Live Web uses a data model that is the dual of the data model that has prevailed on the static Web. The static Web is built around interactive Web sites that leverage pools of static data held in databases. Interactive Web sites are built with languages like PHP and Ruby on Rails, which are designed to take user interaction and formulate SQL queries against databases. The static Web works by making dynamic queries against static data. In contrast, the Live Web is based on static queries against dynamic data.

Streams of real-time data are becoming more and more common online. Years ago, such data streams were just a trickle, but the advent of technologies like RSS and Atom and the appearance of services like Twitter and Facebook have turned this trickle into a raging torrent. And this is just the beginning.

The only way you can hope to make use of all this data is to filter it and automate your responses to it as much as possible. As will be discussed in detail in Chapter 4, "Telling Stories on the Live Web," the task is greater than mere filtering. The task is correlating these events contextually. Correlating events provides power well beyond merely using filters to tame the data torrent.

This chapter introduces in detail the pattern language, called *event expressions*, used to match against streams of events. Event expressions are an important way to match events with context. Event expressions are the language used to write static queries for the dynamic data of the Live Web. Together with language structures I'll introduce later, event expressions provide SQL-like functionality for dynamic streams of data. While the details of event expressions can be quite technical, I hope that non-technical readers will come away from this chapter with an appreciation for the kinds of patterns that can be matched and the power of using a pattern language against streams of real-time data.

PATTERNS AND FILTERING

When I was first introduced to the UNIX operating system in 1986, one of the most interesting and powerful commands was something called grep,[1] which is used to find all the lines in a file that match a user-supplied pattern. Consequently, grep is very useful for finding specific patterns of strings in files. Along with file globbing (the ability in the UNIX command line to apply a command to files that match a pattern called a *file glob*), grep allows large numbers of files to be searched for complex string patterns in a matter of seconds. Even today, I use grep almost daily.

The simplest pattern is an exact match. The following command prints out all the lines in a file named file.txt that contain the string "foo":

```
grep foo file.txt
```

As shown in Figure 3.1, this would match any sequence of characters that contain the subset "foo." So, the string "food" would match, as would "buffoon."

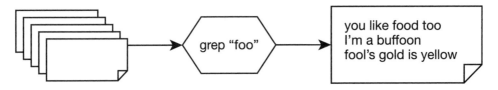

Figure 3.1
Using grep to select strings from a group of files that match the pattern "foo."

Things get more interesting when you supply patterns that are more complex. Patterns in grep can be full-on regular expressions, or regexes. This makes grep a very powerful tool for finding specific items. Here are a few examples of regular expressions and what they would match:

- **\bfoo.** Strings that contain words starting with "foo." This pattern would match "food" and "fool" but not "buffoon."

- **fo+.** Strings that contain a character sequence that starts with the character "f" that is followed by one or more occurrences of the character "o." This pattern would match "food" and "fool" but not "baffled."

- **foo[^d].** Strings that contain the sequence "foo" where it is not followed by "d." This pattern would match "buffoon" but not "food."

- **$\d+\.\d\d.** Strings that contains a dollar sign followed by any positive number of digits followed by a decimal point, followed by exactly two digits. This pattern would match "$15.59" and "$0.00" but not "+5.44" or "$5.666."

By using patterns, you can filter large amounts of data while being very specific about what you want to find. Pattern languages, like regular expressions, provide a convenient, succinct, and unambiguous way to express complex ideas. Writing a standalone program to find patterns in strings that look like currency amounts ($d+\.\d\d) isn't rocket science, but I don't want to do it every time I need to find something in a file. With regular expressions, I express the pattern declaratively and another program translates the pattern into a program for finding the pattern.

A Pattern Language for Events

Similarly, writing a program to look at streams of events and pick out specific patterns isn't hard, but it gets tiresome when you want to do it over and over again. In the same way you use regular expressions to find patterns in strings, you can use a declarative language to express patterns in event streams and then automatically translate those patterns into the programs that search for them.

I will call patterns in this language *event expressions* or *eventexes*. As you'll see in later chapters, eventexes are used in KRL for selecting rules when a particular event pattern is present in the event stream. The processing system for KRL also uses eventexes to determine what events are salient for a particular rule set.

An effective event expression language will have the following properties:[2]

- Power of expression
- Notational simplicity
- Precise semantics
- Scalable pattern matching

There is a trade-off between some of these properties. One can easily imagine powerful event-expression languages that are not scalable or simple to write. The event expressions described in this chapter achieve the goal of being quite powerful while retaining their implementability, scalability, and simplicity.

Eventexes have the following benefits over natural-language descriptions and standalone programs for recognizing the same pattern:

- Eventexes save time. Eventexes are succinct. Writing an eventex is shorter than writing the equivalent program in a general-purpose programming language, reducing tedium and mistakes at the same time.

■ Eventexes provide a common foundation for communication. Eventexes are unambiguous. Programmers describing interesting patterns can be sure they are expressing the same concept when they use the same eventex. Similarly, programmers can be more sure that the program they are writing means what they think it does.

■ Event processors can translate eventexes into programs to programmatically recognize specified patterns.

■ Event generators can use eventexes to determine which events are of interest to the event processor, thereby making the event network more efficient.

I'll begin by discussing the patterns that you can use to select individual events and then move on to more complex event expressions that look for patterns over streams of events. Appendix D, "Event Semantics," contains a more formal description of event expressions used in this book, including the syntax and semantics of the types of eventexes explored informally in this chapter.

Finding Individual Events

As you saw in Chapter 2, "Events on the Live Web," events have structure. They have a type and attributes that have values. Events also include a domain that can be used to group events together—forming a two-tier hierarchy. The way this structure is expressed in event instances isn't important now; for the time being, I'll ignore it. (Chapter 5, "Architecting the Live Web," discusses the specifics of how event generators format and transmit events.) Instead, we will concentrate on writing patterns that can match the components of this structure using primitive event expressions to recognize the occurrence of individual events.

Exact Matches

The simplest pattern for selecting an event from an event stream is just an event type. The following eventex selects events that have the type pageview. (The keywords select when denote the beginning of an event expression. You'll see how this fits with KRL in Chapter 6, "Live Web Rules.")

```
select when pageview
```

If you wanted to include a domain to ensure you were looking at events in a specific group, you could do so:

```
select when web pageview
```

This would ignore pageview events unless they also included the domain web.

While grep can be used with complex regular expressions, I suspect that in more than 90 percent of cases, people use it for simple, exact matches, as you saw in the first example. In the same way, simple type-only patterns may not seem powerful; however, they are among the most frequently used event expressions. That's because, for much of what you want to do, simply matching the type is sufficient.

Attribute Matching

When exact matches aren't enough, the next step in expressive power is garnered through attribute matching. Eventexes for attribute matching are formulated in the same way as exact matching eventexes, adding as many attribute-regex pairs as needed to specify the precise events that should match.

The following eventex matches a pageview event and applies a regex to the event attribute url:

```
select when pageview url re#/archives/\d{4}#
```

This pattern will match all events in the event stream that contain an attribute named url that has a value that contains the string /archives/ followed by four digits. This particular event would indicate that the user has viewed a Web page that has a URL matching the regex.

Note

> The regex shown uses the hash character (#) to delimit the regular expression instead of the more common (and acceptable) slash (/) because the slash is a frequently used character in URL paths. This removes the need to quote the slash with backslashes: re/\/archives\/\d{4}\//. Using alternate delimiters makes the regex more readable and thus communicates its meaning more clearly.

You can test more than one attribute by simply including them in the eventex. Multiple attribute-regex pairs are evaluated. All of them must be true for the event expressions to match. For example:

```
select when pageview url re#/archives/\d{4}/#
                   title re#iphone#i
```

This represents a subset of the events selected by the preceding eventex to include only those from the archive path that contain the word "iphone" in the title of the page. The trailing i in the regex indicates that case shouldn't be taken into consideration in matching the title.

Capturing Values

Regular expressions inside an eventex can be used to capture values and assign them to a variable for later use. You indicate that you want to capture a value in a regex by enclosing the part of the pattern you wish to capture in parentheses. Event expressions can use an optional setting clause to indicate the variable names for any captured values. Values are assigned to named variables in the order the captures appear in the regexes.

The following eventex would select the same events as the one in the preceding example, but also capture the digits of the archive path from the URL and the value of the word following "iphone" in the title:

```
select when pageview url re#/archives/(\d{4})/#
                  title re#iphone (\w*)#i
        setting(year, next)
```

Suppose the actual event is a page view on the path /archives/2005/ with the page title "Singing the iPhone Blues." When the given eventex matches such an event, the variable year will contain the value 2005 and the variable next will contain the value Blues.

As another example, consider the following eventex that sets the variable user_id from the "from" address in an incoming email message:

```
select when mail received from re#(.*)@windley.com#
  setting(user_id)
```

The ability to select events not just by type and domain, but also by regex matches against their individual attributes along with binding part or all of the matching values to variables, provides a powerful means of selecting events from the event stream.

When you need to use parentheses for grouping inside a regular expression but don't wish to capture the value, you can add ?: to the front of the grouping:

```
select when pageview re#/(?:archives|logs)/(\d+)/(\d+)/#
        setting (year,month)
```

The ?: inside the first expression in parentheses keeps that match from being captured so that the year and month are still set correctly. If you capture more values than you have variables in the setting clause, the extra captured values will be ignored.

Attribute Expressions

As powerful as regex matching is, there are times when you need a more freeform expression to precisely select the events in which you are interested. Instead of following the eventex type with a series of attribute-regex pairs to match attributes, the type can be followed with a single expression. (Expressions will be formally introduced in Chapter 6 and are described in greater detail in Appendix E, "The KRL Expression Language.") If the type and domain match and the expression's value is true, then the eventex matches. Attribute names can be used as variables in the expression.

Attribute expressions are introduced to a primitive eventex with the `where` keyword. For example, the following two eventexes mean the same thing:

```
select when pageview where url.match(re#/archives/\d{4}/#)
```

```
select when pageview url re#/archives/\d{4}/#
```

But suppose you only want to match events when the year in the archive path of the URL is greater than 2003? You could express that using regexes, but it gets messy. The following eventex accomplishes that:

```
select when pageview
          where url.extract(re#/archives/(\d{4})/#).head() > 2003
```

The `extract` operator in this expression returns an array of matches in the regex. The `head()` operator returns the first element in the array for use in the inequality test.

While only a single attribute expression can be used in a primitive eventex, you can use Boolean operators to test scenarios that are more complex. The following eventex not only matches articles after 2003 but also requires that the title contain the string "Utah":

```
select when pageview where
        url.extract(re#/archives/(\d{4})/#).head() > 2003 &&
        title.match("Utah")
```

Attribute expressions provide a powerful and flexible way to match individual events.

Event Scenarios

Responding to individual events is useful, but event expressions are even more powerful when used to correlate events contextually. A contextually meaningful, related group of events is called an *event scenario*. Systems that deal with event scenarios are said to do "complex event processing."

For example, consider the simple scenario shown in Figure 3.2. As you drive through town, your phone notifies you that the DVD you added to your Amazon wish list this morning is available and on sale at the Best Buy you're passing. You can't realize this scenario by recognizing an event that says you added something to your wish list or an event that indicates you're driving past Best Buy. To realize this scenario, you

Figure 3.2
Your DVD's at Best Buy! (Image used with permission from Best Buy.)

have to recognize the pattern of a DVD being added to the wish list before you drive past Best Buy. Combined, the two events automatically provide information that you'd otherwise have to synthesize yourself.

Complex event scenarios like this are not unusual. In fact, they make up the most interesting interactions one might have on the Live Web. You might be interested in knowing when someone is viewing a particular sequence of pages on your site or calling your support line after having sent a question by email. But creating these kinds of interactions is prohibitively expensive or even impossible using the old client-server model, with its silos of data. Complex event expressions that describe event scenarios make them easy to recognize.

Event scenarios provide much of the filtering necessary to make the potentially over-whelming streams of real-time data and events manageable. Without eventexes, the most common way to deal with complex scenarios programmatically is to build ad hoc logic that recognizes the event scenario and dispatches procedures to handle each scenario. Most modern Web applications have a chunk of logic for keeping track of the user's state in the application and then getting the user to the right functionality.

But you needn't approach this important task in an ad hoc fashion. As you've seen, eventexes provide a declarative means of recognizing individual events. Event expression language allows you to combine primitive event expressions to form compound event expressions that can be used to match the patterns of events that are common in complex event scenarios. By combining primitive events into event scenarios, developers can create sophisticated applications without needing them to manage the state machine that would be necessary to recognize those scenarios.

COMPOUND EVENTS

Compound event expressions allow you to combine primitive events to form event scenarios. Event expressions provide a robust, precise notation for expressing complex patterns on event streams. Complex event expressions are not new; they have been the subject of research in database trigger languages since the 1990s and have been used since then in event engines in a variety of disciplines. (For a list of papers and other resources related to complex event expressions, see Appendix B, "Resources.") What *is* new is their application to real-time data streams on the Web.

Event Operators

Event operators combine event expressions into even more complex event expressions using operators that relate subexpressions to each other. Bear in mind that you're not interested in a forensic exercise in which you examine logs of event occurrences. Rather, you apply event patterns to live, real-time event streams. This colors the semantics slightly.

The following binary event operators are available:

- **A or B.** Eventex A matches or eventex B matches. There is no expectation of order. If either subexpression matches, then the entire expression matches. In the following example, the expression would match if the user viewed a page with the string "bar.html" in its URL or received a phone call from a number with area code 801.

```
select when pageview url re#bar.html#
        or phone inbound_call from re#801\d+#
```

- **A and B.** Eventex A matches and eventex B matches in any order. In the following example, the expression would match if the user viewed a page that contained the string "bar.html" in its URL and viewed another page that contained the string "foo.html." There are two events, both of which must occur independently for this match to occur.

```
select when pageview url re#bar.html#
        and pageview url re#foo.html#
```

■ **A before B.** Eventex A matches before eventex B matches. Another way to understand this is that event A appears before event B in the event stream. The compound event matches when event B occurs. There may be intervening events between A and B. The following eventex would match if the user viewed a page with the right URL before the `inbound_call` event is received. Both events have to occur before this eventex matches.

```
select when pageview url re#bar.html#
        before phone inbound_call
```

■ **A then B.** Eventex A matches, then eventex B matches with no intervening salient events. The following eventex would match if the user viewed a page with the right URL and the next event signals an `inbound_call`. Both events have to occur before this eventex matches.

```
select when pageview url re#bar.html#
        then phone inbound_call
```

■ **A after B.** Eventex matches if A occurs after B. This is equivalent to B before A. The following eventex would match if the user viewed a page with the right URL after the `inbound_call` event is received. Both events have to occur before this eventex matches.

```
select when pageview url re#bar.html#
        after phone inbound_call
```

■ **A between(B, C).** Eventex A matches between eventex B matching and eventex C matching. The compound event matches when event C occurs. In the following example, the eventex would match if the user viewed a page with a URL that contains the string "mid.html" between viewing pages that have URLs that contain the strings "first.html" and "last.html," respectively. Note that this eventex will match only after the page view with "last.html" occurs.

```
select when pageview url re#mid.html#
            between(pageview url re#first.html#,
                    pageview url re#last.html#)
```

■ **A not between(B, C).** Eventex A did not match between eventex B matching and eventex C matching. The compound event matches when event C occurs. The following eventex would match if the user did not view a page with a URL that contains the string "mid.html" between viewing pages that have URLs that contain the strings "first.html" and "last.html," respectively. Note that this eventex will match only after the page view with "last.html" occurs.

```
select when pageview url re#/mid.html#
           not between(pageview url re#first.html#,
                       pageview url re#last.html#)
```

Variables are not captured in compound eventexes. Variables can be set based on regex captures for primitive eventexes as part of the primitive event.

```
select when pageview url #mid.html#
           not between(pageview url re#(\d+).html# setting(b),
                       pageview url re#(\d+).html# setting(c))
```

For simplicity, the preceding examples use a single primitive eventex (`pageview`) but there's no restriction on using different event types from different event domains in an eventex. In fact, the most interesting eventexes usually involve more than one event type:

```
select when inbound_call
           from re#(\d{3})\d+# setting(area_code)
   between(pageview url re#custserv_page.html#,
           pageview url re#homepage.html#)
```

Of course, compound eventexes can be nested. Parentheses specify order where precedent is not apparent.

```
select when pageview url re#/mid.html#
        between(pageview url re#\d+.html#,
                pageview url re#\d+.html#)
     before pageview url re#/archives/(\d+)/foo.html# setting (year)
```

Time

Time is an important component of many events. There are three ways to use time:

- As an explicit condition on primitive eventexes
- As an absolute event that is raised at an explicit point in time
- As a relative comparison of the timestamps on the components of an event expression

Explicit Time Expressions

As you saw in Chapter 2, events can contain a `timestamp` attribute. You can use the `timestamp` attribute in explicit conditions on primitive events. Because the `timestamp` attribute is a datetime object, the time module operators can be used to manipulate the timestamp as part of the attribute expression of a primitive eventex. (The built-in operator `time:new()` is used to convert strings into datetime objects.)

For example, suppose your car raised an event each time it was started. You could create an eventex that only selects when the car is started before 8 a.m. as follows:

```
select when car started where
    time:compare(timestamp,time:new("8:00:00")) < 0
```

The `time:compare()` function returns −1 if the first argument is less than the second, 0 if they are equal, and 1 if the first argument is greater than the second.

Absolute Time Events

Absolute time events are similar to `cron` jobs in the UNIX operating system. They are not comparisons, but events that are raised at a particular time. When you create an eventex that contains an absolute time event, you are setting an alarm that will go off at that point in time. When you use them in an eventex, the eventex will not match until that alarm occurs.

Absolute time events are set using the `at` operator:

```
at(<datetime>)
```

This creates an alarm that will raise an event at the given datetime. The eventex matches at that specified absolute time. The parameter (`<datetime>`) is specified using datetime objects from the KRL time module of the expression language.

You could specify a page view event in between 8 a.m. and 5 p.m. as follows:

```
select when pageview
        between(at(time:new("8:00:00")),
                at(time:new("17:00:00")))
```

Note

You might be wondering, "8 a.m. in what time zone, and in reference to what?" Relative alarms are referenced to the location of the user for whom the event was raised. These kinds of alarms require an endpoint on the user's smartphone or other location-sensitive device that uses salience data to determine what alarms the user cares about and raises those events.

Note that this eventex doesn't match when the page view occurs, but rather when the alarm occurs at 5 p.m.

Here are a few other examples along with an explanation of their semantics:

```
select when at(time:new("8:00:00"))
```

Match at 8 a.m. every morning.

```
select when at(time:new("Friday, 7:00:00"))
```

Match at 7 a.m. every Friday.

```
select when at(time:new("2012 May 15 7:00:00"))
```

Match at 7 a.m. on May 15, 2012.

```
select when at(time:new({day: 15}))
```

Match on the 15th of the month, every month.

You can use `before` and `after` operators with `at` to specify time delineations:

```
select when pageview
        after at(time:new("Jan 15 2011 8:00:00"))
```

When the date in a datetime string is not fully specified, you disambiguate it by assuming today. Thus, the following eventex matches any page view after 8 a.m. today:

```
select when pageview after at(time:new("8:00:00"))
```

Relative Event Expressions

Relative event expressions compare the timestamps of the event subexpressions. The `within` operator is used:

```
A <eventop> B within n <period>
```

This eventex matches only if the compound event expression A `<eventop>` B happens within the specified period. The `<eventop>` can be any of the event operators from the preceding section. (Note that the `within` semantics don't make sense for the `or` operator. Using it in that context is not syntactically wrong, but accomplishes nothing.) The `<period>` can be one of `seconds`, `minutes`, `hours`, `days`, or `weeks`. For example:

```
select when pageview url re#custserv_page.html#
        before pageview url re#homepage.html#
        within 3 hours
```

This eventex would match an event stream where a page view with a URL for the customer-service page came before the page view with a URL for the home page as long as those two events occurred within three hours of each other.

If the `within` clause is applied to a nested event, the period tested is between the first match and the last match of the entire nested eventex. For example:

```
select when inbound_call from re#^801-\d+#
    before(pageview url re#custserv_page.html# and
        pageview url re#homepage.html#)
    within 3 hours
```

This eventex would match an event stream where the page view with a URL for the customer-service page and the page view with a URL for the home page occurred after a phone call from the 801 area code, as long as the final page view occurred within three hours of the inbound call.

Conditions and Alarms

Be careful not to confuse timestamp conditions with absolute time eventexes. For example, the following two eventexes are not equivalent:

```
select when car started where
    time:compare(timestamp,time:new("8:00:00")) < 0
```

```
select when car started
        before at(time:new("8:00:00"))
```

The first will match as soon as the car is started, as long as the car is started before 8 a.m. The second will match at 8 a.m. if the car was started any time prior to 8 a.m. that same day.

Variable Arity Event Operators

The compound event operators used previously were given as infix, binary operators. (The term *infix* describes operators that are placed syntactically between their operands.) Event expressions also allow variable arity event operators that provide more convenient methods of expressing patterns over large numbers of events. (The term *arity* refers to the number of parameters a function takes. Variable arity functions can take a variable number of parameters.) Using compound operators in this way follows this pattern:

```
select when <eventop>(E₁,...Eₙ)
```

In the previous example, `<eventop>` is one of `or`, `and`, `before`, `after`, or `then`. Variable arity functions are merely a convenience because their semantics can be expressed using the binary operators. For example, the following two `select` statements are equivalent:

```
select when or(A, B, C, D, E)
```

```
select when A or (B or (C or (D or E)))
```

Note that `or` is commutative and associative. Consequently, the order of the arguments is not important for the `or` variable arity operator.

Note

Because of the way eventexes are translated to finite state machines in the current KRE implementation, the binary and operator is not associative. Specifically, the following are not equivalent as you might expect from your experience with Boolean logic:

```
select when (A and B) and C
select when A and (B and C)
```

The first will match the event sequence C;A;B but the second one will not. The second will match the event sequence A;C;B, but the first will not. The variable arity and operator has been implemented such that the sequence of events does not matter, so it should be used instead of the binary and operator when matching multiple events where sequence insensitivity is important. Future implementations of KRE could automatically collapse nested binary and operators into the variable arity and operator at compile time.

Group Operators

There are three group operators:

- **any** *n* **(E$_1$,...,E$_m$)**. This matches if any *n* of eventexes E$_1$ through E$_m$ match. In this eventex, *n* must be less than or equal to *m*. When *n* is not less than *m*, any behaves in the same way as a variable arity and operator, checking for matches of all the subexpressions. The following example shows how any can be used:

```
select when any 2 (web pageview url re#customer_support.htm#,
                phone inbound_call to re#801-649-4069#,
                email received subject re#\[help\]#)
```

This eventex would match if any two of the three enclosed simple eventexes matched. The preceding eventex has the same semantics as this compound eventex:

```
select when (web pageview url re#customer_support.htm# and
        phone inbound_call to re#801-649-4069#)
     or
        (phone inbound_call to re#801-649-4069# and
        email received subject re#\[help\]#)
     or
        (web pageview url re#customer_support.htm# and
        email received subject re#\[help\]#)
```

I think you'll agree that the first eventex is clearer than the second one is!

- **count** *n* **(E)**. This matches after *n* of eventex E have matched. When the count eventex matches, the counter is reset and the expression begins looking for n more of eventex E. Consider the following eventex:

```
select when count 3 (E)
```

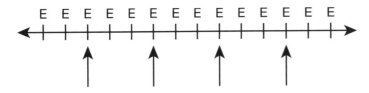

Figure 3.3
Event stream showing matches for `count(3, E)`.

The arrows on the event stream in Figure 3.3 show where this eventex would match.

■ **repeat** n **(E).** This matches after *n* of eventex E have matched. When the repeat eventex matches, the counter is not reset, and the eventex matches using a sliding window on the event stream, always matching the last *n* of the eventex given in the subexpression. Consider the following eventex:

```
select when repeat 3 (E)
```

The arrows on the event stream in Figure 3.4 show where this eventex would match.

The `repeat` operator is not particularly interesting by itself, but is mostly used in concert with aggregators introduced in the next section.

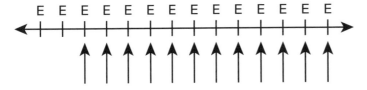

Figure 3.4
Event stream showing matches for `repeat 3 (E)`.

You can use relative time bounds with group operators, as shown in the following example:

```
select when any 2 (pageview url re#customer_support.html#,
                   inbound_call to re#801-649-4069#,
                   email received subject re#\[help\]#)
           within 3 minutes
```

This event expression has the same semantics as the `any` example given earlier, except the matches of the subexpressions must occur within three minutes.

To use absolute time bounds, the `between` operator is used:

```
select when any 2 (pageview url re#customer_support.html#,
                   inbound_call to re#801-649-4069#,
                   email received subject re#\[help\]#)
       between(at(time:new("8:00:00")),
               at(time:new("17:00:00"))))
```

This eventex would match when the events matches occurred between 8 a.m. and 5 p.m.

Variable Correlation Between Eventexes

You've seen that the `setting` clause can be used to capture values in regular expressions and bind them to variables in primitive events. When a value is bound to a variable, it can be used in subsequent subexpressions in the same eventex. (To be less ambiguous, variables bound in one eventex can be used in enclosing eventexes. Parentheses can be used to ensure that the nesting of event subexpressions is what the developer desires.) For example, suppose you want to see if someone has viewed the same page twice without having to specify the page. You don't care which page they view, as long as they view it twice.

```
select when pageview url re#/archives/(.*)#) setting (a)
     before pageview url.match(("#/archives/"+a+"#").as("regex"))
```

This eventex takes advantage of the expression language's type coercion operator, `as`, to construct a string using the value from the first eventex and then turn it into a regex for the second match.

Aggregators

For the `count` and `repeat` operators, you sometimes want to aggregate values from the enclosed subexpression. The following clauses can be used to accumulate values:

- **E max(<var>).** Accumulate the maximum value of the captured value in the variable <var>. The following eventex will match using a sliding window of five withdrawal events and set the variable m to have the maximum amount:

  ```
  select when repeat 5 (withdrawal amount re#$(\d+\.\d\d)#) max(m)
  ```

  As you saw earlier, the `repeat` operator will continue to match for every withdrawal event after the first five. The variable m will always contain the maximum value of the last five withdrawal events.

- **E min(<var>).** Accumulate the minimum value of the captured value in the variable <var>. The following eventex will match five withdrawal events using a sliding window and set the variable m to have the minimum amount:

  ```
  select when repeat 5 (withdrawal amount re#$(\d+\.\d\d)#) min(m)
  ```

- **E sum(<var>).** Accumulate the sum of the captured values in the variable <var>. The following eventex will match five withdrawal events and set the variable m to have the sum of the amounts:

```
select when count 5 (withdrawal amount re#$(\d+\.\d\d)#) sum(m)
```

Because count was used rather than repeat, the eventex will sum the amounts of every five withdrawals rather than the last five.

- **E avg(<var>).** Accumulate the average of the captured values in the variable <var>. The following eventex will match five withdrawal events and set the variable m to have the average of the amounts:

```
select when repeat 5 (withdrawal amount re#$(\d+\.\d\d)#) avg(m)
```

- **E push(<var>).** Append the captured values to the variable <var>. The following eventex will match five withdrawal events and set the variable m to the array containing the amounts:

```
select when repeat 5 (withdrawal amount re#$(\d+\.\d\d)#) push(m)
```

If the eventex to which the aggregator is attached captures more than one variable, the first variable captured is used in the aggregator. Only one aggregator can be used in an event expression.

EVENTEX EXAMPLES

The following examples give scenarios and sample eventexes that might be used to recognize each scenario. All these assume the presence of endpoints that can recognize events of interest and that are properly configured.

Example 1: Large Withdrawals

This scenario is fairly common and a feature built into many banking sites. The eventex selects when there is a withdrawal event where the parameter amount is over a certain limit.

```
select when bank withdrawal where amount > 100
```

Example 2: Too Many Withdrawals

You may be interested to know when the number of withdrawals from an account passes a certain threshold during the business day:

```
select when count 4 (bank withdrawal)
    between(at(time:new("8:00:00 MST")),
            at(time:new("17:00:00 MST"))))
```

Example 3: Too Many Withdrawals in 24 Hours

Rather than focusing on the business day, which might be too specific for a world of ATMs, you can use a relative time expression to match when there are four withdrawals in a 24-hour period:

```
select when count 4 (bank withdrawal) within 24 hours
```

Example 4: Too Many Withdrawals over a Limit

You can add a limit to match only a specific number of withdrawals that are over a threshold ($100 in this case):

```
select when count 4 (bank withdrawal where amount > 100) within 24 hours
```

Example 5: Withdrawal after a Deposit

A withdrawal following a deposit matches when the withdrawal amount is greater than the deposit:

```
select when bank deposit amount re#(\d+)# setting(dep_amt)
    before bank withdrawal where amount > dep_amt
```

Example 6: Withdrawal after a Deposit with a Limit

A withdrawal following a deposit matches when the withdrawal amount is greater than the deposit or greater than a threshold:

```
select when bank deposit amount re#(\d+)# setting(dep_amt)
    before bank withdrawal where amount > dep_amt || amount > 100
```

Example 7: Phone Call with a Follow-Up SMS

You are interested in knowing when a phone call is received within one hour of an SMS being received from the same number:

```
select when inbound_call from re#(.*)# setting (num)
    and sms_received where from.match("/#{num}/".as("regex"))
  within 1 hour
```

Example 8: Too Many Phone Calls

Match when there is more than a threshold number of phone calls in a given time period:

```
select when repeat 5 (phone inbound_call) within 20 minutes
```

Example 9: Too Many Phone Calls from One Number

Match when there is more than a threshold number of phone calls from the same number in a given time period:

```
select when repeat 5 (phone inbound_call from re#.*#) push(nums)
        within 20 minutes
```

Note

> You don't actually check that the numbers are the same in the eventex; you merely push them onto an array. A condition in the rule associated with this eventex can check to ensure they're the same. This is a good example that some complicated event scenarios require more complicated processing than can be accomplished in an eventex alone. See Chapter 6 for more information on rules.

Example 10: Looking at Travel Sites

Match `pageview` events that appear to be focusing on travel-related sites:

```
select when any 2 (pageview url #orbitz#,
        pageview url re#kayak#,
        pageview url re#priceline#,
        pageview url re#travelocity#,
        pageview url re#expedia#)
```

Example 11: Looking for Support

Match when the user calls the support number within one day of visiting the support Web site:

```
select when phone inbound_call from app:support_number
        and pageview where url.match(app:support_website)
        within 1 day
```

Note that this example uses application variables for the support number and Web site regular expressions. The use of the and operator means that either could happen first.

Example 12: Find News Articles That Affect Stock Price

Match when an RSS feed contains a story that includes a stock-ticker symbol and the price of that same stock goes up by more than 2 percent within 10 minutes:

```
select when rss item content re#Stock Symbol: (\w+)# setting (symbol)
        before stock price_change
            where direction eq "up" && ticker eq symbol && percent > 2
        within 10 minutes
```

MATCHING SCENARIOS

The examples from the preceding section show some of the power of using eventexes to match complex event scenarios. Eventexes make expressing the desired scenarios succinct and unambiguous.

The use of eventexes enables you to create dynamic queries that can filter the stream of real-time event data, matching only the event scenarios that are relevant to the task at hand. Being able to look for relevant event patterns is the first step toward managing and harnessing a deluge of real-time events. In coming chapters, you'll discover the power of not only matching event scenarios, but also processing them to achieve the user's purpose.

ENDNOTES

1. For a history of `grep`, see the Wikipedia article at http://en.wikipedia.org/wiki/ Grep.
2. Luckham, David. (2002). *The Power of Events*. Addison-Wesley.

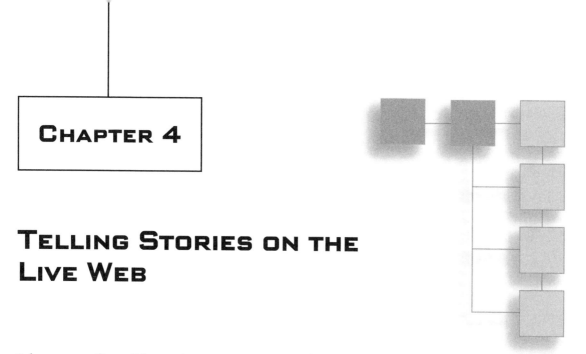

CHAPTER 4

TELLING STORIES ON THE LIVE WEB

I love campfires. I love singing songs around the campfire. I love the quiet time of reflection, as the coals burn low. And I love the campfire stories. The best campfire stories involve the audience in how the story plays out.

The Live Web is full of stories. And the best part is that, like a good campfire story, Live Web stories aren't just written by the developer. Users participate and, in the process, help create new stories that the developer could never have imagined.

In *Storytime on the Interwebs*,[1] Venkatesh Rao makes an important connection between "plural, interconnected and dynamic 'mesh' experiences"—what we'd call Live Web applications—and stories. The relationship is more than analogy. Every Live Web experience is a story. Knowing that, you can use the techniques of storytelling to better understand the Live Web.

Every story has certain components. Stories have a purpose, intent, or moral—the thing that defines them. Stories also have a context that creates a model of what information is relevant. They need a tempo to move them along and define the timeframe. Stories have a narrative structure that connects things together through the beginning, middle, and end, as well as connecting past, present, and future. And stories have characters—protagonists, antagonists, and supporting roles.

Building applications is, at its best, storytelling. The best application developers are storytellers. That's why techniques like storyboarding work as well in designing software as they do in creating books or movies. The exciting thing about the Live Web is that it gives people an opportunity to tell better stories than ever before.

ME AND MY DATA

The Live Web is, of necessity, more personal that the static Web. Good identity is foundational to the Live Web's support for great user participation, which is to say great storytelling. Identity supports the story's characters and is the basis for much of the story's context and content.

Identity has been part of computer applications since timesharing on mainframes. Recently, however, identity's gotten a face-lift that's been dubbed *user-controlled identity*. User-controlled identity provides the Live Web with better, more comprehensive information about the story's protagonists, their intent, and their context.

When I speak to an audience, I often include a slide that I title "A brief (and mostly wrong) history of digital identity." The slide has two bullets:

- 1993: There wasn't any.
- 1995: Cookies were invented and we said "good enough."

While this is said tongue in cheek, it always gets a laugh because many people relate to it. Cookies have provided the primary means of establishing online identity.

Cookies get a lot of bad press, but in fact, they are simply a way of creating context in a stateless protocol like HTTP. Cookies are a form of unauthenticated pseudonymous identity. The RESTful nature of the Web dictates that clients are responsible for maintaining context and sending it along with every request. The server reconstitutes the state for any given request each time, as shown in Figure 4.1. This may sound wasteful, but it's a key driver of the loosely coupled nature of the Web.

Note

> REST is short for REpresentational State Transfer, and is a description of the architecture of the Web. The term was introduced by Roy Fielding, one of the principal authors of the HTTP specification. RESTful systems have certain properties, including the requirement that servers not be responsible for maintaining session state.

I will call the subject of an identifier an *entity* to be as general as possible. Entities can be people, organizations, software programs, Web services, or even machines. In the world of security, we often think of entities laying claim to an identity to gain access to one resource or another. On the Live Web, identity is necessary to correlate information *for* the entity, which does involve accessing resources, but the resource itself is not the end goal.

Entities usually have multiple online identities. Identities usually have an associated set of attributes, preferences, and traits. On the static Web, with its overreliance on

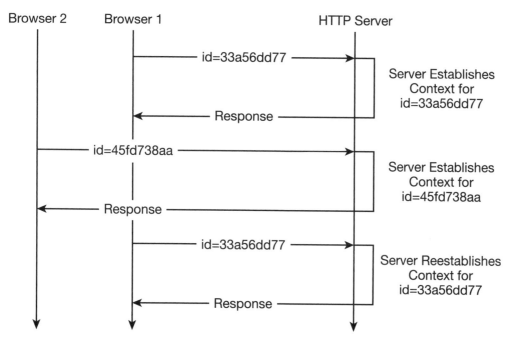

Figure 4.1
Web clients maintain identity context, and servers reconstitute it each time.

cookies, people are inundated with multiple online identities. This has led not only to a problem of too many passwords, but also to an issue with duplicate attributes—often out of date—that have to be reentered at each new site. To be effective, the Live Web must solve the static Web's "multiple personality disorder."

User-Controlled Identity

One of the hottest trends of the last several years is user-controlled identity. User-controlled identity places the user structurally inside decisions regarding the user's identity information. This is a sharp contrast to how enterprise systems usually talk about users behind their back.

User-controlled identity systems are coming along just in time. Organizations are finding more and more that storing and managing personal data is expensive, prone to errors and inaccuracies, and undermines rather than strengthens the relationship of trust they want with their customers.

Examples of user-controlled identity technologies include Information Cards, OpenID, Webfinger, and OAuth. The last is familiar—in operation, if not in name—to anyone who's linked their Twitter or Facebook profiles to one of the many ancillary services that have sprung up. For example, I use a blogging service called Posterous. Whenever

I post something on my Posterous blog, I want the post to be automatically sent to Twitter. Twitter uses OAuth to allow this kind of linking so that I don't have to give Posterous my Twitter login credentials and they don't have to store them. When I ask Posterous to link to my Twitter account, I am redirected to Twitter and asked if they should grant Posterous access to my account, as shown in Figure 4.2. Behind the scenes, OAuth is being used to conduct the ceremony in a secure and private way. Each time I post something to my Posterous blog, Posterous uses OAuth credentials to update my Twitter status. I can easily revoke a credential for one link without upsetting the others. A few years ago, this kind of interaction was completely ad hoc, and thus too complicated to do reliably and repeatedly. Now, with OAuth, such interactions between online services are easy and commonplace.

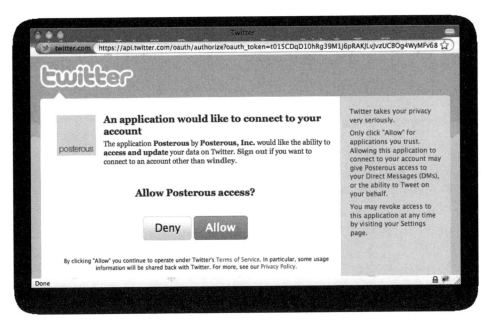

Figure 4.2
The Twitter OAuth page, asking if I will grant Posterous access to my Twitter account.

User-controlled identity protocols will get more sophisticated. The User-Managed Access (UMA) standard, for example, promises even more user control by enabling users to manage access they've granted various services from one central console as well as by giving users increased say over what is accessed and when.

The ability to link the data you care about and then grant access to the right pieces of that data provides Live Web applications with a more complete picture of who you are and what's important to you—context.

Personal Data

People usually speak of identity in the singular, but in fact, everyone has multiple identities. I view all of my accounts as linked together, and they seem like different facets of my overall identity. The problem is that the only thing linking them together is me, the person. From the outside looking in, they appear disjointed and incomplete. My bank sees one set of attributes and my employer sees another. Occasionally they link up, such as when I give my employer my checking-account number for direct deposit, but they mostly exist in frustrating isolation.

This may seem like a good thing from a privacy standpoint, but everyone's suffered the hassle of having data in one place that they can't use somewhere else. The overall message of user-controlled identity is this: You don't have to sacrifice privacy for convenience. You can link all this data through an online agent under your control.

With the advent of user-controlled identity services, one can envision a future in which users more freely link together their personal data, stored in online services. Personal data has the power to make online interactions more meaningful, and user-controlled identity will make such sharing more private and secure. As a simple example, imagine a world in which online ads are random compared to a world in which they are based on things that interest you. Laying aside privacy concerns, most people would rather see relevant ads than random ones.

People are already becoming socialized to the idea of keeping data about themselves online through services like Facebook and LinkedIn. If you want someone's current email address or phone number, chances are they've kept their Facebook page up to date but haven't contacted you so you can update your personal list. The idea that there will be one place for canonical versions of personal data is gaining momentum.

OAuth and more-sophisticated protocols like UMA enable people to assemble virtual "stores" of personal data from the various services they use around the Web. These virtual stores also enable you to augment the attributes that various services keep about you and assemble as complete a picture as you'd like, keeping your data under your control.

Better Golf Through Software

Better access to personal data promises to completely change multiple aspects of people's lives. For example, David Siegel describes a golfing scenario in which your clubs, bags, and even the balls and green cups communicate with each other, transmitting information about your game to a personal data store in the cloud.[2] In this scenario, shown in Figure 4.3, the score is calculated as data comes in during your game. You see the score on your phone. You don't calculate the strokes; rather, your strokes—and even how far your ball is from the hole—are calculated for you. Your phone can even help you find your ball in the tall grass. After the game, you can replay it on a map of the course and get analysis about how you could have played better. While the system doesn't guarantee that your game will improve, it will keep your fellow golfers honest about their game. If this scenario seems far-fetched, think back to the last time you went bowling. Bowling is almost to this point. No doubt golf, on which people spend millions of dollars a year, will find its way to being completely instrumented.

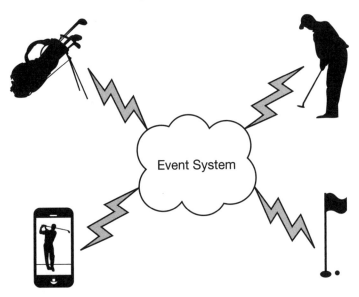

Figure 4.3
Better golf through software.

As this example illustrates, even the most mundane personal data is likely to find its way online. Endomondo records information about my bike rides and puts it online. The Withings Bodyscale has WiFi built in and pushes your weight to the Web every time you weigh yourself. A FitBit will record your daily activity and push it to an online account. As the world becomes increasingly instrumented, more and more of this kind of data will find its way into the cloud.

Even greater instrumentation is only as far away as your phone. Most of today's smart phones are really sophisticated mobile "sensing" platforms that also happen to make calls. App stores are full of software that uses those sensors to collect data on the user's behalf and then push it into the cloud.

It's All Semantics

Beyond linking data, you also need to understand it. Consider the golfing example. Suppose my Calloway driver uses the term "swing," but my Ping putter uses the term "stroke." If you don't know those two terms mean the same thing, then linking them does no good because there will be no way to reliably use the data.

When people talk about the Semantic Web, they are referring to this problem: creating a clear understanding of what a name means in a specific context. For data to be semantic, terms must be tagged in an unambiguous way. (Some also impose the condition that the format be royalty free.) Thousands of people have been working to make the semantic markup of data a reality.

To illustrate, suppose the golfer from the previous example also enjoys dancing. How do you know that "swing" means "stroke" in one context, but is the same thing as "hop" in another? That's the job of ontologies, or semantic dictionaries. The context of the link determines which is the correct answer. (See Figure 4.4.)

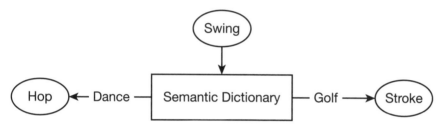

Figure 4.4
Semantic markup can link terms like "swing" and "stroke."

As I write this, very little of the Semantic Web exists, although work has been ongoing for a decade. The good news is, you don't have to wait. Most of what you want to achieve in creating the Live Web can still be done, albeit with a little more work in understanding and translating proprietary formats. More importantly, the Live Web will create use cases that demand semantic markup and thus drive development in practical ways with real-world examples.

Purpose and Intent

Since its inception, the primary metaphor of the Web has been location. But people don't get online to go to a server. They get online to get something done—to achieve a purpose. Application developers have long understood the importance of purpose, or intent, in creating applications that meet users' needs.

Consider the word processor I'm using. In building the word-processing program, the designer anticipated my intent to write and designed a program that would meet that need. Software applications are designed as a collection of use cases, where the coarse-grained intention is broken down into smaller operations that provide for the smaller goals a user meets as part of accomplishing the larger task.

Use cases anticipate the user's intent. My word processor has use cases like "enter text," "spell check," "format," "review," and so on. Designers strive to create user interfaces that make the program's features meet users' intentions in the most natural way possible.

When to Bind

Most of the time, designers fail to perfectly understand the user's intent. This might manifest itself as a missing feature or a feature that fails to fully meet the user's need. People are often baffled and hindered by a software designer's failure to understand and meet their particular needs and intent.

The problem is twofold:

- The designer is working months, maybe years, in advance of when the user will use the application. Plug-ins and patches are one way that software attempts to mitigate this problem.
- The designer has to please everyone, not any particular person, leading to the "least common denominator" problem. Menus and preferences are methods for letting people personalize applications and how they work.

You can think of this problem as an early-binding problem. The designer is choosing (binding) a solution well in advance of when the user actually has a problem and trying to anticipate the problem as closely as possible. In contrast, a late-binding approach chooses the solution as near as possible to when the user wants a problem solved in hopes of more closely matching her intent. Plug-ins and configuration are ways that designers move decisions about how an application will act closer to the time the user wants a problem solved.

Coupling

Coupling between software components is one of the primary reasons for inflexible applications. Whenever a software module references a class, object, method, procedure, variable, or constant from another module, a coupling is created between them. Coupling makes software systems more difficult to maintain and understand.

Coupling is just as big a problem for data as it is for programs. The golf scenario I described earlier provides an example. If you have to get everyone to agree up front that they're going to use the word "stroke" instead of "swing," you've created a tightly bound situation for the data interactions.

You can never remove all coupling in a computer system. Coupling is necessary to make computer systems perform useful work. Nevertheless, the kind of coupling used makes a great difference in the application's flexibility and fitness for your individual purposes.

Software systems are defined as tightly or loosely coupled—nomenclature that makes the problem seem like a simple choice along a single dimension.[3] In fact, over the course of designing any software system, myriad decisions are made that affect the level of coupling.

While coupling is inevitable, some forms of coupling are more pernicious than others. Live Web applications reduce coupling between components in a software system by relying on interaction strategies that produce more desirable coupling. These interaction strategies produce applications that are more responsible, personalized, and flexible. Here are a few examples of these interaction strategies:

- Live Web applications use an event-based interface rather than relying solely on the Web's traditional user-driven, request-response interface.

- Live Web applications are dynamically coupled through the event-based interface, providing for the late binding of components interested in a particular event.

- References on the Live Web are pattern-based. The eventexes in Chapter 3, "Event Expressions: Filtering the Event Stream," provide patterns that query the event stream in real-time. Data references, where possible, are made unambiguous through semantic descriptions.

- Semantic descriptions provide for names that are self-describing rather than requiring that everyone agree up front on what names to use and what they mean.

- Interactions on the Live Web are brokered through intermediaries, where possible, to allow actors to join or leave a particular interaction without unnecessary connection overhead.

- Evaluation sequence on the Live Web is emergent. This is in contrast to evaluation on the static Web, where it is explicit. Again, this is a consequence of the event model of evaluation, in which components can listen to the event stream and interpret events as they see fit. Because the specific arrangement of components in an evented system is fluid, so is the sequence in which the evaluations that are performed.

- Components on the Live Web react to events as they occur rather than interacting in a pre-planned manner.

- The coordination of components on the Live Web is distributed and depends on a number of factors. These include what components are taking part in the computation and what data elements are available.

These strategies are summarized in Table 4.1. As you employ these strategies on the Live Web, you create applications that are more loosely coupled and consequently more flexible in meeting the user's intent.

Table 4.1   Coupling on the Static Web vs. the Live Web[4]

	Static Web	Live Web
Interface	Request-response	Event-based
Binding	Early, static	Late, dynamic
References	Procedure call, named	Pattern-based, semantic
Ontology (interpretation)	By prior agreement	Self-describing
Interaction	Direct	Brokered
Evaluation (sequencing)	Explicit	Emergent
Behavior	Planned	Reactive
Coordination	Centrally managed	Distributed

CONTEXT AND CORRELATION

Understanding what information is relevant to a particular story is critical to creating a story that is compelling and interesting. Context isn't just about what you include, it's also about what you leave out. In the article mentioned at the start of this chapter, Rao says the following:

> When my sister and I were kids, she used to ask apparently odd questions about scenes in movies. Say two people are chatting over tea on the screen. Cut to a scene where one of them is no longer holding a teacup. My sister would ask, "What happened to the teacup?"
>
> The answer is, "Who cares?"
>
> Presumably the character put it down, and somebody later washed it. It doesn't matter. If the teacup *were* significant, the storyteller would usually foreshadow events to come by noting it without explanation (such as a close-up shot of the cup after the people have left the room; perhaps signaling a potential poisoning).
>
> So context is not merely about retaining developing momentum, it is about doing so selectively. You have to decide what is significant in the story.

Context is the model we use to make sense of the overabundance of information that any system faces. Context is related to intent. For example, if I show you a handful of

URLs, you will interpret them differently if I tell you my intent is to plan a trip than if I tell you my intent is to write a research report for my international relations class. The context changes, and with that change, so, too, does the relevance of other information we might run across.

When people tell stories on the Live Web, they use context to relate events to each other in meaningful ways. One of the real powers of event-based programming is the ability to contextually correlate events. Correlation goes beyond filtering because it enables you to look for patterns in the event stream that are meaningful for a particular purpose.

While single events, like `web:pageview()`, `mail:received()`, or `phone:inbound_call()` are interesting, you can create even more interesting applications when you start to correlate one event with another. This is analogous to building Web applications. While there are plenty of Web applications that don't require that a Web site maintain any kind of state or context between service calls, most interesting Web applications do. In the case of the Web site, you correlate requests to the server to group those requests and relate them to each other. (Think of a shopping cart, for example.)

When people speak of correlating things, they're talking about finding the relationship between them. When they correlate data in statistics, they're looking to see how strongly two or more data values (like price and volume sold) are related to each other. Often, you can even find clues about the nature of the relationship between the things being correlated.

On the Live Web, you're looking for a series of events that have a meaningful relationship. You can correlate events in at least three ways:

- **Events can be correlated by entity.** All the events for a particular person, corporation, or thing can be related to each other.

- **Events can be correlated explicitly through event expressions (or eventexes).** Eventexes declare specific relationships between their constituent events.

- **Events can be correlated implicitly through shared data.** When a user installs multiple applications that have data in common (say, a to-do list, a Google calendar, or an email account), the events for those applications become implicitly linked through a shared context.

Entity Correlation

Entity correlation is the most obvious type. Correlating events by entity requires that you identify, at least pseudonymously, on whose behalf the events are being raised. I say "on whose behalf" because entities rarely raise events by themselves. There is usually a client of some kind involved. Because the word *client* is closely associated with the notion of client-server computing, we say "endpoint" instead.

One of the primary responsibilities of an endpoint is managing the identity context. An entity controls a number of endpoints. Those endpoints maintain information about the entity for whom they work. As endpoints raise events, they also identify the entity with which they are associated.

Even when the endpoint isn't configured to specifically know about the entity's identity, events can often be correlated with an entity using information contained in the event. For example a `phone:inbound_call()` will contain the number of the calling person, which might be used to correlate the call with an established context.

Correlating events for an entity enables personalization of the interaction and provides a thread upon which otherwise disconnected events can be strung. Entity data is also useful for bringing relevant information to a context. A particular entity owns certain email accounts, calendars, and so on. Interacting with those APIs enriches the context of the interaction.

The correlation of events by entity is the key idea in a personal event network. Endpoints raise events that other things that belong to you see. Your things raise events in *your event network*. The Live Web apps activated on your personal event network represent your intentions and interests—your story. These apps choreograph the interactions among the products and services you own and use. A personal event network does entity correlation automatically at the infrastructure level, freeing developers from this task.

But as powerful as correlating events by entity is, there might be thousands of events raised in a day for any given entity. Consequently, entity correlation is simply the first step. Developers must look for a stronger correlation than mere entity correlation when creating Live Web applications.

Explicit Eventex Correlation

As you saw in Chapter 3, an event expression, or eventex, describes an explicit relationship between two or more events. Whether or not those events are correlated through an entity, an eventex established the conditions that correlate those events. For example, consider the following eventex:

```
select when web pageview "support/main.html"
   before mail received subject "\[help\]"
```

The intent of this eventex is to select a pattern of events where the user has visited the main support page before sending an email that has [help] in the subject. Entity correlation is necessary for this eventex to be meaningful. After all, it's hard to think of why you'd want to know when a person emails support after someone else has visited that Web page. But entity correlation is insufficient to convey the complete requirement. The eventex further correlates web:pageview() and mail: received() temporally, stating that one must come before the other.

As another example, consider the following eventex:

```
select when web pageview "/archives/(\w+).html"
           setting(pagename)
  before web pageview "/archives/#{pagename}.html"
```

This eventex not only correlates the two page views by entity (the default behavior) and temporally through the eventex operator before, it also correlates the two page views by requiring that they be to the same page. The eventex doesn't care which page is visited, only that it's visited twice.

Eventexes are analogous to SQL. SQL statements are declarative and give patterns in a pool of static data that are meaningful. Similarly, an eventex is declarative and gives patterns that describe meaningful sequences of events. Correlating events establishes context for the Live Web.

Implicit Correlation Through Context

While eventexes establish context by describing patterns of meaningful events, context can also be used to correlate events implicitly. In many ways, implicit event correlation is the most powerful because it can enable serendipitous interactions. Serendipitous interactions provide for use cases that designers didn't—and perhaps couldn't—anticipate. The inherent loose coupling of event-based systems and their resilience in the face of errors enables serendipitous interaction and is one of the primary ways that Live Web applications respond dynamically and flexibly to user intent.

Context is not explicitly bound to a specific process or event stream. Rather, context is relevant to multiple processes through implicit relationships. Knowing, for example, the time of day, the weather, the prime rate, the commodity prices, or that it's Super Bowl Sunday provides information that can be used to correlate events. When developers create Live Web applications, the logic of the code provides for these correlations.

As you've seen, one of the significant benefits of event-based systems is that they exhibit extreme loose coupling. To understand this, consider the situation in which you want your DVD player to pause when you get a phone call. Assuming each has an API, programming your phone to send a "pause" command to the DVD is easy enough. Now suppose you decide you want to also raise the room lights when the phone call comes in; in that case, you have to program the phone to also send a "raise lights" command to the room lights. Each new interaction requires a point-to-point connection and an explicit command from one system to another. For n endpoints, there would be $n^2/2$ possible interactions that would need to be explicitly managed. These tightly coupled connections make changes difficult. Change out the DVD player with a new Blu-Ray player, and every device sending commands has to be reprogrammed.

Now, as discussed before, imagine instead that the phone merely raises a `phone:inbound_call()` event. The DVD and lights can both listen for such events and do the right thing. Add something else to the mix, and it, too, can easily listen for the `phone:inbound_call()` event and do whatever is right for it. Nothing else needs to be reprogrammed or even told the new device is there as long as it can listen for events of interest. Each actor in the event-driven system interprets the event according to its own context and purpose—the semantics of the device are more completely encapsulated within it. With an evented system, the number of interactions is linear for a given number of endpoints. Loose coupling leads to simpler, more flexible systems that are also more tolerant of errors, including configuration mistakes.

In an event-driven architecture, the responsibility for flow control shifts from the event source, or sender, to the listener. Event-driven architectures distribute and delegate flow control to event listeners. This method for creating Web applications represents a substantial departure from the traditional way that developers have scripted them. In fact, scripted is the wrong way to think about event-based systems. Any given application is scripted to a particular set of use cases, anticipated by the developer. But the interaction of applications on the event network of the Live Web isn't scripted; rather, it emerges from the individual behavior of the several actors.

Live Web applications don't execute in a vacuum. Instead, they operate in an environment with other applications, endpoints, APIs, and data sources. These various actors consume and propagate events according to their individual programmed functionality. Thus, an event can become correlated—entangled—with other events through the interaction of the various actors in the environment. Changing the environment by replacing one component or adding another has an impact on the overall behavior and thus the correlation of events.

At first, this may seem like a recipe for disaster. But some of that trepidation is born of our experience with tightly coupled systems. Creating event-based systems that respond in a certain way is a talent more akin to throwing a really good party than that of directing a play. You have less control over what happens at the party, but you also have less chance of things going completely off the rails and crashing or falling flat.

An event-based system in which something isn't quite right is more likely to do most things well, some things okay, and a few things poorly. A request-response system in which something isn't quite right is more likely to just not work at all. Event-driven systems are more resilient. Their failures are more linear. That is, small mistakes are likely to result in small, rather than large, failures. This property allows for greater flexibility and later binding of system components because their interactions don't have to be planned, scripted, and otherwise carefully considered to prevent utter failure.

An Example

Consider the event-driven system shown in Figure 4.5. The system is composed of two Live Web applications: one for managing a to-do list and one for watching emails. In addition to the two apps, there's the to-do list itself, a cloud-based service with an API that has the ability to raise events.

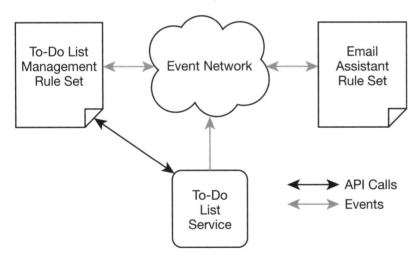

Figure 4.5
Interactions with a to-do service.

The to-do list service isn't a Web application; it's just a Web service with a management API and the ability to raise events when certain things happen in the to-do list (todo:added_item(), todo:deleted_item(), etc.). The to-do list management application is fairly straightforward, offering ways to add items to the to-do list and cross them off or reschedule them. Most of the events it processes would be related to the interface (not shown) that the user manipulates to manage the list. This could be a Web site, a mobile app, a desktop application, or all of these.

The email assistant application listens for `mail:received()` events. When the message contains a to-do item, it raises an event called `todo:new_item()` that contains the to-do item and other relevant information, such as the message ID. (The email parsing application might use microformats, RDFa, or some other semantic markup technology to recognize to-do items in email messages.)

The to-do list management application sees the `todo:new_item()` event and adds it to the to-do list via the API. When that is complete, the to-do list service raises the `todo:added_item()` event. The email assistant application has been programmed to look for those events and reacts by creating a draft email responding to the original email.

The user is also notified (using yet another event) that the draft has been created and needs approval. Because the system notifies the user with an event rather than by directly sending an email or SMS, the user can choose the means used to respond to that event. Perhaps an SMS message is sent. Perhaps the event is merely logged. Once the user has modified and approved the draft email, it will sit in the Draft folder, and will be automatically sent when the email assistant sees the `todo:deleted_item()` event for that to-do item.

Now, imagine that the user adds a to-do item "Send an email to Bob Jones about the company party." Of course, the email assistant can listen for the `todo:new_item()` event and automatically create a draft to Bob with the right subject and have it waiting for the user in the Draft folder when she's ready to work on this task. The email assistant can also know, via the event's parameters, which to-do item is associated with the task and, when the email is sent, send a `todo:done_item()` event. The to-do list management rule set sees the event and automatically marks the to-do item as "done" via the API.

In this example, the to-do list management application and to-do list service function perfectly well with or without the email assistant. In fact, they never know the email assistant exists or that it's listening to events from the to-do list. If it fails, the to-do list system keeps working.

On the other hand, the email assistant knows there may be a to-do list available and uses events to listen for its workings and to interact with it. The email assistant doesn't know about the to-do list service or its API, only the events. Presumably, the email assistant does things other than interact with the to-do system. Consequently, while it won't be as useful without a to-do list application installed, it will keep working because any to-do events it raises will simply be ignored, and none of the to-do events for which it's listening will ever be raised.

When both applications are installed, events that are otherwise only entity correlated, such as `mail:received()` and `todo:new_item()`, are implicitly correlated by the context established through the interaction of the two applications and the to-do service. The correlation occurs because of the particular applications the user has installed and how they interact.

Impromptu Theater

One of the most important lessons of the World Wide Web is that there is real power and value in the emergent behavior of loosely coupled actors. That power has not yet been fully realized for Web applications. Contextually correlated events can bring that power to applications.

Individual Live Web applications use context to correlate events in ways that meet the user's intent. Because of the loosely coupled, dynamic, late-binding nature of the Live Web, suites of applications can combine to serendipitously meet the user's purpose.

The use of events allows developers to create Live Web applications that are more robust than with the request-response architectures of the static Web. While explicit event correlation by entity or event expressions can create interesting applications, the implicit correlations that emerge from the interaction of the actors in the event-based system are very compelling.

I started off using storytelling as a metaphor for application development. By this point, you may have realized that while the story is there, correlating events through context is often more extemporaneous than it is carefully scripted. While there's a story, the developer is only partly in charge. The developer's role is more akin to the way a director might get the ball rolling in impromptu theater and then let the actors develop the story within certain guidelines.

Event-based systems are inherently powerful because of the likelihood of emergent behavior. This is new territory for developers who are used to scripting a precise story, but the most interesting behaviors will emerge from unanticipated interactions between actors.

Endnotes

1. Rao, Venkatesh. (2011). Storytime on the Interwebs. *Building 43 Blog.* http://www.building43.com/blogs/2011/01/14/storytime-on-the-interwebs.
2. Siegel, David. (2009). *Pull: The Power of the Semantic Web to Transform Your Business.* Portfolio Hardcover.

3. For a thorough treatment of coupling in software systems, see Chapter 1 of Ted Faison's *Event-Based Programming: Taking Events to the Limit*, Apress, 2006.

4. Carlos Perez used a table like this to capture the differences between tightly coupled and loosely coupled SOA architectures in "Principles of Loosely Coupled APIs," July 3, 2003. http://www.artima.com/weblogs/viewpost.jsp?thread=6544.

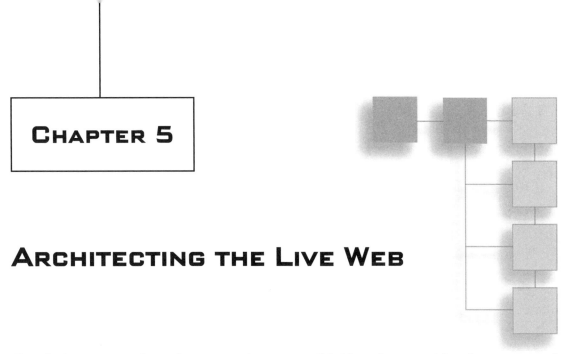

CHAPTER 5

ARCHITECTING THE LIVE WEB

Correlating events through context is a powerful idea that provides the conceptual framework for the Live Web. Making these concepts real and actionable requires an operational model, a system, that embodies these concepts and provides an architecture for achieving your goals.

In his influential dissertation describing the architecture of the Web, Roy Fielding made the following observations about software architectures:[1]

- A software architecture is an abstraction of the run-time elements of a software system during some phase of its operation. A system may be composed of many levels of abstraction and many phases of operation, each with its own software architecture.

- A software architecture is defined by a configuration of architectural elements— components, connectors, and data—constrained in their relationships to achieve a desired set of architectural properties.

This chapter defines the components, connectors, and data, along with their configuration, that comprise a functional architecture for personal event networks and, as a result, the Live Web.

REQUIREMENTS OF THE LIVE WEB

The preceding chapters have laid out the primary requirements for building Live Web applications. By way of review, here is a summary:

- **Evented.** Events provide for loose coupling. Loose coupling provides for components that work together with less configuration and less management.

Event-based models match the real world and people's expectations of temporal relations.

- **Entity-centric.** In many cases, correlating events requires that you know the relevance of that event to a particular entity. The Live Web is built on identity. Entity-centric events give rise to personal event networks. Without entity-centricity you cannot create Live Web applications that respond to things people find interesting, important, or relevant.

- **Extensible.** Participation in the Live Web will come from every quarter. All participants must be able to extend the underlying model in ways that suit their particular needs. Extensibility is a critical property for reducing coupling.

- **Scalable.** The Live Web must scale to include every person and organization, along with everything that they deem important.

- **Semantic.** No central authority can determine a single ontology for events and their attributes. The only hope for creating loosely coupled applications that work together without centralized planning is to rely on semantic technologies to achieve linkage between similar concepts with different names.

- **Universal.** Events and context can come from any device and any system. Because your goal is to create contextual continuity throughout an entire experience, the Live Web should work across Web sites and across devices. The Live Web should enable participation of things you don't think of as "being on the Web" right now.

Requirements in Action

You can more fully appreciate these requirements by viewing them in light of the event-driven scenario involving phone calls and stereos presented in Chapter 2, "Events on the Live Web":

> The entertainment system was belting out the Beatles' "We Can Work It Out" when the phone rang. When Pete answered, his phone broadcasted a message to all local devices that indicated it had received a call. His stereo responded by turning down the volume. His sister, Lucy, was on the line from the doctor's office….

Let's extend the scenario somewhat and assume Pete has a DVR that works this way too: When he gets a phone call, the show that's playing is automatically paused.

- **Evented.** Pete's phone sent events rather than making explicit requests.

- **Entity-centric.** Pete's stereo responded to his event, not his neighbor's.

- **Extensible.** Pete bought the phone, stereo, and his DVR at different times and from different vendors. This isn't a package.

- **Scalable.** Pete isn't the only person who has this system. Anyone can buy the event-driven components and use them. Millions of people might own systems like this. Manufacturers, developers, and others are free to build systems that interact with it.

- **Semantic.** Pete bought the stereo and DVR from different manufacturers. One understands an `inbound_call` event, while the other is listening for a `call_received` event. Semantic information ensured that these were interpreted unambiguously.

- **Universal.** Pete's system consisted of myriad devices that did not come as part of a "system." They participate as equals on the Live Web.

Practical Considerations

In addition to the preceding list of requirements for the Live Web, there are also several practical requirements for a functional architecture for the Live Web:

- **Efficiency.** When you consider all the participants in even modest evented scenarios, efficiency is paramount for the Live Web to be practical. An event network can contain large numbers of event messages. Many of these are irrelevant to a given application. Filtering the event stream ensures that salient messages are transmitted to processors that care.

- **Openness.** For the Live Web to be useful, it must be ubiquitous. For the Live Web to be ubiquitous, it needs an open architecture so that anyone can participate without license restrictions.

- **Security.** The creation of an event-driven architecture has unique security requirements. You wouldn't want unauthorized events to control your devices or services.

- **Accommodation.** The Live Web will be built one piece at a time. It will not spring up at once from nothing. It must be accommodating of existing computing models and data services.

THE KINETIC EVENT ARCHITECTURE

The Kinetic Event Architecture (KEA) is a concrete architecture designed to meet the aforementioned requirements. KEA is an open-source event system for the Live Web. KEA has anticipated and made allowances for most of the issues you'll face in creating evented systems that put people and their context on a level playing field with other participants on the Web.

Certainly, KEA isn't the only way to solve this problem. As with any architecture, KEA has made certain assumptions that, if changed, would result in a different end result. But KEA will provide a structured basis for discussion and building examples in the coming chapters.

Event-processing systems enable programmatic reactions to events. The abstract event-processing architecture described in Chapter 2 includes event producers that are responsible for raising events, event channels that provide messaging of events, and event processors that listen for and handle events. The concrete components of KEA that correspond to these abstract event-processing system concepts are shown in Figure 5.1.

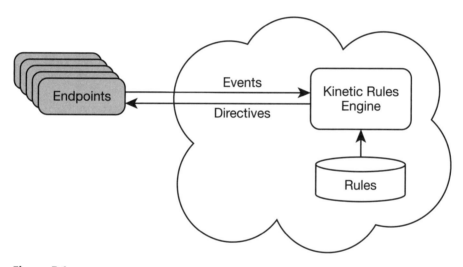

Figure 5.1
The Kinetic Event Architecture.

In KEA, event producers are called endpoints. An endpoint takes note of relevant state changes and signals an event. Event processing is shared between an event engine that processes the event and the endpoints that are responsible for responding to directives returned from the event engine. The event engine selects processing actions based on the event expression language described in Chapter 3, "Event Expressions: Filtering the Event Stream," and returns directives to endpoints as described in the next section. The processing actions in the engine may be defined using any method the engine accepts. This book describes and uses an open-source event engine called the Kinetic Rule Engine, or KRE. KRE runs programs written in a programming language called the Kinetic Rule Language (KRL). KRE is the reference implementation for the Live Web architecture presented in this book. (For more information on running KRL programs as well as installing and using the Kinetic Rule Engine, see Appendix C, "Getting Started with KRL.")

Endpoints can communicate with the event engine using a variety of protocols. KRE uses HTTP (and its underlying request-response model) as a channel for signaling that an event has happened. The Evented API specification (see Appendix F "The Evented API Specification" for details) describes how events can be layered on top of HTTP and defines how endpoints and KRE communicate. For generality, the Evented API specification does not require that events be entity specific, but the KRE implementation of the Evented API specification includes identity tokens as part of the event signal so that identity can be used to establish the context within which events are raised and directives processed. Where appropriate, this context can extend to user data derived through API calls to other services.

In KEA, each endpoint is assigned to a single instance of KRE and signals events by sending the event to that KRE. If the event is to be propagated further, the KRE instance is responsible for doing so.

The following sections discuss this architecture in detail. Understanding how the KEA raises and handles events is critical to understanding how you can build applications for the Live Web.

ENDPOINTS

An event must be observed and communicated to be useful. In KEA, events are generated by endpoints. An endpoint that generates an event may be observing some activity directly and reporting salient state changes, or it might just be reporting or transforming event data from another source (e.g., a Web hook).

Endpoints are responsible for the following tasks:

- Raising relevant events to the event processor
- Responding to directives from the event processor
- Maintaining state to link separate interactions with the event processor in meaningful ways to create context

Not every endpoint will do all three. Some endpoints may just raise events. Others may only take directives. All endpoints will at least raise events or respond to directives. Some endpoints will not be entity specific and thus won't maintain state for the entity.

Endpoints are often specific to a class of events. For example, endpoints exist for the browser, email, telephony, and so on. But that needn't be the case. An endpoint on a mobile device, for example, might raise events for various system, application, and sensor occurrences. The following sections discuss the specifics of events in KEA and then describe how endpoints in KEA accomplish the three aforementioned tasks.

As shown in Figure 5.2, endpoints have varied relationships with the applications and devices with which they interface.

- An endpoint might be built into a client application, such as an iPhone application.

- An endpoint might operate independently of the client application and use its API to affect it.

- An endpoint might be built into a device like a Wi-Fi hub or even a toaster.

- An endpoint might merely transform a data stream, such as the user's Twitter feed, into a series of events.

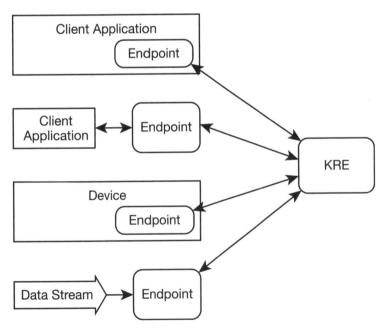

Figure 5.2
The relations of endpoints to client applications.

Raising Events in KEA

Events are the key concept in KEA. They are the common means of communicating between endpoints and KRE. Chapter 2 described events as the notification of a detectable condition in a computer system.

Raising an event requires three steps:

1. Observe a salient state change.

2. Encode the event properly by event domain and type, including needed attributes.

3. Send the event to the Kinetic Rule Engine.

In general, observing an activity and noticing a relevant state change is straightforward. For example, an email endpoint that uses the IMAP protocol to interact with an email account will easily see when an email is received, sent, forwarded, and so on. In some cases, the endpoint may need to maintain state about the activity it is observing so that it knows when that state changes.

Observation of an activity shouldn't interfere with the activity itself. Endpoints should be designed to fail open so that their failure doesn't compromise the behavior of the system under observation.

Events in KEA have a common structure that includes the following attributes:

- **Event domain.** This describes the general domain of the event. Some event domains—like web and email—are predefined, but most are freeform strings used to describe the event domain.

- **Event type.** This describes the event. Some event types are predefined (see the upcoming section "Predefined Events"), but most are freeform strings that describe the event.

The event domain and type form a hierarchy for classifying events within a given event system.

In addition to these common attributes in the event structure, events can have a number of optional attributes that further distinguish them:

- **Attributes.** Any given event type in a particular domain can include attributes that are meaningful to the event. For example, many of the examples you've seen used a pageview event (in the web domain) with a attribute URL indicating the URL of the page that was viewed.

- **Identifying token.** The Kinetic Entity Number (KEN) identifies the entity on whose behalf the event is being raised. Endpoints are given tokens that map to the KEN. By giving endpoints a token rather than the KEN itself, endpoints can be deauthorized without invalidating the KEN and every other endpoint. Not every event is raised on behalf of an entity.

- **Globally unique identifier (GUID).** This is the identifier used to distinguish one event from another. This is usually inferred in KRE.

- **Timestamp.** This indicates the time at which the event was signaled. This is usually inferred in KRE from the time the request was received.

- **Endpoint identifier.** Endpoints that raise an event may include an identifier to indicate their type, version, and so on.

- **Endpoint location.** The location of the endpoint can be important for certain interactions. When raising events on behalf of an entity, transmittal of location data should be by permission.

- **Priority.** The endpoint may indicate the priority for an event. Event engines are not required to respect a priority request. Consequently, the event engine determines the action taken in response to a priority indicator.

- **Event history.** The event history consists of a list of GUIDs of aggregated events. This information is added by the server to the event.

Table 5.1 shows these special KEA event attributes, their canonical names, and their accepted value. Special event attributes are denoted by a leading underscore (not shown in the table). Endpoints should avoid using a leading underscore for their event attributes.

Table 5.1 Special Event Attributes

Attribute	Canonical Name	Accepted Values
ID token	`idt`	String
Event domain	`domain`	Alphanumeric string with underscore, dot, dash, and hyphen
Event type	`type`	Alphanumeric string with underscore, dot, dash, and hyphen
Endpoint identifier	`epi`	String with name, major version, and minor version separated by semicolons
Endpoint location	`epl`	Lat-long coordinates or place name as a string
Priority	`priority`	One of urgent, `high`, `normal`, `low`
Event history	`evhist`	Semicolon separated list of GUIDs

Event Examples

Occurrences such as viewing a Web page, sending an email, or arriving at a new location are seen as events. The following examples give state change and the likely structure of the event representing that state change. (As you'll learn shortly, events in KEA are usually signaled by a URI, but they're shown in a structure that is not encoded as a URL here for convenience and clarity.)

Example 1: John Opens a Web Page

John is using his Web browser with an extension installed that acts as a KEA endpoint. When John opens the URL www.windley.com in his browser, the endpoint signals an event that has the following structure:

```
web:pageview(timestamp: 1294180908,
             idt: "277738884884",
             URL: "http://www.windley.com",
             title: "Windley's Technometria")
```

This event signifies that John opened a page at a particular URL. This event is classified in the web domain and has type pageview. The idt attribute is the token associated with John's KEN. The browser extension maintains this token on John's behalf since it is an identification parameter used to link context across events. The URL attribute indicates which page John opened. All these attributes, except title, are required for this event type.

Example 2: Mary Arrives at BestBuy

Mary has installed an app on her iPhone that functions as a KEA endpoint. The endpoint signals a location event when Mary goes into the store:

```
mobile:location(timestamp: 1294180908,
                idt: "277738884884",
                epl: "40.37695,-111.68701",
                store_id: "138")
```

This event signifies that Mary arrived at a particular store. The fact that this event has an attribute named store_id is a clue that it was raised by an endpoint supplied to Mary by BestBuy. A more general endpoint might just signal the location and rely on the KRL code to map the location to a store name using an API of some kind.

Example 3: Jim Receives an Email

Jim has installed an endpoint that monitors an email address. The endpoint signals an event when an email is received:

```
email:received(timestamp: 1294180908,
               from: "support@amazon.com",
               to: "jim@gmail.com",
               subj: "Book Order # 12788992")
```

This event signifies Jim received an email. The lack of an optional idt attribute indicates that this event was not raised on behalf of a particular user. The other attributes are sent by the endpoint to indicate relevant information about the email. Obviously, there are other attributes, which might be included on an optional basis. These include the body of the message itself, the message ID, and so on.

Example 4: Lynne Receives a Phone Call

Lynne has installed an endpoint that monitors her phone number. The endpoint sends the following event when an inbound telephone call is detected:

```
phone:inbound_call(timestamp: 1294180908,
                   from: "8015551212",
                   to: "4125551212")
```

This event signifies a call being received at a particular number. Again, the lack of an optional idt attribute indicates that this event was not raised on behalf of a particular user. The event processor might be able to use the to attribute to correlate this event with other events that Lynne cares about.

Predefined Events

While event domains and types are freeform in KEA, there are several that are predefined in KRE. The primitive event domains web and email are predefined with semantics and pre-built endpoints for raising them.

The web Event Domain

The Live Web won't displace the existing Web, but will augment it. Reacting to events in the browser with KEA provides significant power to correlate the user's actions across Web sites.

KEA began life as an event system for interacting with the Web. Consequently, the portions of KEA that deal with the Web are very well developed. KEA contains an endpoint, defined by means of a browser extension and a runtime library written in JavaScript.

Note

A browser extension isn't the only way to activate the JavaScript-based browser endpoint. The tags to include the runtime can be placed by an HTTP proxy in certain pages. This is useful for devices, like the iPhone and iPad, that don't allow browser extensions or for broad-based endpoint deployment such as at a conference or in a coffee shop.

The tags to deploy the JavaScript runtime can also be placed in the page when the server returns it. This is useful for using KEA to respond to all the Web events for a given Web site. For example, if you visit my blog at www.windley.com, KEA is used to render many of the components there. (You'll learn to build a simple blog in KRL in Chapter 12, "Advanced KRL Programming.")

JavaScript has long supported the use of events in the browser for creating dynamic Web pages. Events in JavaScript are raised when browser users take specific actions. A JavaScript program running in the browser can listen for these events and take appropriate action.

Events in the web domain of KEA are similar in that they are raised when the user takes specific actions. But instead of being handled in the browser, events in the web domain are raised to KRE. The web domain includes a number of predefined event types on the Web:

- **pageview.** A pageview event occurs when a user views a page in a Web browser. pageview events are not necessarily raised for every page viewed; the browser extension uses information about what pages a rule set is interested in—what we call *salience data*—to pre-filter the event stream.

- **submit.** A submit event occurs when a user clicks a Submit button. Again, not every Submit button click will raise events. As you'll see in Chapter 7, "Creating Contextual Web Experiences," there are specific mechanisms in KRL for developers to place event listeners that indicate salience.

- **click.** A click event occurs when the user clicks a salient page element.

- **change.** A change event occurs when the user changes a salient form element.

The email *Event Domain*

Similar to the Web, email provides an opportunity to consistently recognize and react to certain kinds of events. Most modern mail clients contain a simple rule-based system for reacting to events in the mail client. For example, I can configure the mail client on my MacBook Pro to automatically file mail messages with certain subjects or certain senders.

Similarly, taking action based on events in the mail domain is a natural fit for the Live Web. Being able to write email rules in a way that correlates them with events in other domains (such as the web domain) and uses data from Web-based APIs significantly increases the power of rule-based email processing.

The email domain includes a number of predefined event types for email:

- **received.** A received event occurs when a user receives an email.

- **sent.** A sent event occurs when a user sends an email.

- **forwarded.** A forwarded event occurs when a user forwards an email.

Raising Events with HTTP

Endpoints raise events in KEA using an HTTP request to a specific instance of KRE. This makes KEA a natural fit for the existing Web and increases the ease with which KEA can be deployed. HTTP is ubiquitous. Almost all firewalls are configured to allow HTTP traffic to pass, so HTTP-based endpoints work almost anywhere.

The downside of using HTTP is that KEA is forced to work within the structure of HTTP and its underlying request-response protocol. While this may seem peculiar given the preceding discussions on the difference between event-based systems and request-based systems, you'll see that the request-response nature of HTTP notwithstanding, an event model fits on top of it quite well. I anticipate that KEA will support other protocols as communication channels in the future.

Endpoints raise events in KEA by encoding them as URLs. This is called the *Evented API*. You can read the details of the Evented API specification in Appendix F. The URL includes the current version of the event API. The current version is "sky." The previous version was "blue." Both are still supported in the KRE code-base. The API version, the keyword event, and the ID token are encoded as part of the URL path as follows:

```
/<version>/event/<id_token>/<eid>/
```

Note

The EID in the path is a random number that endpoints can append to the path to ensure that the URL is different from others the endpoint has used. This ensures that requests will be treated as unique by HTTP (commonly called *cache busting*). The EID will be returned to the endpoint in the response from KRE so the endpoint can correlate responses with requests.

Rule sets are used to process events in KEA. KRE normally uses the ID token to determine which rule sets the user has activated. If the endpoint wants a specific set of rule sets to be executed in response to the event, it can specify them using the _rids attribute as a semicolon delimited string or rule-set identifiers (RIDs). In general, endpoints won't specify RIDs because that enables new rule sets to be activated by the user without the endpoint having to be reconfigured.

The endpoint may signal the event using either an HTTP GET or HTTP POST method. Technically, POST is correct (and negates the need for cache busting), but some applications, such as browser endpoints in JavaScript, do not allow a POST, so the engine will respond to either. A POST doesn't run into problems with URL length restrictions that some HTTP components impose on a GET.

Event attributes are included as URL-encoded parameters in the URL query string for a GET or as a form-encoded or JSON-encoded body for a POST. Two types of attributes can be passed:

- **Event attributes.** These are given as regular URL parameters.
- **Rule-set attributes.** These are given as URL parameters with the name of the attribute having the form <rid>:<name>. These attributes are visible only to the rule set with the given RID. Rule-set attributes are generally only useful when the endpoint has specified the rule sets.

One important example of a rule-set attribute is the method an endpoint can use to indicate which version of a rule set KRE should execute. Including the following as an argument will run the development version of the application:

```
{rid}:kinetic_app_version=<version>
```

The version can be the version number, prod indicating the production version or dev indicating the latest version. When the endpoint doesn't specify the RIDs, the information that KRE receives back indicating what rule sets the user has activated also includes version information.

URL Encoding Example

To see how URL encoding works, consider the first of the four examples we used before, "John Opens a Web Page." The structure used was as follows:

```
web:pageview(timestamp: 1294180908,
             idt: "277738884884",
             URL: "http://www.windley.com",
             title: "Windley's Technometria")
```

This would be encoded as a URL as follows. (I am ignoring the domain name portion of the URL and assuming rule sets a16x64 and a8x55 have been configured in the endpoint. Line feeds and spaces have been added for wrapping in print.)

```
/sky/event/277738884884/<eid>?
 _domain=web&
 _type=pageview&
 _rids= a16x64;a8x55&
 timestamp=1294180908&
 URL=http%3A%2F%2Fwww.windley.com&
 title=Windley%27s%20Technometria
```

If this event were raised, the following eventex (among others) would select for it:

```
select when web pageview title re#Windley#
```

Note that the event domain and type are directly correlated to the event information in the URL and that any of the event attributes can be used as filters in the eventex. (Here, we used the filter `title re#Windley#`.)

Maintaining Context

Context matters on the Live Web because applications use context to correlate events. But my context is different from your context. Consequently, endpoints are a key player in maintaining context because they can act on behalf of a specific entity.

Endpoints usually raise events and respond to action requests on behalf of a user or, more generally, an entity. One of the key differences between KEA and other event-processing systems is that KEA is architected from the ground up to understand entities and to associate events with entity context. Endpoints play a key role in linking entity identity to the events that each entity raises.

When an endpoint raises events, it usually identifies which entity it represents. As you've seen, endpoints indicate the identity of the entity using an ID token that can be mapped to the KEN by the system. In some cases, the endpoint may be hard-coded to represent a particular entity. In most cases, the endpoint will be flexible enough to represent any entity, and the entity will have to identify itself to the endpoint through configuration or authentication.

Endpoints can be installed applications on a computer, phone, or other computing device. The browser endpoint I've mentioned is one example. The browser endpoint is configured when the user associates it with an online account. Endpoints can also be Web services, such as the KEA email endpoint service. In such cases, the user establishes an identity when he or she creates the endpoint.

Endpoints can be built into a device and configured. The device itself might be functioning as the entity, or it may be associated with another entity through an online account. In some cases, the entity may be a simple device, such as a toaster, and be configured by a dial.

In addition to maintaining entity information as part of the endpoint state, endpoints must also manage salience information. The KEA dispatch API returns salience information for a given rule set. Salience information indicates event relevance and can be used by the endpoint to pre-filter events. For example, KRL developers can indicate which Web sites, by domain name, their application is intended to run against. The browser extension endpoint uses that data to only raise events for those particular domains, greatly increasing the efficiency of the system by not raising irrelevant events. Endpoints are not required to use the salience information returned from the dispatch API, but are encouraged to do so.

Chapter 3 discussed event expressions. As you'll see in the next chapter, the primary use of an eventex is to select rules for responding to particular event patterns. Eventexes are also used to create rich salience data that endpoints can use to pre-filter the event stream to only those primitive events that are relevant to a given application.

As the rule sets that a given entity has activated increase or decrease, salience data gives endpoints information about what events to raise. Salience data enables endpoints to only raise events that matter to an entity.

Responding to Directives

If the Live Web is to succeed in helping people achieve their purpose, then events must be translated into action. Sometimes, the desired action is to change a value in some database somewhere on the Web. Often, however, the desired action is to affect what the user is doing right now. That might mean changing the Web page the user is viewing to add relevant information based on the user's context, processing an incoming email, or redirecting a phone call.

The term *directive* is used as a general name for the set of instructions that a rule-set evaluation returns to the endpoint. Endpoints are responsible for taking action on the user's behalf according to directives that they receive from KRE. Exactly what actions an endpoint is capable of depends on the endpoint's design and implementation. Some endpoints will have more capabilities than others.

Endpoints process directives. On the Web, these directives are JavaScript programs. The JavaScript runtime that works with the standard KEA browser endpoint is capable of responding to a large number of directives that affect the DOM of the page being viewed. In other domains, the response is frequently a JSON data structure but can be structured in other formats as appropriate to the endpoint. The endpoint is responsible for interpreting any directive it receives. Here are some examples:

- A browser extension serving as an endpoint responds to directives, the most important being to execute the returned JavaScript in the context of the page.

- An email endpoint responds to directives that include actions like `delete`, `forward`, `reply`, and so on.

- An endpoint for the Twilio cloud-based telephony service receives and processes directives specific to Twilio that are encoded as XML.

Directive documents delivered as JSON take the following form:

```
{"directives":
[{"name":<directive_name>,
 "options":{<name>:<value>[,<name>:<value>]*},
 "meta":{"rule_name":<rule_name>,
         "txn_id":<txn_id>,
         "rid":<rid>,
         "eid":<eid>
         }
 }
 ...
 ]}
```

The primary component is a list of directives that have three pieces:

- A name that identifies the directive

- A list of options that take the form of name-value pairs

- Meta information, including the name of the rule that generated the directive, the transaction identifier, the rule-set identifier, and the EID

For each object in the directives array, the endpoint uses the directive name and options to take a particular action. The transaction ID is guaranteed to be globally unique and is the same for every directive in every directive document produced by a particular event-processing episode.

Some specific examples of directive documents are given in the example in the section "Building an Endpoint."

PROCESSING EVENTS

When an endpoint raises an event in KEA, the event is handled by one or more rule sets. You can think of KRE as a set of dynamic event loops. An *event loop* is a message dispatcher. Event loops are constantly waiting for specific events and taking appropriate action.

The event loop chooses the rule sets that will handle a particular event depending on several factors:

- The entity for which the endpoint is raising the event
- The salience of the event to particular rule sets
- Whether or not the endpoint specified particular rule sets to handle the event

The engine uses the following algorithm to determine which rule sets will handle the event:

1. If the endpoint specified rule sets when it raised the event, add those rule sets to the schedule.

2. If not, and the entity is known, add any rule set to the schedule that the entity has installed and that has salient rules.

3. Otherwise, add any rule sets to the schedule that have registered a specific interest in events of this type.

This algorithm constructs the initial schedule for the rule engine. Further rule sets can be added to the schedule as rules are processed if those rules raise explicit events.

After the rule sets have been scheduled, the event is checked against the eventexes in each rule of each rule set. (KRE uses salience data to make this process more efficient than simply checking each rule.) Depending on the current event and past events that the eventex has seen for the subject entity, a given eventex might be satisfied or not. If it is, that rule is added to the schedule. Once the schedule has been built, it is executed. The result of executing a schedule is usually a set of directives that are returned to the endpoint. (In the current version of KEA, only the endpoint that raised the event received directives. Future versions of KEA will allow more general communication to other endpoints so they may be involved in the computation.)

BUILDING AN ENDPOINT

Building a simple endpoint is fairly straightforward. In this section, you will learn to build an endpoint that raises events in the echo domain. The following Perl code functions as an endpoint[2]:

```
#!/usr/bin/perl -w
use strict;
use Getopt::Std;
use LWP::Simple;
use JSON::XS;
use Kinetic::Raise;
```

```perl
    # global options
use vars qw/ %opt /;
my $opt_string = 'h?e:m:';
getopts( "$opt_string", \%opt );
my $event_type = $opt{'e'} || 'hello';
my $message = $opt{'m'} || '';
my $event = Kinetic::Raise->new('echo',
                                  $event_type,
                                  'a16x66',
                                  {'host' => '127.0.0.1'});
my $response = $event->raise({'input' => $message});
foreach my $d (@{$response->{'directives'}}) {
  if ($d->{'name'} eq 'say') {
    print $d->{'options'}->{'something'}, "\n";
  }
}
```

This simple script uses a module called Kinetic::Raise, that takes the relevant information about the event, creates the right URL for the Kinetic event API, raises the event by calling the URL, and processes the response. You can see that it has the possibility of taking the event type from the command line with the -e switch. If none is given, the event type defaults to hello.

Suppose the variable $response in the preceding Perl code contained the following directive after raising the event message:

```
{"directives":
    [{"options":{"something":"Hello World"},
    "name":"say",
    "meta":{
     "rule_name":"hello_world",
     "txn_id":"8FF45D92-7EDB-11DF-B34A-4BA9F4723EB4",
     "rid":"a16x66"
     }
   }
  ]
 }
```

The foreach loop would process the directive list, find a directive with the name say, and print the contents of the option something: "Hello World." To make this happen, you need rules that respond to the possible events and return appropriate directives. Here are two such rules:

```
rule hello_world {
    select when echo hello
```

```
    send_directive("say") with
      something = "Hello World";
}

rule echo {
  select when echo message input re#(.*)# setting(m)
  send_directive("say") with
    something = m;
}
```

Note

Rules will be introduced formally in the next chapter. You likely have enough background with eventexes and directives at this point that these simple rules make sense.

The rule `hello_world` responds to the `hello` event by sending the `say` directive with the attribute `something` set to `"Hello World"`. The rule `echo` responds to an `echo` event with an `input` attribute. The entire value of the input is captured and bound to the variable m. The `echo` rule sends a `say` directive with the attribute `something` set to the value m. Here are a few examples of running this program from the command line:

```
$ ./demo.pl
Hello World
$ ./demo.pl -e message -m "The Live Web"
The Live Web
```

It's critical to note that the KRE engine doesn't know anything about the event domain `echo` or the event types `hello` and `message`. You could define these to be anything you wanted and the example would work the same. KRE is merely receiving events, selecting appropriate rules, and returning whatever directives they indicate.

SMALL PIECES LOOSELY JOINED

In his book *Small Pieces, Loosely Joined*, David Weinberger celebrates the ability of the simple building blocks of the Web to change the world. The example from the last section may have left you shaking your head. An `echo` service hardly seems grand enough to justify the claims and vision of the preceding chapters! From the small pieces represented by endpoints, events, and rules, however, you can construct complex systems of loosely coupled applications that have the power to give people control of things they never before imagined.

Endnotes

1. Fielding, Roy. (2000). *Architectural Styles and the Design of Network-Based Software Architectures*. Ph.D. Dissertation, University of California, Irvine.

2. The code for the `Kinetic::Raise` perl module can be found on Github: https://github.com/windley/Raise.pm.

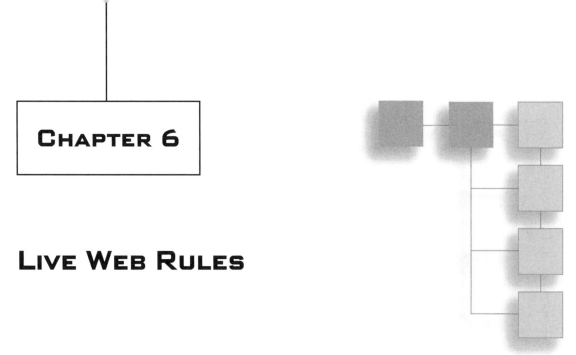

CHAPTER 6

LIVE WEB RULES

You've seen that event-based systems differ markedly from request-based systems (see Table 6.1 for a summary). Event-based and request-based systems are duals of each other. Whereas the receipt of a request triggers the action of a request-response system, the receipt of an event triggers event-driven systems. The nature of an event is different from that of a request. A request says, "Do this for me." In contrast, an event says, "This happened." In a request-driven system, the sender chooses what action to take. In an event-driven system, the sender merely says that something happened. Event processors have no obligation to the endpoint. Endpoints are obligated to report events and respond to directives. Conversely, a client in a request-driven system has no obligation to the server. It can make a request or not. Servers are expected to fulfill requests.

As discussed, event processors interpret what an event means. A request, on the other hand, implies that the interpretation—what should happen—has already occurred. You can think of this as receiver, instead of sender, determinism.

Because of these differences, the flow control of event-processing systems is very different from that of request-response systems. Consequently, applications are constructed differently in event-driven systems. The language at the heart of KEA, the Kinetic Rule Language, is optimized for building reactive, event-based applications.

RULES FOR EVENTS

Let's consider the idea of receiver determinism and its impact on programming event-based systems more closely. Consider the stereo example from Chapter 2, "Events on the Live Web":

Table 6.1   Request-Based Versus Event-Based Systems

	Request-Based	Event-Based
Signal	Request receipt	Event receipt
Nature	"Do this"	"Something happened"
Obligation	At server	At endpoint (client)
Interpretation	On client	On server

> The entertainment system was belting out the Beatles' "We Can Work It Out" when the phone rang. When Pete answered, his phone broadcast a message to all local devices indicating it had received a call. His stereo responded by turning down the volume….

The message that Pete's phone sends is an event. That event—let's call it phone: inbound_call—doesn't say what should happen. Rather, the event processors that happen to be listening for that event make that determination. They *react* to the event.

Event processors take the form of rules. Rules are a natural way to build reactive systems because they allow behavior to be layered. In the stereo example, two rules—one for the stereo and one for the DVR—could be listening for the phone: inbound_call event and take what action is appropriate in their context. Adding another listener simply means adding another rule. The rule defines what should happen when a particular event pattern occurs. The rules determine the response.

The basic pattern for a rule is shown in the following pseudo code:

```
when   an event occurs
if     some condition is true
then   take some action
```

This pattern is called the event-condition-action, or ECA, pattern. Many rule languages use this pattern. The ECA pattern is typical for most business rule systems. Rule languages based on this pattern are a widely accepted way to build reactive systems.

Separating events from conditions is a key concept in ECA rule languages. As you've seen, events represent a state transition. Conditions, on the other hand, are used to determine if the current state has specific properties. For example, the phone: inbound_call event signals that the phone system has detected a phone call (i.e., the state changed from one in which no phone call was happening to one in which a phone call was happening). Conditions can be used to check properties of the new state, such as "is the call from the 801 area code?" "Is it after 5 p.m.?" or "Does the user's Google calendar show that she's busy right now?" The separation of events from conditions provides a clear distinction between when (event), what (condition), and how (action).[1]

Note

Don't confuse ECA rule languages with the kinds of rule languages that have been heavily used in planning and reasoning systems, including expert systems and natural language processing. They are very different.

THE KINETIC RULE LANGUAGE

The Kinetic Rule Language (KRL) is an ECA rule language. KRL is a programming language for creating applications on the Live Web. KRL programs, or rule sets, comprise a number of rules that respond to particular events.

Besides a collection of rules, KRL rule sets also contain a `meta` section for specifying information about the rule set, a `dispatch` section for providing clues about event salience, and a `global` section for global definitions.

Each rule conforms to the aforementioned pattern for ECA rule languages with some significant additions. The basic structure of a KRL rule is as follows:

```
rule <name> {
    select when <eventex>
    pre {
     <declarations>
    }
    if <expr> then
     <action>
    fired {
     <effects>
    } else {
     <effects>
    }
}
```

Only the name and eventex are required, so most rules are simpler than this template. (Obviously, a rule with only a name and eventex wouldn't accomplish anything, so meaningful rules include at least an action or a postlude in addition to the required components.) The prelude contains a list of variable declarations that allow computation of values for the condition and action based on global values and event attributes. Later, this chapter will discuss the KRL expression language in greater detail.

Actions specify the reaction that the rule makes to the event. Actions take two general forms:

- Actions produce directive documents that are sent to endpoints causing them to do something. For example, an email endpoint might receive a directive telling it to delete a specific message.

- Actions invoke operations in network APIs that produce some desired side effect. For example, an action might cause a Twitter update to be made to the user's status.

The section after the action is called the postlude. It allows for effects. Effects are an important addition to the ECA pattern. Effects differ from actions in that they do not result in directive documents being sent to the endpoint. Instead, they cause side effects on the KRE system. Examples of effects include the following:

- **Persistent variables.** An effect might cause a permanent change to a persistent variable. Persistent variables allow context to be automatically maintained for an entity or an application across separate invocations of a rule set.

- **Control statements.** Sometimes, you need to affect the normal execution order. For example, the last statement causes the execution of the rule set to terminate after the current rule.

- **Explicit events.** Explicit events allow a rule set to raise an event in response to incoming events. This effect is so useful and powerful, there is an entire chapter devoted to it: Chapter 11, "Building Event Networks."

- **Exception handling and logging.** Rules can raise error events that other rules respond to for handling exceptions. Also, an effect might direct the system to log something.

Your First Rule

The following example shows a simple KRL rule:

```
rule good_morning {
  select when web pageview url re#exampley.com#
  if time:morning() then
    notify("Welcome!", "Good morning!")
}
```

This rule would send a "good morning" notification to visitors of a specific Web site (as denoted by the URL path) if it is morning where the user is.

In the example, the rule has a name: good_morning. Note the ECA pattern:

- **Event.** The select keyword denotes the event expression that describes salient events for this rule. In this case, when the user views a page (i.e., a pageview event occurs) that matches a specific URL pattern (i.e., using a regular expression re#exampley.com#), the rule will be selected.

- **Condition.** The if keyword denotes the condition controlling whether the rule will fire—in this case, if it's morning. Note that because rules are executed on behalf of an entity, time:morning() is evaluated in that entity's context and will only be true if it's morning where the entity is located.

- **Action.** The then keyword denotes the action to take (i.e., notify) if the rule fires. In this case, the rule would return a directive that causes the browser to place a notification on the current page with the message shown.

This rule has no prelude or postlude.

When a user with a browser extension endpoint visits the site with domain exampley.com, 'a pageview event will be raised to KRE. (Readers familiar with regular expressions will know that this rule will be selected if any part of the URL, such as the query string, has the string exampley.com embedded within it. To ensure you only selected the rule based on the domain name, you'd have to be more specific in the regular expression.) This rule will be scheduled and executed. The result of that execution will be the placement of a notification box in the upper left-hand corner of the page, as shown in Figure 6.1.

RULES ARE SIMPLY CONDITIONAL ACTIONS

As the rule in the previous section shows, rules are conditional actions. The action can be anything appropriate to the domain. For a browser extension endpoint, actions usually modify the DOM and consequently affect how the page is rendered in the browser. (The DOM, short for Document Object Model, is the data structure representing the page that the browser maintains to render it. Changing the DOM dynamically changes what the user sees displayed in the browser.) For an email endpoint, the actions are appropriate to managing email.

As you saw in Chapter 3, "Event Expressions: Filtering the Event Stream," event expressions can be used to specify complex event patterns. A rule is selected when the eventex in the rule's select statement matches events in the rule set's event stream.

Once selected, the rule's prelude is executed and the condition, if any, is evaluated. If the condition is true, the action is taken; we say the rule fired. Empty conditions are

Figure 6.1
Notification on exampley.com as a result of a simple rule firing.

trivially true. Because you can write a selector that always selects and the conditional is optional, some rules will always fire. But most interesting rule sets will contain rules that only fire under certain circumstances. After the action has been generated, the rule's postlude statement is evaluated. (Note that actions are not necessarily sent to endpoints as they are taken, but are queued for delivery when the entire event evaluation has completed for more efficient execution.)

Condition expressions may not have anything to do with the events that led to the rule being selected. They could, for example, check a data source for the weather or a stock price. A condition is valid over a period of time. Events are atomic with respect to time. Being in a state is a condition, and the state transition that got you there is the event.

The best way to think of a rule's condition is as a guard on the action. Programmers new to KRL frequently want an else clause on the conditional. But there is a distinction between choosing an action and determining when an action should fire. The condition is used to determine whether an action should fire, not which action. Which action to fire is generally determined by which rule is selected.

Event Attributes, Conditions, and Filters

You saw in Chapter 3 that event expressions can use filters to further distinguish one event from another. For example, the following eventex matches `pageview` events where the URL has a particular format:

```
rule url_in_filter {
  select when pageview where url.match(#/archives/\d{4}/#)
  notify(...)
}
```

Suppose, instead, that you had written the URL filter as a condition in a rule using the event attribute function:

```
rule url_in_condition {
  select when pageview
  if event:attr("url").match(#/archives/\d{4}/#)
  then notify(...)
}
```

These are, mostly, equivalent, but there are several subtle differences:

- The second rule will be selected more than the first, but fire in the same circumstances. This has implications for system efficiency but not for the overall effect of the rule.

- Eventex filters are useful when you use compound expressions. This is especially true with aggregators. For example, the following eventex will match using a sliding window of five `withdrawal` events and set the variable m to have the maximum amount when that amount is above a threshold:

```
select when repeat(5,
              withdrawal amount.match(#$(\d+\.\d\d)#) &&
                  amount > 100) max(m)
```

  Expressed in KRL, this concept would be more verbose and difficult to understand.

- Salience hints, harvested from the eventexes of a rule set, contain more useful data when the eventex include filters. This makes the network more efficient because endpoints can be written that only raise relevant events.

Rule conditions have the advantage of being able to take other data, aside from the events and attributes, into consideration when determining whether a rule should fire. As you'll see in Chapter 8, "Using the Cloud," KRL makes it easy to access data from cloud-based APIs. In addition, a number of intrinsic functions and libraries offer additional data to a KRL rule set. Consequently, conditions are important for making decisions based on user context because there's more of it available to conditions than there is in an eventex, regardless of sophistication.

What Happens When an Event Is Raised?

When an event is raised, it touches off a series of rule-set evaluations. In Chapter 5, "Architecting the Live Web," you learned that KRE is responsible for determining what rule sets need to be evaluated for a given event. I say "evaluated" rather than "executed" because an event may not result in any rules being executed unless they are selected based on their eventex and the past pattern of events.

Every rule that has a matching eventex will be added to the execution schedule. KRE guarantees that rules in a given rule set will be scheduled in order, but does not give any guarantees about the execution order of rule sets themselves.

Note

> The current version of the Kinetic Event API guarantees sequential execution of rules in a given rule set. Future versions may provide other mechanisms for rule ordering and conflict resolution. Managing and envisioning rule ordering in a rule language is complex. KEA mitigates this by defaulting to what programmers are used to, static ordering, in an effort to make transitioning from other programming languages easier. As Kinetic applications become more complicated, this strategy will likely not suffice.

After the schedule has been created, KRE executes it. Execution results in the creation of one or more directive documents. Note that it is possible to have an execution cycle that does not take any action if all the scheduled rules simply produce effects and have no actions. A directive document is still produced in that case, but the list of directives is empty.

Because rules can raise events, one event can result in a rule executing that causes another event. Rules can raise events directly in the rule postlude. (We will discuss explicit events, as these are called, much more closely in Chapter 11, "Building Event Networks.") In that case, for efficiency reasons, the event is examined and the schedule updated during the same execution cycle. All the directives in this case will have the same transaction ID.

Rules can also raise new events by directing the endpoint to do so. When this happens, the endpoint raises the event afresh and KRE treats it as independent, creating a new schedule. The new schedule will create a separate directive document with a new transaction ID. Again, we'll discuss this in Chapter 11.

TAKING ACTION

Taking action is the primary reason for executing rules. Ironically, the basis for this most basic and important part of KRL is surprisingly simple. There are just a few fundamental actions. The rest are built from these.

Before I describe the specific actions, you need to understand the structure of actions. Actions have a name, a set of required parameters, and a set of optional parameters. Optional parameters are specified using a `with` clause followed by a list of name-value pairs. The name and value are paired using an equal sign (=) and the name-value pairs are separated with the keyword `and`:

```
foo("hello", 5) with
    x = "world" and
    y = 6 + 5
```

This action has a name, `foo`, and two parameters, `"hello"` and 5. The action also has two optional parameters: x with the value `"world"` and y with the value 11. The parameters, required and optional, can be any valid KRL expression and will be evaluated prior to the action being taken. More formally, parameters are evaluated in applicative order.

The following basic actions are available in KRL:

- **send_directive(<expr>).** This returns a directive with the name given by the expression <expr>. (Don't confuse action names—send_directive in this case—and directive names given as the required parameter to the action.) Optional parameters provided to send_directive are passed through to the options structure of the directive as name-value pairs. This action is the primary means of creating directive documents for endpoints. For example, the following action produces the directive document below it:

```
send_directive("say") with
    something = "Hello World"

{"directives":
  [{"options":{"something":"Hello World"},
    "name":"say",
    "meta":{
      "rule_name":"hello_world",
      "txn_id":"8FF45D92-7EDB-11DF-B34A-4BA9F4723EB4",
      "rid":"a16x66"
      }}]}
```

- **send_javascript(<expr>).** This returns its argument as a JavaScript closure application whose body is given by <expr>. The names of any optional parameters are used as parameters in the closure. The closure is applied to the values of any optional parameters. This action is used for communicating with browser endpoints. For example, the following action produces the JavaScript below it. (The <|...|> syntax, called clown hats, is a type of KRL extended quote for producing JavaScript. Values in clown hats are assumed to be JavaScript. White space is not necessarily preserved and templating mechanisms are available.)

```
send_javascript(<|x + y|>) with
    x = 5 and
    y = 6
(function(x, y) { x + y } (5, 6));
```

- **http:post(<expr>).** This makes an HTTP POST to the URL given by <expr>. Any optional parameters are added as name-value pairs in the query string of the URL. This action is useful for interacting with Web services that aren't formally part of KEA. For example, the following action makes an HTTP POST to the given URL, form-encoding the optional parameter q and sending it as the body of the POST:

```
http:post("http://google.com/search") with
  q = "hello"
```

- **send_raw(<expr>).** This returns its argument exactly as given after <expr> is evaluated. The result is not wrapped in a directive document. The send_raw directive takes a single, optional parameter, mime_type, that sets the content-type header in the response. Other optional parameters are ignored. This action is useful for producing responses to endpoints that don't understand directive documents. For example, the following action returns the value below it. (The <<...>> syntax, called chevrons, is a KRL extended quote for producing strings with HTML and XML that includes a templating mechanism. Unlike clown hats, white space is preserved in chevrons.)

```
send_raw(<< <book>
                <title>The Live Web</title>
                <author>Phillip J. Windley</author>
                <rating>5 stars</rating>
        </book> >>)
<book>
    <title>The Live Web</title>
    <author>Phillip J. Windley</author>
    <rating>5 stars</rating>
</book>
```

Chapter 7, "Creating Contextual Web Experiences," discusses actions that are specific to the Web. Chapter 8, "Using the Cloud," discusses modules and composite actions, as well as how to create more complicated actions from these primary actions.

COMPOUND ACTIONS

A rule can take more than one action using a compound action. The most frequently used kind of compound action is the every compound action. The every compound action takes every action listed in order. The actions are listed inside curly braces with semicolon separators:

```
if x > 5 then
  every {
    notify("Hello World!", "This is my first message!");
    notify("Hello Again!", "This is my second message!");
}
```

This would place two notification boxes on the page.

Because this is so common, the keyword every is optional, and so this could be written as

```
if x > 5 then {
    notify("Hello World!", "This is my first message!");
    notify("Hello Again!", "This is my second message!");
}
```

There is no limit to the number of actions that can be placed inside a compound action. While there is no linguistic restriction on mixing actions that send JavaScript and those that send directives, no current endpoint understands both directives and JavaScript, so that is not typically done.

The other kind of compound action is the choose compound action. A choose action takes a list of actions like every, but instead of executing them all, it randomly picks one to execute. So, for example, the following would either send "This is one message!" or "This is another message!" randomly. The key reason for taking random action is to easily accommodate A/B behavior testing.

```
if x > 5 then
  choose {
    notify("Hello World!", "This is one message!");
    notify("Hello World!", "This is another message!");
}
```

The `choose` action can also be used to actually choose a specific action, like a case statement:

```
if x > 5 then
  choose some_var {
    A => notify("Hello World!", "This is one message!");
    B => notify("Hello World!", "This is another message!");
  }
```

Notice that a variable, `some_var`, has been inserted after `choose`. Its value will be compared to the action labels (A or B) in the action list, and the actions associated with labels that match exactly will be taken. Action labels are alphanumeric identifiers for specific actions. If `some_var` does not match any label, then no action is taken—as if the action statement were missing.

EXPRESSIONS

KRL contains a complete expression language for performing computations on event attributes and other data, computing conditionals, and computing action parameters. The upcoming "Declarations" section will show how to bind the value of an expression to a name in the `pre` block.

Comments

Comments start with a double slash (`//`) and end with a new line.

Literals

KRL expressions can be as simple as literal values like strings, numbers, and Boolean values. KRL is dynamically typed. Numbers, strings, and Booleans are automatically converted between types when the meaning is clear from the context. KRL expressions also allow literal array and mapping structures (i.e., associative arrays or hashes) that use JSON syntax (except that names do not have to be quoted). For example, the following is a valid KRL expression:

```
{x: 5,
y: ["hello", "world"],
z: {a: 6, b: "hello again"}
}
```

Array values can be accessed by index. (Components of maps are accessed using the `pick` operator, described in Chapter 8.) The following would return the sixth value (zero-based indexing) from the array `a`:

```
a[5]
```

Arithmetic, String, and Boolean Expressions

KRL includes standard arithmetic operators with the usual infix notation:

```
5 + 6
7 - 3.2
8 * 5
7.6 / 3
```

KRL allows string concatenation using the infix operator +:

```
"hello " + "world"
```

Equality and inequality can be tested using commonly accepted operators:

```
"hello" eq "world"
"hello" neq "world"
5 == 6
5 != 6
3 < 4
4 <= 4
5 > 4
5 >= 6
```

Boolean expressions can be created using negation (not), conjunction (&&), and disjunction (||):

```
(x > y || 4 < z) eq not(x = y && 4 <= z)
```

Conditional Expressions

KRL allows conditional expressions. The following expression returns 5 if x is less than 4, and 6 otherwise:

```
x < 4 => 5
     | 6
```

Conditional expressions nest nicely:

```
x < 4  => 5
x < 10 => 6
x < 15 => 7
        | 8
```

The expressions in the consequent and antecedent of the conditional expression are not evaluated until after the conditional expression has been evaluated and a decision has been made on which arm to pursue. For example, in the following conditional expression, only one of the HTTP GET operations would be performed, depending on the value of the condition:

```
x < 4 => http:get("http://example.com/api1")
       | http:get("http://example.com/api2")
```

Operators

KRL has numerous built-in operators for manipulating arrays, maps, strings, sets, HTML, and other values. Operators use postfix notation and can have parameters. While the full gamut of operators is too extensive to discuss here, I will introduce a few to demonstrate the syntax and semantics operators in KRL. I introduce others as they are needed in later chapters. Appendix E, "The KRL Expression Language," offers a more complete description.

Three operators are used to perform regular-expression operations on strings. The simplest is match, which returns a Boolean value depending on whether the regular expression given as its parameter matches the string that is the target of the operator. For example, suppose the variable x contains the string "This is a string". The following would return true:

```
x.match(re#string#)
```

On the other hand, the following expression would return false:

```
x.match(re#rooster#)
```

The extract operator also uses regular expressions, but returns an array of the values captured in the regular expression. Assuming the same value in x as before, the following expression would return the array in the comment shown below it.

```
x.extract(re#(i\w)#g)
// returns ["is", "is", "in"]
```

This example captures any two-letter sequence starting with an *i*. The following expression returns the array in the comment shown below it:

```
x.extract(re#\w(i\w)#g)
// returns ["is", "in"]
```

The two-letter sequence must be preceded by a letter (no space allowed) in this example. Consequently, the word *is* doesn't match.

The replace operator replaces the substring matched by the regular expression that is the first argument with the string in the second argument. Any instance of the special sequential variables $1, $2, $3, and so on in the second argument is replaced by any captured values from the regular expression. Suppose x contains the string

"This is a string"; the following expressions would return the value in the comment below them:

```
x.replace(re#is#,"ese")
// returns 'These is a string'

x.replace(re#Th(is)#,"Nothing $1")
// returns 'Nothing is is a string'
```

Another useful operator is join. I introduce it here to show how operators form processing pipelines. The join operator concatenates the values of an array into a string, placing a value between them. So, if x contains the array ["hello", "world"], the following expression returns the string "hello world" (note the space between the words):

```
x.join(" ")
```

A string operator, uc, will uppercase all the characters in a given string. Using the variable from the previous example, the following example would return the string "HELLO WORLD":

```
x.join(" ").uc()
```

Other, more powerful operators will be introduced in coming chapters as you encounter applicable problems.

Event Attributes

Event attributes are one of the most important sources of data for computation in a rule because they convey information about the context of the event. In Chapter 3, you saw how eventexes can use expressions on event attributes as filters for which events match a given primitive eventex. Event attributes can also be used in KRL expressions. To avoid conflict with user-declared variables names, event attributes are namespaced using the keyword event. (Namespaces are formed in KRL by prepending the namespace name and a colon to a variable.)

Assume that a rule has been selected based on a pageview event with an event attribute url. The following KRL expression could be used to extract the domain name from the url attribute:

```
event:url.extract(#http://([^/?]+)#)
```

DECLARATIONS

Declarations bind names to values. Variables are declared inside the global section of the rule set, the rule prelude, functions, and user-defined actions. A semicolon separates declarations. The following example shows a prelude that declares two variables, x and y:

```
pre {
  x = 5;
  y = event:url.extract(#http://([^/?]+)#)
}
```

KRL is statically scoped. Each place where an identifier is bound in a program corresponds to a region of the program text within which the binding is visible. The region is determined by the particular programmatic context where the binding is made:

- Each rule set is a binding scope and the bindings constructed within a rule-set evaluation are only visible within that rule-set execution. Any declarations made in the global section of a rule set will be visible for the execution of any rules in that rule set.

- Each rule is also a binding scope. Values bound to names in the setting clause of an eventex and values bound in the prelude are visible throughout the execution of that particular rule.

KRL variable declarations are not variable assignments. Neither can KRL expressions cause persistent side effects. For example, the second declaration in the following prelude does not change the value to which x is bound. Rather, it results in two bindings of x, one of which is hidden (shadowed) by the other:

```
pre {
  x = 5;
  x = 6;
}
```

Developers should avoid treating declarations as assignments because they will invariably be surprised by the resulting semantics in subtle ways.

FUNCTIONS

KRL allows user-defined functions. Only anonymous functions are allowed in the expression language, but they can be bound to variables in declarations. Functions have the following form:

```
function(<parameters>) {
  <declarations>
  <expression>
}
```

The parameter list can be empty, as can the list of declarations. The expression is evaluated, and its value is returned as the value of the function.

The following prelude declares a function that squares its argument and then uses the function to calculate the square of 5:

```
pre {
  sqr = function(x) { x * x };
  y = sqr(5)
}
```

KRL functions can be recursive. The following function declaration defines the factorial function:

```
pre {
  fact = function(x) {
           (x == 0) => 1
                       | x * fact(x - 1)
         };
  y = fact(5)
}
```

Declarations in a function can be used to compute intermediate results. The following example defines a sum-of-squares function that defines square internally for its own use:

```
pre {
  sos = function(x,y) {
          sqr = function(x) { x * x };
          sqr(x) + sqr(y)
        };
  y = sos(5,6)
}
```

The definition of sqr is within the scope of the function sos and not available for use outside the sos function.

Functions are first-class values in KRL. These can be passed to and returned from other functions. For example, a number of operators on arrays take functions as parameters. The filter operator, for instance, takes a function that has a single parameter. The function is applied to each member of the array, and any members for whom the function is false are removed.

Assume that c is bound to the array [3,4,5]. The following expression would return the array [3,4]:

```
c.filter(function(x){x<5})
```

PERSISTENT VARIABLES

Earlier, I made note of the fact that KRL declarations do not cause side effects. That doesn't mean KRL rule sets can't cause persistent changes that are available from one rule-set execution to another. KRL has persistent variables that can be used inside any expression in a rule set and can be changed in the postlude.

KRL has three types of persistent variables. (Persistent variables are currently limited to approximately 1,000,000 characters each.)

- **Entity variables.** These are used to record persistent data about individuals interacting with rules. Entity variables are identified by the namespace ent. KRL programs keep each user's persistent entity variables separate. KRL programs are multi-tenanted automatically.

- **Application variables.** These are used to record persistent data about the application or rule set. Application variables are identified by the namespace app.

Entity, application, and request variables share the same syntax and operations. They differ primarily in the scope of their definition. An analogy might help: Entity variables are similar to instance variables, and application variables are similar to class variables in object-oriented languages.

Persistent variables take four forms:

- **Flags.** Flags store Boolean values. Operations on flags allow the flag to be set or cleared.

- **Counters.** Counters store numeric values. Operations on counters allow them to be incremented, decremented, and tested.

- **Trails.** Trails function like stacks. Operations on trails allow values to be pushed onto the trail, forgotten, and tested. (The name *trail* is historical. As originally envisioned, trails were used to keep track of the URLs an entity visited.)

- **Literals.** Literals can be numbers, strings, arrays, or maps, and admit operations on those values.

Using Persistents in Preludes

Flags, counters, and literal value persistent variables can be used inside prelude expressions like any other variable. If the persistent variable does not exist before it is used, the default value is 0. For example, the following declaration would add 3 to the value stored in the entity counter ent:fizz, storing the result in x:

```
pre {
  x = ent:fizz + 3
}
```

KRL includes special built-in functions for accessing individual places in a trail:

- **history.** This takes an expression and a persistent variable as arguments. If the expression evaluates to n, then the history function will return the nth place on the trail. The most recent place is at history location 0. If *n* is larger than the length of the trail, the history function returns the empty string.

```
pre {
  x = history 1 ent:another_trail;
}
```

- **current.** This takes a persistent variable as its argument. The current function performs the same operation as the history function with a location of 0. That is, it returns the most recent place on the trail.

```
pre {
  x = current ent:another_trail;
}
```

Using Persistents in Conditions

Persistents in condition statements are accessed in the same way as in the prelude. The following action will fire when the persistent variable ent:archive_pages is greater than 3:

```
if ent:archive_pages > 3 then
  notify(...)
```

Persistent flags and counters can also be tested with an associated timeframe. For example, the following action will fire when persistent variable ent:archive_pages is greater than 3 and the last time it was set was within the last two hours:

```
if ent:archive_pages > 3 within 2 hours then
  notify(...)
```

The syntax of timeframe-limited predicates is as follows:

```
<pvar> (<= | >= | < | > | == | !=) <expr>
  within <expr> (weeks| days| hours | minutes| seconds)
```

where `<pvar>` is a persistent flag or counter and `<expr>` is any valid KRL expression that returns a number.

Persistent trails can be tested using the seen predicate. There are two forms. The first form asks whether a regular expression has been seen within an optional timeframe (specified exactly as above). So, you can say:

```
if seen re#/archive/2006# in ent:my_trail then
  notify(...)
```

or

```
if seen re#/archive/2006# in ent:my_trail
   within 3 days then
     notify(...)
```

The second form of special predicates for trails allows for checking whether a match of one regular expression appears before an item matched by another. This example would fire the action when a place matching the regular expression re#/archive/2006# was put on the trail before a place matching the regular expression re#/archive/2007#.

```
if seen re#/archive/2006# before re#/archive/2007#
   in ent:my_trail then
     notify(...)
```

Note that before in the preceding conditional is not the same as the before operator in an eventex event, although they share the same name.

Mutating Persistents in the Postlude

To be useful, persistent variables must be mutated. Persistents can only be mutated in the postlude. The following statements mutate persistent variables:

- **clear <pvar>.** This clears (sets to nil) the persistent variable <pvar>.

- **set <pvar>.** This sets (sets to true) the persistent variable <pvar>, making it a flag.

- **set <pvar> <expr>.** This sets the value of <pvar> to the value of the expression (literal). If the persistent variable is bound to a complex data structure (i.e., maps and arrays), <pvar> can contain a hash path referencing part of the structure. The KRL documentation (http://docs.kynetx.com) has additional information.

- **<pvar> (+=|-=) <expr> from <expr>.** This increments (or decrements) the persistent variable <pvar> by the value given by the first expression. If the value is null when the statement executes, the value of the second expression is used to initialize the persistent.

- **mark <pvar> with <expr>.** This marks the trail <pvar> using the value of the expression as the place.

- **forget <regexp> in <pvar>.** This forgets any places in the trail matched by the regular expression.

Using Persistents

The following rule uses a counter to fire an action when an individual has visited a collection of Web pages (anything in the archive directory) more than twice in the last three days:

```
rule frequent_archive_visitor {
  select when pageview url re#/archives/#
  pre {
   c = ent:archive_pages;
  }
  if ent:archive_pages > 2 within 3 days then
    notify("You win the prize!",
        "You've seen " + c + " archive pages")
  fired {
   clear ent:archive_pages;
  } else {
   ent:archive_pages += 1 from 1;
  }
}
```

There are several interesting items in the preceding code:

The entity variable ent:archive_pages is a counter.

- The counter is referenced in an expression in the prelude.

- The rule condition checks the value of the counter and can also impose a time constraint on the check using the within 3 days clause.

- The counter is cleared when the rule fires, resetting and starting the count over again, and otherwise increments the counter by 1.

- Because the counter is an entity variable, a separate count will be maintained automatically for each individual on whose behalf the selecting event was raised, without specific instructions from the programmer.

To see the difference between entity variables and application variables, consider the following example that places a page counter on a page, indicating how often it's been visited:

```
rule count_archive_visitors {
  select when pageview url re#/archives/#
  pre {
   c = app:visitor_count;
   res = << <div id="page_count">#{c}</div> >>
  }
```

```
replace_html("#page_count", res)
always {
  app:visitor_count += 1 from 1;
 }
}
```

The preceding code has several features to point out:

- The rule has no condition and so, if selected, will always fire.

- The `replace_html` action replaces a DOM element that has the ID `page_count` with the contents of the variable `res`.

- The variable `res` is constructed using extended quotes and contains a beesting (`#{c}`). As such, it acts as a template. (A *beesting* can contain any valid KRL expression. The value of the expression is substituted for the beesting. Beestings can appear in extended quotes—think clown hats and chevrons—as well as strings.)

- The application variable `app:visitor_count` is never cleared, only incremented in this rule. A different rule, in the same rule set, however, could clear the counter, because all rules of a rule set can see the rule set's application and entity variables.

- Because this rule uses an application rather than an entity variable, the variable is incremented for all entities, making it perfect for recording information relevant to the application as a whole.

The following rule uses an entity variable to store the URLs of the pages a user visits in an array, excluding sites that the user has already visited:

```
rule make_history {
  select when pageview url re#(.*)# setting (url)
  pre {
    sites = ent:my_sites || [];
    new_array = sites.union(url)
  }
  if (not sites.has(url)) then {
    noop();
  }
  fired {
    set ent:my_sites new_array
  }
}
```

Again, there are several things to point out about the preceding rule:

- The URL of the page being visited is captured and bound to the `url` variable.

- Two KRL set operators (`union` and `has`) manage an array of sites that have been visited.

- Because the postlude of the rule cannot have a general conditional expression but merely piggybacks off the rule's condition with the `fired` statement, the rule tests a condition but takes no action by using a `noop` action.

- The postlude sets (assigns) the new array to be the value of `ent:my_sites`.

Note

You may want to try converting this rule to use trails instead of an array to test your knowledge of persistent variables.

There's an alternate way to write this rule that doesn't require a `noop` action and results in cleaner code:

```
rule make_history {
  select when pageview url #(.*)# setting (url)
  pre {
    sites = ent:my_sites || [];
    new_array = sites.union(url)
  }
  always {
    set ent:my_sites new_array if (not sites.has(url))
  }
}
```

In this rule, the action is left out entirely. The `always` statement in the postlude is always executed. Updating variable `ent:my_sites` is guarded by the `if` statement in the postlude. Any statement in the postlude can have a guard.

PROGRAMMING IN KRL

Although building applications in KRL may require learning new language elements, developers gain access to events, opening a whole world of possibilities. The design of the expression language in KRL is purposely kept familiar, so this new language should not seem too foreign.

As discussed, event-based applications are different from request-based applications. Event-based systems react to occurrences such as a person visiting a Web page, receiving an email, or placing a call. A KRL application is the result of multiple, possibly interdependent, conditional actions taking place over a series of reactions to events. Rules are a natural way to structure programs that react to events.

KRL has declarative structures that reduce programmer burden:

- Eventexes provide a declarative means of specifying the event scenarios to which a rule applies. Developers should plan the eventexes they use in their applications with care.

- Conditions declare the contextual conditions under which actions should be taken. KRL's expression language provides a very capable means for computing the context.

- The embedded little languages for regular expressions, JSONPath and HTML DOM Query, are all declarative methods for computing results.

Developing a KRL application requires understanding the relevant events, their attributes, and determining the correct reactions to those events. More than one rule, even in a single rule set, might fire in response to a given event and the conditions that surround it. A KRL developer should plan the actions a rule takes so they play nice with each other. This is especially important when you realize that a user might have rule sets from other developers installed that respond to the same event and send directives to the same endpoints.

Because rule sets execute each rule once, in order, for any given event, developers can use the instincts they honed working with other statically scoped languages to understand their rule sets and the rules within them.

As you've seen, persistents provide a means of creating data values that are available across rule and rule-set executions. Normal KRL expressions do not have the ability to cause side effects in values. This is slightly more restrictive than what developers are used to from their experience with most programming languages, but limits effects to just the postlude.

Persistents are not currently available outside of a single rule set. Sharing data between rule sets requires using an outside data service or an explicit event (see Chapter 11). This prevents most problems where data isolation would be required to maintain the integrity of data values. Future versions of KRL will deal with concurrent data changes between rule sets as part of the language.

As mentioned, event languages like KRL can build applications that exhibit extreme loose coupling. Each rule is clearly identifiable with a specific portion of the experience based on its eventex, condition, and action.

Rules build experience layer upon layer. As more and more rules are added, they add to the overall experience. Where possible, KRL has been designed to ensure rules work together. Of course, that can't be guaranteed, but the goal is to allow rules to be added in ways that build the experience for the end user. As a consequence, when planning actions for rules, developers should strive to create actions that are idempotent and independent wherever possible:

- Idempotent operations can be carried out more than once without affecting the final value. Adding zero to a number is idempotent because no matter how many times you do it, you get the same result. When rule actions are idempotent, multiple rule applications from a single event create the desired result.

- Independent operations are careful to take actions that won't interfere with other actions in the same domain.

Idempotent and independent actions are not always possible. In addition, some domains are more prone to these types of actions than others. For example, in the domain of Web pages, it's fairly easy to make changes to the DOM in such a way that multiple actions will result in good results and also preserve the DOM structure so that other rules can fire without interference. In the email domain, on the other hand, while deleting an email by message ID is idempotent, forwarding it isn't. Further, deleting an email interferes with a latter action that forwards the same email.

In coming chapters, you'll explore the use of KRL in various domains and see patterns for KRL programming that make solving common problems easier.

WHY USE THE KINETIC RULE LANGUAGE?

A natural question is, "Why a new programming language?" KRL is a cloud-based programming language designed specifically for building applications that respond to events on behalf of individuals. Before I deal with the "new programming language" question, let's handle a more basic one: why a programming language at all? Why not just build a menu-based user interface that allows people to configure the actions the system takes in response to certain event scenarios?

User interfaces are inherently limiting because they provide a fixed menu of choices and little opportunity to combine features from one submenu with another. The whole idea of a menu is to limit choices in order to gain simplicity. In contrast, languages are combinatorial in their expressiveness. Good programming languages have orthogonality, which means that features are independent and thus can be combined together in ways that open up a geometric explosion of possible outcomes. This gives programming language nearly unlimited expressive power. In my career, I've built dozens of user interfaces (UIs) and several programming languages. No one has ever surprised me with what they accomplished with a UI, but I'm constantly amazed at what people achieve with languages.

I believe that languages promote "creative laziness," to borrow a phrase from Douglas Crockford.[2] By creating a domain-specific notation, we encourage programmers to be lazy in ways that save effort and enhance effectiveness. Moreover, notations mold the thought patterns of programmers. Anyone who experienced a wildly different language from the ones they're familiar with such as Erlang or Lisp knows that you have to change the way you think to effectively use such a language. This is often a feature rather than a bug.

Current Web-programming languages are optimized for the dynamic query, static data (DQSD) problems of traditional Web sites. PHP, for example, was specifically designed for building interactive Web sites that depended on a database for their operation. Later, Ruby on Rails came along and improved on that model. In contrast, KRL is optimized for dynamic data, static query (DDSQ) problems and the event model of the Live Web.

In addition to handling events well, any programming language for the Live Web must also manage and manipulate entity context effectively. As you saw in Chapter 4, "Telling Stories on the Web," one of the goals of the Live Web is to bring individuals onto common ground with every other online entity. That means identity and the methods for linking identities must be built into the tools and frameworks used to create the Live Web.

A language that provides intrinsic identity for entities can abstract away much of the overhead that current online identity solutions require. Programmers spend far too much time managing identities and often do it poorly due to the limited expressive power most languages have for dealing with this particular problem domain. KRL has the notion of "entity" built-in from the ground up, and the architecture of KEA supports that abstraction.

Why did programmers adopt Ruby when it's functionally equivalent to existing languages? Why did Rails become popular when it's just written in Ruby? New languages become popular because they solve current problems in a better, more efficient way than existing languages and platforms.

KRL is a new language because developers were frustrated trying to solve evented problems with tools ill-suited to the task. KRL is specifically built to program systems that react to events in the Live Web. Using KRL, a programmer can construct intelligent filters that look for complex patterns in multiple event streams and prompt further action.

ENDNOTES

1. Chakravarthy, Sharma and Deepak Mishra. Snoop: An Expressive Event Specification Language for Active Databases. *Journal of Data Knowledge Engineering*, November 1994.

2. Crockford, Douglas. (2010). Gluing Together Wet Cats in a Crowd. Gluecon 2010. http://www.slideshare.net/douglascrockford/gluecon.

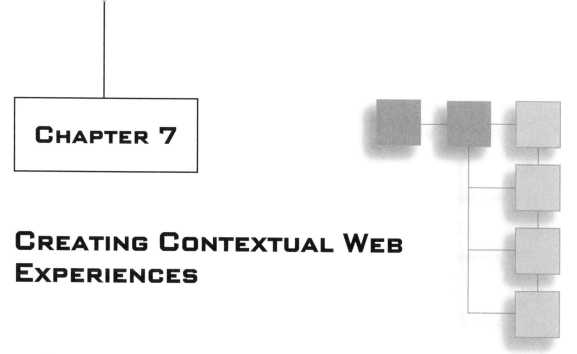

CHAPTER 7

CREATING CONTEXTUAL WEB EXPERIENCES

People spend a great deal of time on the Web in a browser such as Firefox, Chrome, Safari, or Internet Explorer. Consequently, creating Live Web experiences necessarily entails working well with existing Web sites and services—in the browser. This chapter explores using KRL and browser-based endpoints to create Live Web experiences on the existing, static Web.

CONTEXT AND BROWSING

One way to keep children entertained is with connect-the-dot pictures like the one shown in Figure 7.1. Only by connecting the dots does the image appear.[1]

Like this picture, most browsing episodes are disconnected. When people go from site to site in a browsing episode with the goal of accomplishing some task, they must connect the dots in their heads. One way to think of the lines that connect the "dots" of individual Web site visits is as "context."

As you saw in Chapter 4, "Telling Stories on the Live Web," context is all the information relevant to a user's task or purpose. In any given browsing episode, context can include the traits, preferences, and attributes of the user; the sites being visited; and historical information from past episodes. The primary challenge of an ad hoc browsing experience is that the user must manage much of the relevant context rather than being able to turn this chore over to the machine. Browsers provide very little help with this task.

Context automation generates a browsing experience that links formerly disconnected experiences and even modifies individual sites to automatically manage portions of the user's context and to help users achieve their goals with less effort.

Figure 7.1
Connect the dots to see the picture. Image courtesy of PrintActivities.com.

CONTEXTUAL WEB EXPERIENCES

Decisions made long ago about Internet and Web architecture created a system in which machines, IP addresses, and resources (as identified by URLs) are primary and people are secondary. Our current Web experience grows out of these decisions.

Compare the current ad hoc situation with a new one where rich context, built on a foundation of independent Web site identity, is used to give people enhanced Web experiences and relationship-based interactions. At the same time, this new paradigm protects people's identity, privacy, and security.

Over the past decade, browser extensions have become increasingly popular. But people don't usually install browser extensions merely to customize their browser. They are customizing their browser for a purpose: to impose order, form, control, and classification to the otherwise ad hoc flow of information that a stock browser provides.

In contrast to ad hoc, contextual Web experiences are:

- **Browser-aided.** The browser—with the added functionality provided by structuring devices like browser extensions—serves as a tool for helping the user manage context and take action based on that context. In this chapter, you'll see examples of how the browser, with help from KRL, can provide contextual experiences on the Web. The browser plays a key role in this task by functioning as the KEA endpoint and by representing the user.

- **Personal.** Context depends on what is relevant to a person. Some people, for example, may care about security, while others might be concerned with saving money. For the security-minded person, the safety of sites is relevant context. For the frugal shopper, the availability of discounts is relevant context. Any system for managing context has to allow for customization at an individual level, without introducing layers of burden for the developer. Companies spend billions of dollars trying to "get personal" without achieving good results due to the difficulty they face in trying to infer this information from scant data. In contrast, real personalization, with the protection of privacy, can be achieved with contextual Web experiences.

- **Bridged.** In the static Web, each Web site has its own context. On the other hand, Live Web applications use data from multiple Web sites as part of a single experience. Bridging the context of individual Web services to bring them together for the user's purpose is a key idea of the Live Web. Later in this chapter, you'll see an example showing how data about what discounts AAA gives and which companies the Better Business Bureau certifies can be placed right in search results—where it's needed and in context.

- **Identity-based.** Individual customization is not enough. With an underlying foundation of an identity system that is designed to protect personally identifying information and secure user data, context automation bolsters the privacy and security of users. For example, the ability to assert that someone is over 25 for purposes of renting a car without actually revealing the person's birthday provides sufficient context without unnecessarily releasing private information.

- **Relationship-supportive.** By creating an individualized, private and secure experience, context automation supports an atmosphere of trust, wherein relationships between service providers and their customers can flourish. Relationships based on trust create loyal, satisfied visitors. Building a relationship with a company or Web site might seem like a funny idea, but in fact everyone has trusted relationships with certain companies—ones that are mutually beneficial to both. Loyalty programs are a cheap alternative to real relationships, making the benefit purely about discounts or free product. In contrast, real relationships provide assurance and comfort based on trust.

KRL AND THE WEB

KRL has a special relationship with the Web. Not only is the Web ubiquitous, but it's also the first domain to which KRL was applied. Consequently, there is a significant number of actions built into the core of KRL that support interacting with Web sites.

The Web represents a special domain of interaction for developers creating Live Web applications because it is extremely flexible and widely used. There are millions of existing Web sites from which people derive significant value. KRL can be easily used to augment these Web sites, pulling them together and mashing up formerly individual services to create Live Web experiences unlike any available on the static Web.

THE WEB ENDPOINT

The standard KEA endpoint for the Web is the browser itself. Modern browsers are, as evidenced by their extensive collections of extensions, platforms in their own right. The KEA endpoint for the Web is implemented as a JavaScript Web Runtime library that runs in the browser. The Web Runtime implements the functionality necessary for the browser to act as an endpoint in KEA.

Loading the Web Runtime is usually accomplished by placing JavaScript tags in the DOM of appropriate pages based on salience data. The Web Runtime has also been deployed in evaluation sandboxes inside the browser extension. Two tags are used. The first tag sets configuration data and the second tag loads the Web Runtime. The following shows the JavaScript for these tags:

```
<script type="text/javascript">
var KOBJ_config ={
  "rids": ["11"],
  "name" : "Phil"
};
</script>
<script type="text/javascript"
  src="http://init.kobj.net/js/shared/kobj-static.js"></script>
```

The simplest configuration contains only a list of the rule sets to be considered as the Web Runtime raises events. Other event parameters can also be set and will be added to any events raised as a result of loading the Web Runtime. In the preceding example, the event parameter name is set with the value Phil.

The Web Runtime URL depends on the installation of KEA. In the example, the URL is for the commercial service run by Kynetx.

Placing Tags

The tags can be placed using several mechanisms. The most common method used to place JavaScript tags is a browser extension. The browser extension can be single purpose, running a fixed set of rule sets, or a universal extension, running whatever rule sets that user configures. KEA includes open-source (MIT license) examples of single-purpose browser extensions for Internet Explorer, Safari, Chrome, and Firefox.

Simple browser extensions that use a fixed set of rule sets are fairly easy to implement for browsers like Firefox and Chrome that include an extension architecture. The Kynetx Browser Extension (KBX) is a commercial service built on top of KEA that provides Web-based support for managing rule sets giving users a common experience across multiple browsers.

Besides browser extensions, there are several other methods for placing JavaScript tags on a Web page:

- **Tags can be placed using a bookmarklet.** A *bookmarklet* is a browser bookmark that runs JavaScript instead of retrieving a page. Most modern browsers support bookmarklets. Selecting the bookmark runs the JavaScript invoking the program. Bookmarklets have several advantages. For one, they do not require a user download. The user determines when the application runs. Sometimes, such explicit user action is desirable. Bookmarklets, however, can be difficult for non-technical users to install. In addition, managing multiple bookmarklets can be a burden.

- **Tags can be placed using a Web proxy.** The proxy places the tags in the HTML content of any relevant HTTP responses as they transit the proxy. The end user does nothing. Proxy deployment has the advantage of not requiring any user download for applications to run. In addition, proxy deployment provides a universal experience for everyone who is downstream from the proxy. In the case of a conference, for example, this can be desirable. Proxy deployment is also an advantage for devices like the iPhone and iPad that have non-extensible browsers. The key disadvantage is that applications aren't user-installed and are thus fixed in the proxy, although allowing users to establish accounts on the proxy and treating pages from different users differently could mitigate this disadvantage.

■ **Tags can be directly embedded in a Web site's pages.** The key advantage of direct tagging is that it allows a site to be customized using Live Web context rather than when it's updated or deployed. I've long had tags embedded in my blog[2] and use them for everything from displaying my tweets to changing content for visitors from search engines.

Because of the limitations of bookmarklets, proxies, and direct tagging, the browser extension has become the preferred method for deploying Live Web applications in the browser. Another important reason for using browser extensions is that there is relevant context that is unavailable to applications deployed strictly through Java-Script running on a page. A browser extension, as part of the browser "chrome," can see things like new tabs being opened, pages being closed, and so on, and raise events as appropriate. A browser extension can also see what other pages are open and make this context available. Finally, the browser extension can aid in establishing strong identity for the user.

Using Salience Data

Making the Live Web work means raising events. To avoid the efficiency problems that would result from the browser extension raising events for every `pageview`, `click`, `submit`, or `change` event that the user generates, the Web Runtime is written so that it determines (with support from the browser extension, if available) which events are salient and only raises those falling within specific bounds.

When a developer creates a rule set in KRL, the primary source of salience data is the event expressions in the rules. In particular, primitive events and their filters provide significant salience data. In addition, the developer can give salience hints using the `dispatch` section of the rule set.

For rule sets listening for Web events, the `dispatch` block is used to indicate domain names for Web sites that should raise `pageview` events. The following `dispatch` block indicates that the rule set is interested in `pageview` events on google.com and bing.com:

```
dispatch {
  domain "google.com"
  domain "bing.com"
}
```

Of course, these could be listed in the regular expression filters in the event expressions, but often it's easier to write regular expressions that don't pay attention to the domain name in the URL and just select based on some other feature of the URL.

The salience API provides endpoints with basic or detailed salience data about the rule set. For browser endpoints, the basic salience API provides just the domain names listed in the `dispatch` block. The detailed salience API provides data on primitive events in the `web` event domain and the filters from the `select` statements of the rule set in addition to information in the basic salience API. The following JSON structure shows the detailed salience data for a single rule set:

```
{"a16x69":{
  "domains":["byu.edu","exampley.com"],
  "events":{
   "web":{
    "submit":[{"pattern":"#my_form","type":"element"}],
    "pageview":[{"pattern":"www.foobar.com","type":"default"},
                {"pattern":".*","type":"default"}]},
   "explicit":{"got_name":[{"pattern":".*","type":".*"}]}}}}
```

The detailed salience information returns the domains but also detailed information about the events in which the rule set is interested, giving information about the event domains, event types, and patterns.

The endpoint uses salience data from the API to reduce its communication with the rules engine. There are also privacy benefits from this arrangement because the user's entire browsing history isn't visible to applications, only those events that are relevant. In addition, salience data can inform users of what Web sites will be affected by the applications they install. Notifying users of which KRL applications are running on a given Web site protects users from malicious applications.

The Web Runtime

The Web Runtime is a JavaScript library that implements a Kinetic endpoint in the browser. The primary duty of the Web Runtime is to raise relevant events for rule sets and respond to the directives sent back from any rules processing those events.

In the case of the browser endpoint, directives take the form of JavaScript code that is executed on the page in the browser where the Web Runtime raised the event. (We'll discuss the specific events that the Web Runtime is capable of raising and the specific actions that it understands later in this chapter.) The browser endpoint is currently the best example of a scriptable endpoint because it can execute the full complement of JavaScript within the browser, making it extremely flexible and capable.

Here's how that works: When a browser makes an HTTP `GET` request for a URL, it usually receives back an HTML document representing the page. The browser parses the HTML document and fetches any referenced images, CSS files, or JavaScript. The result of this process is a data structure called a document object model (DOM) that the browser uses to render a page.

One of the amazing things about browsers is that they respond, in real time, to changes in the DOM. Thus, if you change the DOM after the browser has rendered the page, the browser will re-render the portion of the page represented by the changed portion of the DOM. This idea is the basis of Dynamic HTML and AJAX technologies that have been made popular by myriad interactive Web applications.

The Kinetic Web Runtime makes use of that property when it takes action on a Web page. The JavaScript returned as a directive from KEA makes use of functions in the Web Runtime to modify the DOM and thus change what the user sees in the browser.

The Kinetic Web Runtime is based on jQuery, a powerful JavaScript framework. Although many KRL programmers will never need to go this far, the full power of jQuery is available within KRL for making changes on the page. One of the most important benefits of using jQuery is that the Web Runtime behaves consistently in all modern browsers.

Note

Modern browsers include Firefox version 3 and above, Chrome, Safari 3 and above, and Internet Explorer version 7 and above. There is limited support in the Web Runtime for Internet Explorer 6.

Developers can load their own JavaScript libraries and CSS descriptions for a page with the use resource pragma in the `meta` section of the rule set. For example, the following would load a JavaScript library from the given URL, which could be used later in the rule set:

```
use javascript resource "http://example.com/a8x62/date.js"
```

Similarly, the following would load a set of CSS directives from the given URL:

```
use css resource "http://example.com/a8x62/dates.css"
```

That CSS is placed on the page and can change stylings on the page or provide CSS definitions for use later in the rule set.

Note

Changing the existing styling of the page in this way isn't robust and can break things on the page, so proceed with caution. Defining CSS for your own use is perfectly safe if you take care to choose names that don't clash.

Note

> Fully understanding and making use of KRL is easier for programmers who understand the DOM, dynamic HTML, CSS, and JavaScript.

The Web Runtime is a JavaScript program that the Web endpoint downloads. For performance reasons, the user's browser caches the library according to the caching parameters set by the server. Different installations can set these parameters differently, but there's generally no need for a time shorter than 24 hours. Because of this caching, you should be aware that changes made to the Web Runtime won't be seen by all users at the same time, but only as their browser expires the old version and reloads the Web Runtime.

Dual-Execution Environment

One of the most important concepts to understand in using the Web endpoint with KRL is the dual-execution environment of the rule set on the Web. When the rules of a rule set are executed in response to a web event, they are executed on the server. The execution of these KRL rules results in a JavaScript program that is then executed on the browser.

This two-stage execution of rules in response to an event confuses some new KRL developers. For many uses, you can ignore the server entirely and just think of the action as an atomic change on the browser. But that is not true in every case. For example, when using the annotation action that decorates lists on a page according to a filter that is using dynamically loaded data, you have to consider how the filter (written in JavaScript) will execute in the browser and what format the data takes. (We'll program an example using annotation later in this chapter.)

The rules engine and the Web Runtime cooperate to make this easier. For example, most declarations made in the prelude of a rule are also made in the JavaScript that is generated. Consequently, in the aforementioned annotation example, the filter you write can make use of values computed in the rule prelude. Scoping in the generated JavaScript matches the scoping in the rule set itself. The JavaScript generated by each rule is wrapped in a closure to properly scope the variables declared in the rule. Similarly, the JavaScript generated by a rule set is also wrapped in a closure to properly scope the variables in its global block. On the Web, it's sometimes useful to think of KRE as a KRL-to-JavaScript translator. KRE takes great pains to maintain semantic consistency between the JavaScript and the KRL from whence it is generated.

Note

> Some KRL expressions cannot be meaningfully translated to JavaScript and thus are not available.

One of the benefits of the dual-execution environment is the protection of user privacy. KRL rules, running on the rules engine, can use data about the individual without revealing it to either the developer or the execution environment in the browser (which can be unfriendly, despite being on the user's desktop). A secure execution environment can protect against leaking sensitive data and exposing it to risk.

WEB EVENTS

As you've seen, endpoints are responsible for raising events. At present, the Web endpoint raises four events:

- `pageview`
- `submit`
- `click`
- `change`

Note

There is nothing magic about these four, but they have proven themselves to be very useful. Over time, this list is likely to expand.

pageview

The primary and most frequently raised event on the Web is `pageview`. A `pageview` event occurs whenever a user visits a page in his or her browser. The event includes the following named parameters:

- **url**. The URL of the page being opened. This is also called `caller` for historical reasons.
- **title**. The title of the page as given in the HTML `<title/>` element.
- **referer**. The URL of the page that referred the page view. This is the page the user came from if he or she clicked a link to generate the current `pageview` event.

Note

The original HTTP specification misspelled "referrer" as "referer," and the mistake has propagated through the Web. I will remain true to the spelling in the HTTP specification.

submit

Whenever the user clicks a salient HTML Submit button, the Web Runtime raises a `submit` event. Applications indicate that any element of a page is salient using the `watch` action (described momentarily).

Submit buttons are typically located inside HTML forms. The `submit` event includes the form-encoded name-value pairs for each of the associated form elements as rule set parameters. While event attributes are available generally to every rule set that responds to an event, rule set parameters are only available to a single rule set. In the case of `submit`, the rule set ID used is the same as the rule set ID that placed the watch on the Submit button.

Note

Presently, because the event is raised using an HTTP GET, the length of these parameters is limited by the length limit for URLs. Future Web endpoints will raise `submit` events using a POST to overcome this limitation.

In addition to the form elements, the event includes an event attribute named `element` that gives the selector (name or identification) of the form that was submitted. This is useful for distinguishing which form has been submitted when more than one form is being watched.

click and change

The `click` event is raised when the user clicks an element being watched. The event also includes the `element` attribute, giving the selector of the DOM element that was clicked. The `change` event is raised when the user changes an input field that is being watched. The event also includes the `element` attribute, giving the selector of the DOM element that was clicked.

Other Event Attributes

In addition to the specific attributes for each event just described, KRE makes other event attributes available that are implicit in raising the event:

- **rid.** The RID of the rule set being evaluated
- **ip.** The IP address of the host of the browser endpoint

The built-in module `useragent` uses the `UserAgent` string sent by the browser to pre-compute several values, including language used by the browser, the browser name and version, the operating system and version, and the selector (endpoint) name and version. For example, the following shows a declaration binding a variable named lc to the language code returned by the browser:

```
lc = useragent:language_code();
```

The built-in module page contains a function url() that can be used to parse the URL of the page into the following components: hostname, URL path portion, domain name, top-level domain, port, and query string. The following binds the variable named d to the domain name of the Web page where the pageview event was raised:

```
d = page:url("domain");
```

These event attributes can be used to determine information about the event and where it came from. Chapter 8, "Using the Cloud," discusses other built-in modules.

ACTIONS IN THE WEB DOMAIN

KRL actions for the Web primarily result in the DOM being changed in some way. Some of these actions are fairly simple, straightforward methods for manipulating the DOM. For example:

- **after(<selector>, <html>).** This places the HTML fragment given by the second argument after the DOM element identified by the jQuery selector given as the first argument.

- **move_to_top(<selector>).** This moves the item identified by the selector in the argument to the top of whatever container it's in.

Note

Appendix E, "The KRL Expression Language," offers a description of the DOM selector syntax and semantics used in the Web Runtime.

Other actions are sophisticated, requiring coordination of resources and data across multiple rules and even rule sets. For example:

- **notify(<header>, <message>).** This places a notification box on the page, similar to Growl notifications in OS X. Multiple notifications stack nicely. notify has numerous options for controlling lifetime, styling, and placement. Figure 7.2 shows a simple notification box placed on a Web site (www.example.com).

- **annotate(<name>).** This annotates a list (such as Google search results). Optional parameters provide a function for filtering which items are annotated,

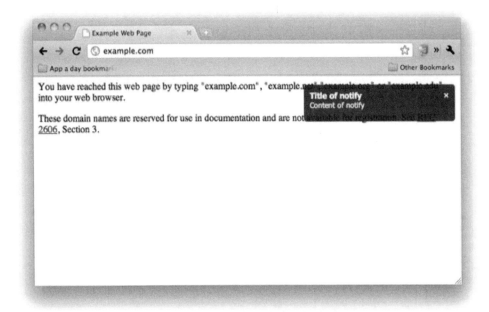

Figure 7.2
A simple notification box on www.example.com.

what the annotation looks like, and how the items are annotated. Figure 7.3 shows Google search results for "shoes" with AAA and Better Business Bureau reminders annotating some results.

The ability to interact with Web pages as they are rendered in the browser provides a powerful way of giving users important data in context. The annotations in Figure 7.3 provide important, valuable information to users right when they need it: as they search. This mashup of data from one or more services on a Web site the user cares about is an effective use for KRL.

Another Web-specific action that plays a key role in Web interactions is watch(). The watch(<selector>, <event>) action attaches a listener to a browser event (don't confuse these with KRL events). The watch() action provides salience information to the Web Runtime. When you watch, say, a form-submission button for a submit event and the user clicks that button, the Web Runtime will raise a web: submit event to KRE and any rules listening for that event will be selected.

Note

The watch action is not strictly necessary because the salience data from a rule set could tell you what browser events to attach listeners to. Future versions of KRL will not need a watch action if the browser endpoint uses salience information to do this automatically.

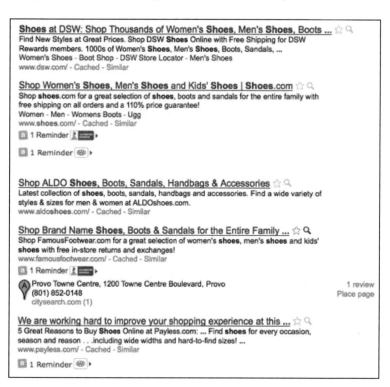

Figure 7.3
Google search results annotated with AAA and BBB reminders.

The Web endpoint understands dozens of actions, some simple and others more complicated. The full list can be found in the KRE documentation online.

Examples of KRL in Action on the Web

It's time for several examples of KRL in action on the Web. First, you'll explore a simple page modification. Next, you'll explore annotating search results with external data. Finally, you'll learn how to process forms using KRL.

Welcoming Searchers to My Blog

All the past articles on my blog are in the `archive` directory. The URL for a given post contains the year and month when the post was written, and ends with the blog post title in lowercase letters, with underscores replacing the spaces. That means a blog post written in June 2009 with the title "Buying an iPhone" will have the following URL path:

```
/archives/2009/06/buying_an_iphone.shtml
```

Suppose you want to display a welcome panel for people coming to the blog post from a search engine on the assumption they're not a regular reader, showing them where to find additional posts about the iPhone. The following rule accomplishes that goal:

```
rule iphone_welcome {
  select when pageview url re#/archives/\d+/\d+/(.+).shtml#
                   setting(pagename)
     pre {
       iphone_invite = < <
<div class="welcomepanel">
 <h2>Want more articles about iPhone?</h2>
 <p>Click <a id="iphonetag" href="/tags/iphone">
 through for related articles</a> about iPhone.</p>
</div>
       >>;
     }
     if (referer:search_engine_referer() &&
        pagename.match(re#iphone#)) then
       replace_html("#kynetx_11", iphone_invite);
     }
}
```

This rule is selected on the URL pattern shown, setting the variable `pagename` to the portion of the URL that contains the title of the blog post. The rule prelude binds a variable called `iphone_invite` to a chunk of HTML that produces the welcome panel. I've removed much of the styling for readability. The rule condition uses the `search_engine_referer()` function from the built-in module `referer` to determine whether the event's `referer` parameter is a commonly known search engine and matches `pagename` against "iphone" using the binary operator `like`. The `replace_html()` action replaces an HTML element with the identifier `kynetx_11` with the HTML in `iphone_invite`. When this rule fires, you see a box like the one shown in Figure 7.4 above the body of the blog posting.

Suppose you wanted to make this example more general so that it would work with several terms. The following rule does the same thing as the previous rule, but usesan array of terms that will trigger the welcome panel:

```
rule welcome_panel {
  select when pageview url re#/archives/.*#
```

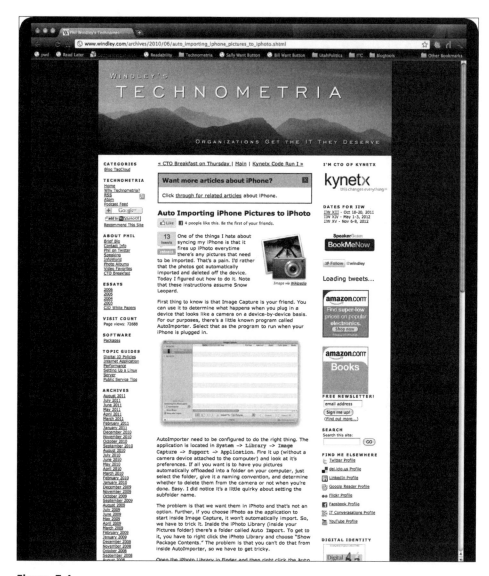

Figure 7.4
A welcome panel appears above the blog posting text for articles about the iPhone.

```
pre {
  keywords = [
    "iphone",
    "google",
    "kynetx"
    ];
  keyword_str = "re#(" + keywords.join("|") + ")#i";
  keyword_re = keyword_str.as("regexp");
```

```
   topic = event:param("title").extract(keyword_re).head();
   invite = <<
<div class="welcomepanel">
 <h2>Want more articles about #{topic}?</h2>
 <p>Click <a id="tag" href="/tags/#{topic.lc()}">
 for related articles</a>about #{topic}.</p>
</div>
   >>;
 }
 if(referer:search_engine_referer() &&
   event:param("title").match(keyword_re) then
      replace_html("#kynetx_11", invite);
 }
}
```

This example is similar to the previous one, except it's been generalized by the introduction of the keywords array. By merely adding words to this list, you can increase the topics for which blog visitors will see a welcome panel. In the next chapter, you'll see how to use external data sources to create dynamic updates to rule behavior.

The primary changes necessary to generalize the rule involve processing the array to create a regular expression and then using that regular expression to get the topic from the page title. You use the real page title rather than information in the URL because you want words, like "iPhone," to have the proper case. Note that because you are getting the topic from the page title now, the filter in the event expression can been simplified.

You create keyword_str, a string representing the regular expression you want to fashion by joining the members of the array with a bar separating them and then wrapping the result in parentheses and hashes. The trailing i ensures that the regular expression will match regardless of case.

The variable keyword_re simply coerces the string representation into a proper regular expression using the as() operator. (I could have created the regular expression all in one step, but I split it up for clarity.) The result is as if you'd typed the following regular expression directly:

re#(iphone|google|kynetx)#i

The regular expression is used with the extract() operator to pick out the topic from the blog post title. The topic is used in creating the invitation text in the panel with beestings. Note that you use the lc() operator in the beesting that creates the tag link because it must be all lowercase. A beesting can contain any KRL expression.

KRL provides the means of manipulating arrays, regular expressions, and other complex data so that the rules that are written are purposeful and powerful.

Search-Result Annotation

Annotation is a good example of a complex KRL action in the Web domain because it is doing much more than simply manipulating the DOM (although there's certainly plenty of that going on, too).

Early in the development of KRL, one of the things people loved was its ability to modify a Web site to better fit the purpose of the user. One of the key uses became annotating Web sites with relevant data from an online data source. And, of course, some of the best sites to annotate were those where people spend an inordinate amount of time: search engines.

We built an action called `annotate()` to annotate lists of data on Web sites—especially search engines. Search-engine annotation presents special challenges:

- Different search engines have different DOM structures, even though the basic idea is similar: Present a list of results. The `annotate()` action functions correctly on the eight most popular search engines.

- The content of the page is dynamic depending on what the query term is, so annotation decisions need to be made after the page has rendered.

- Some search results, like Google, also dynamically update the results without a page refresh. Consequently, there will be no subsequent event to KRE to rerun the rule. The JavaScript in the browser must manage the refresh.

KRL's `annotate()` action takes all these design-space issues into account, making annotation of search results easy and fast. In addition, the `annotate()` action works on any list structure—not just those on search engines—so it can be used to annotate tweets, Facebook pages, and any other page with a list structure.

Annotation relies on a user-supplied JavaScript function to determine which list items to annotate and what form the annotation should take. You can write the function, place it in an HTTP accessible file, and load it using the use resource pragma you saw earlier. However, often—especially during development—this is too much work. An easier way is to use the `emit` action. The `emit` action takes a chunk of JavaScript, delimited with clown hats, as its argument. The JavaScript is emitted in place as part of the JavaScript directive sent to the browser endpoint.

The function can be named anything you like, but should take exactly three parameters:

- The item in the list to annotate
- The wrapper `<div/>` element that you will modify to produce the annotation
- A data object that contains information about the item being annotated

The item and wrapper are given as jQuery objects. When the annotate() action runs on the page, it will call this function, with the appropriate arguments, once for each item being annotated.

The annotate() action itself takes a single argument: a name that is used to coordinate annotation among several cooperating rule sets. The name is used to name the wrapper <div/>. If two rule sets use the same name, they will be given the same wrapper to modify.

The following example shows the annotation of items from www.windley.com in search-engine results with the string "READ THIS!" in red on Google, Bing, and Yahoo!.

```
rule annotate_windley {
  select when pageview url
    #google.com|bing.com|search.yahoo.com#
  every {
    emit <|
      function anno_windley(toAnnotate, wrapper, data) {
        if(data.domain == "www.windley.com") {
          wrapper.append(
            "<span style='color: red'>READ THIS!</span>"
          );
          wrapper.show();
        }
      };
      KOBJ.anno_windley = anno_windley;
    |>;
    annotate:annotate("windley") with
      annotator = <|KOBJ.anno_windley|>;
  }
}
```

The first thing to notice about this rule is that the action is a compound action created with the every structure. Each of the actions in the every structure will be taken when the rule fires. In this case, the emit action is used to define the annotation filter function in JavaScript and then use it with the annotate:annotate() action. (This notation indicates that annotate() is an action in the built-in annotate module.)

The JavaScript function, anno_windley(), is structured as described previously. Remember that annotate() will apply this function to each item in the result list in turn, setting the arguments according to the current item. The data argument will contain a map that, among other things, contains a field called domain that holds the domain name of the item in the result list.

The domain is tested to see if it's equal to www.windley.com. If so, a <span/> element containing the desired text is appended to the wrapper that annotate()

supplied. I also show the wrapper since it's hidden by default. The `append()` operation is part of jQuery, which is included in the Web Runtime and thus always available. While I merely appended some text, you could also display a graphic or anything else that you can create with HTML.

I didn't use the `toAnnotate` argument in the function. Because this argument refers to the JavaScript object representing the item in the result list, performing operations on the `toAnnotate` argument will modify the result itself, not merely annotate it, as I have done.

When this rule fires, it will annotate any search results from www.windley.com. Figure 7.5 shows a portion of the Google search results for the query "kynetx rule language modules" annotated using the preceding rule. Note that the results from www.windley.com are annotated with a red "READ THIS!" string.

Figure 7.5
Google search results for "kynetx rule language modules" showing annotations for www.windley.com.

Note

The `annotate()` action is sophisticated and has options and uses that are not covered here. The KRL documentation (see Appendix B, "Resources") has more information.

Using Web Forms with KRL

Forms are all over the Web, and every non-trivial Web application uses them. This example shows how to use forms in KRL along with persistent variables to gather, remember, and use user-supplied data.

The rule set you will create follows a basic KRL pattern: Initialize and populate. The idea is to use one rule to initialize a canvas on the page and use the remaining rules to paint content onto the canvas. You will use a persistent trail to store the user data. If the trail is empty, the user will be presented with a form to enter his or her name. If not, the contents of the trail will be displayed on the canvas. When the form is processed, you'll store the name in the trail.

Because the order of the rules in a rule sets is important, I will discuss them in order. There are five rules altogether:

- `clear_name`
- `initialize`
- `send_form`
- `respond_submit`
- `replace_with_name`

clear_name

The first rule simply clears the entity variable `ent:username` when someone visits a particular Web page. This allows you to reset the application to its initial state. You could, of course, do this under user control using a form submission or some other mechanism, but this is an easy way to clear the data.

```
rule clear_name {
  select when pageview re#\?reset#
  always {
    clear ent:username;
    last
  }
}
```

This rule has no action. If the rule is selected (the page URL has a query string that starts with the string `reset`), then the entity variable is cleared and this is the last rule executed in this rule set.

initialize

As mentioned, the initialize and modify pattern first initializes the page with a canvas so that different rules can do different things to the area as needed, without each rule having to do the setup. The `initialize` rule simply puts up an empty notification box with a `<div/>` element named #my_div that will be used in later rules.

```
rule initialize {
  select when pageview url re#.*#
  pre {
      blank_div = << <div id="my_div"></div> >>;
  }
  notify("Hello Example", blank_div)
    with sticky=true;
}
```

The optional parameter for the `notify()` action, `sticky=true`, causes the notification box to remain visible on the page. I've made the URL pattern in this and other rules selected by a `pageview` event as general as possible (re#.*#). In a production rule set, the filters would likely be much more restrictive. Also, while I'm placing this form in a notify box, you could easily place it inside the page as well with a `replace_html()` action, making it fit in better with the Web site.

send_form

This rule puts the form into the `div` you initialized in the previous rule if the entity variable `ent:username` is empty. The primary action is to append the form to the blank `<div/>` element placed in the canvas at initialization. The rule also sets a watcher on that form. If this rule fires (i.e., the rule is selected *and* the condition is true), then this will be the last rule executed in this rule set based on the control statement in the postlude.

```
rule send_form {
  select when pageview url #.*#
  pre {
    a_form = <<
<form id="my_form" onsubmit="return false">
<input type="text" name="first"/>
<input type="text" name="last"/>
<input type="submit" value="Submit" />
```

```
</form>
>>;
  }
  if(not ent:username) then {
   append("#my_div", a_form);
   watch("#my_form", "submit");
  }
  fired {
    last;
  }
}
```

When this rule fires, you get a notification box that looks like the one shown in Figure 7.6.

Figure 7.6
The form placed on top of a Web site.

respond_submit

You need a rule to listen for the submit event and process the content of the form. The rule, respond_submit, uses a select statement that looks for the submit event and filters on the form name.

```
rule respond_submit {
  select when web submit "#my_form"
  pre {
    username = event:attr("first")+" "+event:attr("last");
  }
  replace_inner("#my_div", "Hello #{username}");
  fired {
    set ent:username username;
  }
}
```

Note

You might notice that the filter in the select statement is not the standard name-filter pairing and that the name of the event parameter, element, is missing. Web events have a historical syntax that assumes particular event parameters.

The action of this rule replaces the contents of the <div/> element with the ID my_div with the name information that was submitted in the canvas. Note that the rule uses the action replace_inner(), which replaces the form in the canvas with the content computed in the prelude. If I had used the append() action, the form would remain with the name below it. The work of storing the form data is done in the postlude, where the name is put in the entity variable ent:username.

replace_with_name

The final rule uses the data in the entity variable to put the user's name in the <div/> placed in the initialize rule. Like the aforementioned respond_submit rule, this rule replaces the contents of the <div/> with the ID my_div with a hello message that includes the name.

```
rule replace_with_name {
  select when web pageview ".*"
  pre {
    username = current ent:username;
  }
  replace_inner("#my_div", "Hello #{username}");
}
```

Note

You might be wondering why this rule doesn't fire after `respond_submit`. The answer is in the `select` statements. `replace_with_name` fires on a `pageview`, not a `submit`. Only rules listening for a `submit` event, like `respond_submit`, will fire on a `submit` event.

When this rule fires, the notification box looks like the one shown in Figure 7.7.

Whenever this rule set is selected in the future, the user will not see the form, but will simply see this box. That's because the system remembers the name stored in the entity variable and has no need to ask for it again. If the data gets cleared, the user is prompted to enter it again.

Figure 7.7
The result after the form is submitted.

Improving the Rule Set

You might object to the need to use `replace_inner()` in two different rules to paint the name data in the canvas. For a simple program like this rule set, using two rules is easy enough, but it isn't good programming practice. If you update the look or style of the content, you'll have to remember to make the changes in both rules.

This problem is actually easy to solve using a slightly more complicated eventex in the last rule. After removing the `replace_inner()` action from the respond_submit rule, you change the `select` statement of the `replace_with_name` rule to the following:

```
select when web pageview ".*"
       or web submit "#my_form"
```

After this change, the only rule painting the name on the canvas is `replace_with_name`; it will do so on either a `pageview` event or a `submit` event.

Chapter 11, "Building Event Networks," explores explicit events and shows how they can be used to chain rules together for cases when the eventex doesn't provide an easy solution, as it does is here.

CONTEXT ENABLES THE LIVE WEB

Because the Web is ubiquitous and browsers have become the default user interface for so many of the applications that people use, KRL provides a number of powerful primitive operations, functions, predicates, and actions for dealing with the Web. The browser endpoint provides a universal experience regardless of the type of browser being used. Because the endpoint is scriptable using JavaScript, it is powerful and flexible.

Being able to knit together multiple Web sites under the influence of a common, universal browser endpoint allows for the creation of context that spans these Web sites. Where context was previously split between them, it can now travel with the user, creating Live Web experiences.

The examples shown in this chapter are only a few of the many possibilities. Developers have created thousands of applications that use the browser to create Live Web experiences. The key to making these experiences truly compelling, however, is the advent and availability of thousands of data APIs. The next chapter explores how these can be used to augment what you've seen in this chapter with dynamic data.

ENDNOTES

1. If you'd rather not deface your book, but are dying of curiosity, it's a frog.
2. Windley's Technometria is found at www.windley.com.

CHAPTER 8

USING THE CLOUD

A Google Trends search shows that while the number of people searching for the term "SaaS" (software as a service) has stayed relatively flat over the past seven years, the use of the search term "cloud computing" has gone from nothing in mid-2007 to surpass the volume of searches for "SaaS" by mid 2010 (see Figure 8.1). Clearly, the concept of cloud computing resonates with people.

Using the cloud—data and services delivered via online APIs—inside an application is a sure way to increase the application's value because it bridges context from one service to another. *Programmable Web,* a directory of cloud services, lists more than 4,000 APIs.[1] Many of these provide valuable sources of context for Live Web applications.

So far, the KRL applications you've built haven't used data and services from the cloud, but that's going to change in this chapter. KRL includes numerous primitives that make using external services easy. You'll finish the chapter by seeing how these primitives can be encapsulated inside abstractions that make them easy to use and share. KRL was designed from the ground up with the cloud in mind.

dataset AND datasource DECLARATIONS

The simplest way to use cloud-based data inside KRL is with `dataset` and `datasource` declarations. Both declarations are made in the rule set's `global` section. The difference between the two is timing. A `dataset` request is processed once, when the rule set begins execution. On the other hand, `datasource` declarations simply declare an operation that can be used to make queries to the data source in other parts of the rule set on demand.

Figure 8.1
Google Trends search for keywords "SaaS" versus "cloud computing" in August, 2011.

`dataset` Declarations

Global declarations can declare a data set for use in the rules of the rule set. `data-set` declarations are preceded by the keyword `dataset` and contain a name to bind the data to as well as a URL where the data resides. These are separated by the small `left-arrow` symbol (`<-`).

```
dataset temps <- http://example.com/UT/SLC/Temps/
```

In this example, the data at the location specified by the URL is downloaded immediately and bound to the variable `temps`.

Doing this each time a rule set runs would be wasteful and inefficient for data that changes infrequently. Consequently, the `dataset` declaration supports an optional caching specification. If a caching specification is not given, the data is assumed to not be cacheable. The caching specification consists of the keyword `cacheable` followed by an optional time period specified as follows:

```
for <num> <period>
```

Note

> To avoid server overload, a minimum caching period (currently 20 minutes) is imposed on all remote data sources in the current implementation of KRE. Specifying caching periods shorter than the minimum will have no effect.

In the specification, `<period>` can be `seconds`, `minutes`, `hours`, `days`, or `weeks`. If the time period is not specified, the caching period defaults to 24 hours.

The following shows examples of `dataset` declarations:

```
global {
  dataset public_data <- "http://example.com/data.json";
  dataset cached_data <- "http://example.com/data.json" cacheable;
  dataset other_data <- "http://example.com/other.json"
     cacheable for 3 hours;
}
```

`dataset` declarations are best used with small to medium sets of data that don't change often and can be cached.

Recall the dual-execution environment that KRL enables on the server and the browser. This also means that data you load will be transferred to the browser as well. The Web Runtime tries to do this as efficiently as possible and uses a separate script to load the data so that the browser can cache it. Different instances of KRE may handle the caching times on the browser differently, so be sure to understand the caching settings of the KRE instance you are working on to ensure good performance from `dataset` declarations.

datasource Declarations

`datasource` declarations are like `dataset` declarations in that they are a way of accessing remote data, but they are queried when needed rather than loaded all at once like `dataset` declarations. Similar to `dataset` declarations, `datasource` declarations are declared in the `global` block using a similar syntax:

```
global {
 datasource library_data <- "http://example.com/solr/?wt=json";
}
```

Later, a data source can be queried as part of any KRL expression. For example, you could query the data source declared previously like so:

```
pre {
 book_data = datasource:library_data("&q="+isbn);
}
```

Note that when you prepend the namespace `datasource:` to the name of the data source and give additional arguments to be added to the query, the following occurs:

■ If the parameter is a string, then it is concatenated with the URL root given in the `datasource` declaration without modification. The string you supply, when appended to the data source root URL, *must* result in exactly the URL that you intend to call.

■ If the parameter is a map of name-value pairs, the map will be converted into a properly formatted query string and appended to the data source URL. Naturally, the map can be computed rather than simply being made up of literals. The composition of the URL is done in an effort to create a valid URL.

`datasource` declarations use the same syntax for specifying cacheability as `dataset` declarations.

Note

If the URL given in the `datasource` declaration contains a question mark, the parameter string created from the map is appended using an ampersand. If it does not, the string is appended using a question mark.

Data Formats

When you use a `dataset` or `datasource` declaration, KRL assumes the data is returned as JSON and tries to parse it accordingly. If the parse fails, the data is returned as a raw string. You can give `dataset` and `datasource` declarations hints about the format of the data being requested if it's not JSON, and KRL will try to parse that data format and return the resulting JSON structure.

Aside from JSON, KRL also supports parsing XML and—as a special case—RSS. You provide the format hint by appending it to the name in the declaration separated by a colon, like so:

```
global {
  dataset news:RSS <- "http://rss.news.yahoo.com/rss/mostviewed";
  dataset dales:XML <- "http://frag.kobj.net/clients/sales.xml";
}
```

Of course, there is no canonical way to convert XML and RSS to JSON. For specifics of how these formats are converted to JSON data structures, see the KRL documentation.

APIs and Built-In Libraries

KRL has a number of built-in libraries that provide access to data and services from across the Web. Where possible, these libraries are designed to give access to data and services related to the entity for which the rule set is executing. Some libraries simply adapt information based on the user's location as determined from information supplied by the endpoint (e.g., time zone). Other libraries use OAuth or other authorization schemes to link the user's identity at the service to the rule set.

One of the most important libraries adds support for HTTP to KRL. I will cover that in detail because it is important to examples discussed later in the book. I will then briefly cover some other built-in libraries. The KRL documentation contains the latest list of all the built-in libraries available.

The HTTP Library

The HTTP library allows more general, flexible access to cloud-based data than `dataset` and `datasource` declarations. The HTTP library supports the primary HTTP methods—GET, POST, PUT, DELETE, HEAD, and PATCH—as both functions and actions.

Note

Using GET to send data to an API is not very RESTful and is not recommended. KRL allows it for cases where the API has been written poorly and using GET is the only way to interact with it.

I'll discuss the `http:get()` function and `http:post()` action in detail to show the general operation and refer you to the KRL documentation for information on the other functions and actions.

The get() Function

The `http:get()` function can be used as part of any KRL expression. The function always returns a map of name-value pairs, so the expression must expect the data in that format. The `http:get()` function takes four arguments (in order):

- **URL.** This is the URL to retrieve.

- **Parameters.** These are contained in a map that will be used to create the URI-encoded query parameters.

- **Headers.** These are contained in an optional map that will be used to create headers for the GET request.

- **Response headers.** These are contained in an optional array that contains the names of headers from the response to pass back in the response.

The result of calling `http:get()` is a map of name-value pairs that has the following structure:

- **content.** The content of the response

- **content_type.** The MIME type of the content

- **content_length.** The number of bytes in the content

- **status_code.** The three-digit HTTP status code

- **status_line.** The complete status string, including the three-digit HTTP status code

In addition, the response map contains any keys given in the fourth optional parameter to the request and their value in the resulting response header.

The following example shows using `http:get()` to call a URL on example.com:

```
pre {
  r = http:get("http://example.com/widgets/printenv.pl",
          {"a": "5",
          "version": "dev"});
}
```

Often, the parameters won't be a literal map (as shown here), but a computed value. This function application would make the call to the example.com URL after fashioning a query string from the parameters in the map in the second argument. The URL called would be:

```
http://example.com/widgets/printenv.pl?a=5&version=dev
```

Suppose you made the same function application, but also included the third and fourth optional arguments:

```
pre {
  r = http:get("http://example.com/widgets/printenv.pl",
            {"a": "5",
             "version": "dev"},
            {"X-proto": "flipper"},
            ["flopper"]);
}
```

When the call is made, the HTTP request will also contain the header:

```
X-proto: flipper
```

The response will contain the map outlined previously, plus a name-value pair with the name `flopper` and a value equal to the value of the header `flopper` in the HTTP response.

HTTP Actions

Interacting with cloud-based services usually involves sending data. To send data, you use the `http:post()` action. The `http:post()` action takes a single argument: the URL of the resource accepting the `POST` request.

The `http:post()` action accepts the following optional parameters (given using the `with` syntax):

- **params.** A map of key-value pairs that will be used as the parameters for the `POST` request. These parameters will be form-encoded and sent in the body of the `POST` request.

- **headers.** A map of the headers to send with the `POST` request.

- **response_headers.** An array of the names of headers from the response to set in the response object.

- **body.** The body of the `POST` request. This is only sent if the `params` parameter is empty or undefined and the `content_type` parameter is set in the headers. This allows for sending raw, unencoded content with the `POST` request.

- **credentials.** A map of key-value pairs that present the credentials for a URL that requires HTTP basic authentication.[2]

- **autoraise.** A string that will be the label applied to the event that this action automatically raises. Explicit events, including automatically raised events, are discussed in Chapter 11, "Building Event Networks."

The http:get() action works in the same manner as http:post(), except that an HTTP GET is used instead of a POST and the parameters are encoded as an HTTP query string.

The following example shows using an http:post() action inside a rule:

```
rule r1 {
  select when pageview url re#/archives/#
  http:post("http://www.example.com/go")
    with params = {"answer": "x"}
}
```

When this rule is selected, it will POST to the specified URL with a form-encoded body containing the name-value pair shown in the params map.

Here's another example showing the use of the http:post() action to POST raw content—XML in this case:

```
rule r2 {
  select when pageview url re#/archives/#
  http:post("http://example.com/printenv.pl")
    with body = << <?xml encoding='UTF-8'?>
                   <feed version='0.3'>
                   </feed> >> and
        headers = {"content-type": "application/xml"};
}
```

The http:post() and http:get() actions support an optional setting clause that gives the name of the variable to which the response to the HTTP request should be bound for later use. This variable is available to any expression executed after the action takes place—expressions in the parameters of later actions or in the postlude of the rule.

The response is a map of the following key-value pairs:

- **content.** The content of the response.
- **content_type.** The MIME type of the content.
- **content_length.** The number of bytes in the content.
- **status_code.** The three-digit HTTP status code.
- **status_line.** The complete status string, including the three-digit HTTP status code.
- **label.** The autoraise label, if autoraise is given as a parameter.

The following rule makes a POST, binding the response to the variable named resp.

```
rule r1 {
  select when pageview url re#/archives/\d+#
  http:post("http://example.com/go") setting(resp)
  fired {
    set app:resp_length resp{"content_length"}
  }
}
```

The content length portion of the response map is bound to an application variable named app:resp_length in the postlude.

Being able to interact with cloud-based services using HTTP is the foundational activity in building Live Web applications that use cloud-based data. We'll use the HTTP library over and over again in this and subsequent chapters.

Other Libraries

KRL also includes other built-in libraries that provide convenient access to APIs. The goal of built-in libraries is to reduce the programming effort necessary to perform these functions by abstracting the interaction and the output so that these actions are easier to use. I will describe some of them briefly. See the KRL documentation for a complete list and description.

The location Library

KRL includes a built-in library, location, for getting GeoIP data about the entity raising the event. The library makes use of a GeoIP database to get approximate locations for the entity based on the IP address presented when the event is raised. Obviously, proxies and gateways can affect the accuracy of the IP address for determining the location of the user, but the data is a good first approximation. The location library contains functions for determining the entity's country (by code or by name), region (i.e., state in the U.S.), city, and postal code. For example, the following KRL would bind the city and state of the user to a variable named address:

```
pre {
  address = location:city() + ", " + location:region();
}
```

The time Library

The time library provides functions for getting the time, manipulating it by adding or subtracting time intervals, or formatting the output for specific applications. The time library also includes predicates for testing the current time. As with all KRL predicates, these tests are done with respect to the entity raising the event (the GeoIP location is used in this calculation for the Web). For example, the following condition would be true if it's morning (between 6 a.m. and 12 p.m.) where the user is:

```
if time:morning() then ...
```

The `twitter` Library

The `twitter` library gives full access to the Twitter API. API access functions are available for retrieving timelines, managing friends, seeing your own tweets, viewing mentions, accessing direct messages, getting geographic information about tweets, and using Twitter search. Actions are available for posting status updates, retweeting, following users, and tracking keywords. Twitter uses OAuth for access to protected resources. I discuss KRL's mechanisms for using OAuth to connect to APIs in a moment, and give a detailed example of how the Twitter API can be used later in this chapter.

The `facebook` Library

Facebook has opened up access to most of its data through its Graph API. This new REST-based interface is simple and straightforward. Using the `facebook` library in KRL, developers can interact with Facebook using KRL.

The `google` Library

Many services at Google provide external access to data and functionality through APIs that utilize the Google Data Protocol, commonly called GData. KRL provides built-in support for the underlying protocol and specific APIs, including calendars and spreadsheets.

The `odata` Library

The Open Data Protocol, commonly called OData, is a Microsoft-inspired Web protocol for querying and updating data. KRL provides the `odata` library for interfacing with OData APIs. OData and GData are very similar. They both aim to provide a rich data interface over the HTTP protocol, using Atom as the data medium.

The `amazon` Library

The `amazon` library implements functions related to Amazon's Product Advertising API (PAA, sometimes referred to as the eCommerce API). PAA provides data about products for sale on Amazon. KRL also supports the Amazon Associates affiliate program.

The oauth Library

The KRL oauth library provides a generic process for making OAuth1.0A authentication and protected resource requests. There are two elements to OAuth1.0A that cause aggravation to developers: request signing and authorization callbacks. Every request for a protected resource needs to be signed with the developer's private key. Even if someone snoops an OAuth1.0A token, it can't be used without that private key. Using the KRL oauth library, Web app developers can make OAuth requests without leaking their private key.

JSONPATH EXPRESSIONS

Because KRL rule sets frequently involve using large sets of data, KRL includes an embedded language specifically designed to make accessing parts of the JSON data structure easy without the need to specifically "walk the entire tree." This language, called JSONPath,[3] is similar in purpose and design to XPath (used for accessing parts of XML documents).

A JSONPath expression (JPex) is a compact specification of the parts of the JSON document to select. JPexes are applied to a JSON data structure using KRL's pick operator.

JSON data structures are usually anonymous and thus don't have a root. JSONPath assigns the abstract name $ to the root of the JSON data structure. Dot notation is used to specify paths in the structure.

Some examples will help make this clear. Suppose the variable book_data has been bound to the following data:

```
{"responseHeader":{"status":0},
 "response":{
  "numFound":2,
  "start":0,
  "docs":[
    {"isbn":"0316160202",
     "price" : 15.99,
     "title":"Eclipse",
     "url":"http://example.com/search/0316160202"
    },
    {"isbn":"0316124929",
     "price" : 23.99,
     "title":"Baker Street",
     "url":"http://example.com/search/0316124929"
    }
  ]}}
```

The following KRL expression would return 2, the value of numFound:

```
book_data.pick("$.response.numFound")
```

You can use descendent notation (..) in a JPex to descend through the JSON data to the first name that matches and make this expression slightly more compact:

```
book_data.pick("$..numFound")
```

JPexes are even more powerful when applied to JSON that includes arrays. The following JPex returns an array containing the titles from both books (as shown after the KRL expression):

```
book_data.pick("$..title") // returns ["Eclipse", "Baker Street"]
```

You can also address specific array values in the JSON data. The following KRL expression returns just the title of the first book (*Eclipse*):

```
book_data.pick("$..docs[0].title")
```

JPex filters allow you to pick out specific parts of a large document according to some condition. Filters are indicated by a prepended ? symbol. In a JPex, the @ symbol represents the current element and can be used in predicate expressions. For example, the following KRL expression would return an array of titles for any books with a price less than $20:

```
book_data.pick("$..docs[?(@.price<20)].title")
```

JSONPath and the `pick` operator provide a succinct way of finding specific values in a complex JSON data structure. JPexes are used frequently in KRL rule sets that make use of cloud-based data.

DON'T BUY THAT BOOK!

Let's take a break from exploring KRL's data features and use them to create a simple application that shows book readers useful data in context about books they want to read.

Book readers often turn to online bookstores to find a book. Many, however, are also patrons of the local library and in many cases would love to check out the book there when it's available. Certainly, one can visit the online bookstore and the local library's Web site separately, but the experience is easier when these two visits are combined into one.

The Minuteman Library Network of Boston, in association with Azigo, created a contextualized experience that does just that. As shown in Figure 8.2, when a member of that network visits Amazon or Barnes and Noble online, a notification is placed on the page when the book they're looking at is available at their local library.

Figure 8.2
Finding a book to read in context.

The KRL for achieving this result is remarkably simple. Suppose you have a data source that returns book data formatted as JSON. You can declare it like so:

```
global {
  datasource library_search <- "http://example.com/library.cgi?";
}
```

When this data source is queried using the ISBN of a particular book, it will return the results for that book.

You can write a rule that fires on Amazon and places a notification showing that the book is available at the library and giving a link to the availability page:

Note

In this and other examples throughout the book, CSS styling has been removed from the HTML for clarity.

```
rule book_notification is active {
  select when pageview url "(/gp/product/|/dp/)(\d+)/"
    setting(path,isbn)
  pre {
    book_data = datasource:library_search("q=" + isbn);
    url = book_data.pick("$..docs[0].url");
    title = book_data.pick("$..docs[0].title");
    msg = <<
     <div>
      <p>#{title}</p>
      <p><a href="#{url}">Check Catalog</a></p>
     </div>
    >>;
    msgtitle = "Book Title Found";
  }
  if (book_data.pick("$..numFound") > 0) then
    notify(msgtitle, msg)
}
```

Amazon (along with other online booksellers) helpfully puts the ISBN number of the book in the URL, so you capture it in the select statement and bind it to the variable isbn. The first thing you do in the prelude is query the library_search data source with the ISBN to get the book data. A few JPexes get the title and URL of the book, and you create an HTML template using extended quotes and beestings. (Note that styling has been removed from the HTML to make it cleaner and easier to understand.)

The action is conditional on whether the number of books found is greater than zero. You don't want to unnecessarily bother the user if nothing was found. But if there are results to show, you place a notification box on the page.

This example shows that even simple rule sets can make the task of finding a book to read more contextual by mashing up the data from multiple Web sites and putting the results in a place that is convenient for the user. You could make this rule set even more useful by including data from Goodreads and other online book resources.

KEY MANAGEMENT

Many cloud services require keys of one sort or another to authenticate and authorize access. Some of these use standardized authorization systems like OAuth; others use custom developer key schemes. Managing and using keys inside rule sets is a critical feature in KRL.

One of the primary reasons for having explicit support for keys in KRL is to promote code sharing. When you share a rule set with others, you'd rather not have your keys—vital secrets—exposed. Redacting them each time you share the rule set is a hassle. By explicitly supporting keys in the language, KRL can automatically redact keys.

Keys are declared in the `meta` section of the rule set using the keyword `key` like so:

```
key errorstack "dakdladaoadoajdoa"
```

This creates a key called `errorstack` with the value shown.

Many times, there is more than one key that a service needs. You can also supply a map of name-value pairs for the key values:

```
key twitter {
  "consumer_key" : "skfjldfajsdkfaj",
  "consumer_secret" : "fjfoiasjf;asdfjdoifjsdopfasdjfoa"
  }
```

This creates a key named `twitter` that has the value shown in the map.

Some libraries (like the `twitter` library) require keys that have specific names and values. When you aren't working with a library that has specific requirements, you will likely need to access the keys to send them to the cloud service you're working with. You can access keys stored in the `meta` section from within KRL expressions using the following syntax:

```
key:<keyname>(<name>)
```

The `<keyname>` is the name given after the keyword `key` in the `meta` block. The `<name>` is optional. If it's missing, the entire value is returned. If it's present, just the value associated with `<name>` in the map is returned (assuming the value is a map). For example, the following KRL declaration would bind the entire map associate with the `twitter` key to the variable `my_key`:

```
pre{
  my_key = keys:twitter();
}
```

On the other hand, the following KRL declaration would bind only the value associated with the name `consumer_secret` to the variable `my_key`:

```
pre{
  my_key = keys:twitter("consumer_secret");
}
```

EXAMPLE: SHOWING TWEETS ON MY BLOG

I have a box on the right side of my blog showing my latest tweets, powered by KRL. In this example, I'll show you how I wrote a simple rule that uses the `twitter` library to access my Twitter timeline and show my latest tweet. The beauty of this method is that it will always show the latest tweet because it's updated, on demand, when the page is loaded, rather than relying on polling and storing the tweet for five or 10 minutes.

The KRL `twitter` library provides two functions you're going to need to make this work:

- **`twitter:authorized()`**. This function uses keys declared with the `meta` section to access Twitter and returns true if that access is authorized and false otherwise. In this case, because I'm just accessing my timeline, I generated single-user access token when I created the application on the Twitter site. (That means the map of key values declared in the `meta` section will have four mappings: the two shown in the preceding example plus `oauth_token` and `oauth_token_secret`.) Authorization status is stored automatically by KRE during the rule set's execution.

- **`twitter:user_timeline()`**. This returns the timeline for the currently authorized user—me, in this case. You can give it an optional argument in the form of a map to limit the number of return results.

In the global declarations, declare a variable that contains the timeline:

```
global {
  tweets =
    twitter:authorized() => twitter:user_timeline({"count" : 1})
                          | [];
}
```

This will put the user's last tweet in the variable `tweets` if access is authorized.

The rule is straightforward:

```
rule publish_tweets {
  select when pageview url ".*"
  pre {
```

```
  res = tweets.pick("$[0]..text");
  img = tweets.pick("$[0]..profile_image_url");
  twit_res = <<
   <div>
    <div>
     <a href="http://twitter.com/windley">
      <img src="#{img}">Phil on Twitter</a>
    </div>
     <div>#{res}</div></div>
   >>
  }
  replace_html("#tweets", twit_res);
}
```

When the rule fires, it replaces the `<div/>` element named `tweets` with the HTML given in `twit_res`. The rule pulls the tweet and my picture from the user timeline returned by Twitter.

Note

Note that this rule is specific to me. If you run it with your Twitter credentials, you'll get your picture and tweets, but the link and name will be mine. One improvement you could make to this rule would be to get the name and Twitter URL from the timeline as well so that it's completely independent of me. Another would be to post-process the text to make any included URLs live.

Using a little KRL, you can accomplish a fairly complex interaction with a cloud-based service like Twitter, including the authorization.

LOOPING IN KRL

When dealing with data, iteration is important. KRL supports implicit and explicit looping. Recognize that the entire rule set can be seen as a big `loop` over the event stream. Seeing event processing as a looping process can help you to design efficient, effective rule sets.

Also, as you've seen, JPexes provide a way of processing arrays in large data sets that amounts to a kind of implicit looping in many cases. Several built-in operators like `filter()` and `map()` loop over data. In addition to these implicit forms of looping, KRL functions support recursion and thus can be used to iterate over arguments.

But with all that, you sometimes need explicit loops. KRL loops are a little different from what your previous programming experience might lead you to expect. The KRL `foreach` statement can only appear just below the `select` statement like so:

```
select when pageview url "/archives/"
 foreach [1, 2, 3] setting (x)
```

This statement would execute the entire rule three times with the variable x bound to 1, 2, and 3 in each successive execution.

The value following the keyword foreach can be any KRL expression that yields an array or map. If the variable f were bound to a JSON data structure, you could use a pick and JPex like so:

```
select when pageview url "/archives/"
  foreach f.pick("$..store") setting (x)
```

To use the foreach statement with a map, you provide two variables in the setting clause that will be bound to the name and value of that entry in the map:

```
select when pageview url "/archives/"
  foreach {"a" : 1, "b" : 2, "c" : 3} setting (n,v)
```

This would bind a, b, and c to n along with 1, 2, and 3 to v on each successive iteration through the loop.

Note

Maps do not have an order like arrays. Consequently, when you loop over a map, the order is non-deterministic. The loop order in the previous example might be c, a, b. If you must have a specific order, you need to use the keys() operators to retrieve the keys from the map, sort them using the sort() operator, and then loop over the resulting array. For example, suppose m is a map containing {"a" : 1, "b" : 2, "c" : 3}. The following code snippet shows how you'd accomplish this if you wanted to process the name-value pairs in alphabetical order:

```
select when pageview url "/archives/"
      foreach m.keys().sort() setting (n)
      pre {
        v = m{n};
        . . .
      }
```

You can have more than one loop in a rule by simply nesting one foreach inside another:

```
select when pageview url "/archives/"
  foreach [1, 2, 3] setting (x)
   foreach ["a", "b", "c"] setting (y)
```

As you'd expect, this would bind a, b, and c to y while x is 1, and then bind a, b, and c to y while x is 2, and so on. Because values being iterated over can be computed, you could use x in computing the array for the second loop.

At first, it may seem restrictive to only be able to loop at the start of a rule, but it fits the rule model very nicely. Because of their structure, rules in KRL become what are called FLWOR (pronounced "flower") statements in XQuery. (FLWOR is an acronym for "`foreach, let, where, order, result`.") Table 8.1 shows which KRL rule features play which part in creating FLWOR statements.

Table 8.1   Comparison of FLWOR and KRL

FLWOR	KRL
foreach	foreach
let	Prelude
where	Rule condition
order	Array filters and operations
result	Action

The entire rule body—everything after `select`—is executed once for every loop. If the premise is true, an action is produced. So a rule with a `foreach` over a three-element array would produce three actions if the premise were true each time.

Note

KRL optimizes rule preludes by automatically moving expressions that don't depend on the variable being set in the `foreach` statement outside the loop during execution so that only those things that really need to be executed multiple times are.

When to Use a Loop

Your instincts might be to use `foreach` loops in places where it's less efficient than using implicit looping. To see when you might want to use a JPex instead of a `foreach` statement, let's walk through an example.

Suppose you have a data set that lists a number of sites by URL and gives some data about each of them. Further, suppose you'd like to annotate sites with the data out of the data set when the URL matches so that you don't have to republish the rule set each time it changes. This kind of data would generally be generated. In this case, however, you just declare it in a variable named `items` in the `global` section:

```
global {
  items = [{"page": "baconsalt.com",
           "content": "Hello World. Go Bacon.",
           "header": "Bacon Salt Test"
           },
```

```
      {"page": "craigburton.com",
       "content": "Hello World. Burtonian methods.",
       "header": "Craig Burton Test"
       },
       {"page": "kynetx.com",
       "content": "Hello World. The World According to Kynetx",
       "header": "Kynetx Test"
       }]
}
```

Using this data, you want to place a notification box on any of the three sites listed in the `page` field. The notification uses the `content` and `header` data out of the data set for any give page.

Your first attempt, using `foreach`, might look something like this:

```
rule using_foreach {
  select when pageview url ".*"
    foreach items setting (d)
    pre {
      h = d.pick("$.header") + " using foreach";
      c = d.pick("$.content");
      site = page:url("domain");
    }
    if(site eq d.pick("$.page")) then
      notify(h,c);
}
```

This does the job, looping through each item (binding its value to d) and using the premise of the rule to check that the current domain is applicable before placing the notification. The problem is that this rule is quite inefficient. You're looping through the data and throwing all the work away in all but one case (where the domain name matches the site you're on). For three items, this isn't a big problem, but what if the data set contained information for thousands of sites? You'd be wasting a lot of processing time.

There are two ways to solve this problem. The first is to use the full power of array filters to cut the array down to just those members meeting the desired criterion:

```
rule using_foreach_with_filter {
  select when pageview url ".*"
    foreach items.filter(
        function(x) {page:url("domain") eq
                       x.pick("$.page")})
      setting (d)
    pre {
      h = d.pick("$.header") + " using foreach";
```

```
    c = d.pick("$.content");
    site = page:url("domain");
  }
  if(site eq d.pick("$.page")) then
    notify(h,c);
}
```

The anonymous function in the `filter` operator compares the page in its argument to the domain of the page against which the rule is running. You could also define this function earlier in the `global` block and just give its name as an argument to `filter`.

In this rule, the array will be filtered to only those items that have a page name that matches the domain of the current page. For this example, that would be an array of one. Consequently, the `foreach` isn't really looping; it's running once. This points you to the second way of making the rule more efficient: Don't use a `foreach` statement at all.

In the following rule, you use the implicit looping and filtering capabilities of a JPex to find just the item you want from the data structure and then pick the pieces you need out of that one item.

```
rule without_foreach {
  select when pageview url ".*"
  pre {
    dom = page:url("domain");
    item = items.pick(
        "$[?(@.page eq '"+dom+"')]");
    content = item.pick("$..content");
    header = item.pick("$..header")
      + " without foreach";
  }
  if(dom eq item.pick("$..page")) then
    notify(header,content);
}
```

This rule uses the domain in constructing the JPex to select the right element of the array of items. The JPex is the secret to how this rule works: The JPex does an implicit loop over the data and only selects the items where `page` matches the domain. Consequently, you don't need the `foreach`.

Loops Drive Multiple Actions

As you've seen, `foreach` causes the same rule to be fired multiple times in a single rule set evaluation. Some actions are better suited to use inside a `foreach` loop than others. For example, issuing multiple redirect() actions from a single rule doesn't usually make sense. But other actions—such as append(), replace(), send_dir-ective(), and so on—are often done over and over with different data. An example illustrates this idea.

Suppose you wanted to make changes to a page based on data you retrieved from an online data source. Assume the datasource query returns data like the following, and you bind it to a variable named replacements:

```
{"desc": "Data set to test foreach",
 "replacements": [
    {"selector":"#categories",
     "text":"This was the cloud tag"
    },
    {"selector":"#friends",
     "text":"This was a list of friends"
    },
    {"selector":".action-stream",
     "text":"This is where the action stream was"
    }
    ]
}
```

In this data, you have an array of replacements, each of which contains a jQuery selector[4] pattern for elements on a Web page and the text you're going to use with the action. The following rule set uses the items in this data structure to prepend the text in each of the preceding items to the element on the page that matches the associated selector pattern:

```
rule prepend {
  select when pageview url "windley.com"
    foreach replacements.pick("$.replacements")
        setting (r)
    pre {
      sel = r.pick("$.selector");
      new_text = r.pick("$.text");
    }
    prepend(sel,new_text);
}
```

This changes the same page multiple times according to the content of the data structure. Change the data and the behavior of the rule will follow.

Using data often requires loops. As you've seen, there are multiple ways to loop in KRL: a rule set is a loop, each rule can loop explicitly using foreach, and implicit looping is accomplished using the pick operator.

Seeing Your Friend's Tweets

You've seen several techniques for using data from the cloud in KRL. Now, it's time to use them together to accomplish a more sophisticated task: showing each user his or her friend's timeline from Twitter. You'll use the `twitter` library, keys with OAuth, and looping with `foreach` to accomplish this task.

Integrating interesting data using KRL is an important part of what makes the language so useful for building Live Web applications that mash up data and user interactions. By allowing users to authenticate to their own account on Twitter (or anywhere else), you also make this application more personal. Every user of this application will see a different behavior.

In this example, you'll use two KRL patterns:

- **Authorize-then-use.** The authorize-then-use pattern is useful for data sources that require authorization before use.

- **Initialize-then-populate.** The initialize-then-populate pattern is common for data that requires looping.

Authorize-then-Use

In the authorize-then-use pattern, a rule is put in place to check whether the app is authorized to take a certain action and, if not, do what is necessary to complete the authorization. You use the `last` control statement in the rule postlude to ensure that the rest of the rules (which presumably rely on the authorization) don't run.

Twitter uses OAuth to allow users to authorize a third-party program (like this application) to access their account without users having to share their password with the third party. To make this work, you have to register the application with Twitter, whereupon you'll be issued a consumer token and consumer secret, keys that you declare in the `meta` section of the rule set.

The OAuth protocol involves redirecting the user to Twitter, where the user has the opportunity to authorize access or reject it. OAuth requires that the application and the service provider (Twitter in this case) interchange various tokens. KRL provides an action in the `twitter` library, `twitter:authorize()`, that abstracts all those interactions.

The following rule shows how to authorize a user to access his or her Twitter account:

```
rule auth {
  select when pageview url ".*"
  if(not twitter:authorized()) then
```

```
twitter:authorize()
  with opacity=1.0 and
      sticky = true
fired {
 last
 }
}
```

Notice that this rule only fires if the predicate `twitter:authorized()` is *false*. The action, `twitter:authorize()`, initiates the OAuth ceremony. The action will pop up a notification in the user's browser as shown in Figure 8.3. The text of the authorization box is restricted to limit the ability of a rule set to fool its users. The name, author, and description are taken from the rule set's `meta` section. For this reason, it is important to accurately name the rule set and author and to carefully write the text in the description so that the user understands what he or she is authorizing.

Figure 8.3
Twitter OAuth ceremony in KRL.

The postlude of the rule runs the `last` statement if the rule fires to ensure that nothing else happens. Of course, if the rule set is authorized, the rule doesn't fire, the OAuth ceremony is *not* initiated, and the `last` statement is never executed, allowing the remaining rules in the rule set to execute. Authorization is automatically stored in the entity's persistent data so that it persists from invocation to invocation.

If the rule set is already authorized, you want to get the user's Friends timeline from Twitter and do something with it. In this example, you'll just place it in a notify box on the page.

Initialize-then-Populate

The initialize-then-populate pattern is important for working with complex data where developers frequently need to do something for each component of an array. As you've seen, the foreach statement does this. The problem is that if you use a foreach to loop over the tweets and use a notify() action to place them on the page, you'll end up with one notification box for each tweet—not exactly what you want. Instead, you want one notification box containing all the tweets.

The way you solve this is to use one rule to place the notification box on the page (the initializer) and another rule to loop over the tweets and place them in the notification box (the populater).

To begin, you have to have a data structure that contains the tweets. You do this in the global block so that it can be used by other rules:

```
global {
  tweets = twitter:authorized() => twitter:friends_timeline()
                                | [];
}
```

The variable tweets will contain a JSON data structure of the latest tweets from the user's friends if Twitter has already been authorized, or an empty list otherwise.

Here's the initialization rule:

```
rule init_tweetdom {
  select when pageview url ".*"
  pre {
    init_div = << <div id="tweet_list"></div> >>
  }
  if(tweets.length() > 0) then
    notify("Friends' Tweets", init_div)
      with sticky=true and
          opacity = 1.0
}
```

This rule simply puts up the notification box with the desired title and an empty <div/> element that will serve as the container for the tweets.

The real work in this pattern is done by the populating rule:

```
rule populate_tweetdom {
  select when pageview url ".*"
    foreach tweets setting (tweet)
      pre {
        text = tweet.pick("$..text");
        div = << <div>#{text}</div> >>;
      }
      append("#tweet_list", div)
}
```

This rule loops over the tweets, picks the right data out of them using a JPex, and then appends the result to the empty `<div/>` you placed in the notification box.

After going through the OAuth ceremony at Twitter, wherever I run this app, I see a box that contains the latest tweets from my friends' Twitter timeline, as shown in Figure 8.4. Of course, if you ran the application, you'd see your friends' latest tweets.

Figure 8.4
Tweets from my friends.

The ability to personalize apps by appealing to personal data elsewhere on the Web without the developer having to create multi-tenanted applications is a huge advantage of KRL.

Abstracting Cloud Services in KRL

KRL has four important abstraction mechanisms that you can use to make using cloud data easier. One, functions, you've already seen. This section talks about two others: user-defined actions and modules. A fourth abstraction mechanism, for events, is introduced in Chapter 11.

Until now, you haven't been able to abstract rule set interactions to make them easier to reuse. Making them available to other programmers would require writing long lists of instructions so they could redo the work you have already done. The combination of user-defined actions and modules allows for developers to write their own KRL interfaces to cloud-based services.

User-Defined Actions

One of the keys to making use of an external API inside KRL is being able to define actions. As you've seen, using data from the API is a powerful way to harness the abilities of APIs inside a rule set. What's more, actions like `send_directive()` and `http:post()` give you the ability to respond to those APIs for a true dialog.

In Chapter 6, "Live Web Rules," you saw how functions are defined. Functions are great when you want to abstract the computation of a value, but they don't work for abstracting the computation of an action. KRL provides a parallel construction for defining actions called *defaction*.

Just as the `function` primitive in KRL defines an anonymous function that can be applied as part of an expression for creating a value, the `defaction` primitive defines an anonymous action that can be applied in an action context to take a user-defined action. Here's a simple example:

```
global {
  send_warning = defaction(msg) {
    notify("Warning!", msg)
      with sticky = true
  }
}
```

This declaration in a rule set `global` section defines an action that will be bound to the variable `send_warning`. The action takes a single parameter, `msg`, and, when applied, takes a `notify()` action with the title pre-filled to "Warning!" and causes the message to stay displayed.

Later, the rule could use this action like so:

```
if error_level > 12 && error_level < 15 then
  send_warning("Abnormal error levels")
```

The ability to abstract how an action works is a key idea in KRL and, like any abstraction, encapsulates behavior so it can be more easily managed. The send_warning() action could be used in several rules in the rule set. If the definition changed, then it would need to be updated in one place to affect all the rules that have used it.

One key difference between functions and defined actions is that defined actions use a configuration clause, along with optional parameters when the action is used, to create flexible behavior and usage.

Suppose that in the previous example, you want the send_warning() action to be sticky by default, but allow the developer to make it transitory when needed. You could add a parameter like so:

```
global {
  send_warning = defaction(msg, transitory) {
    notify("Warning!", msg)
      with sticky = not transitory
    }
}
```

But this requires that the developer always supply the argument indicating whether to make the warning sticky or transitory. A better option is to use a configuration variable like so:

```
global {
  send_warning = defaction(msg) {
    configure using transitory = false
    notify("Warning!", msg)
      with sticky = not transitory
  }
}
```

The configure clause defines a variable and its default value. The value can be any KRL expression. Multiple name-value pairs can be given, separated using the keyword and (the same syntax as optional action parameters):

```
global {
  send_warning = defaction(msg) {
    configure using transitory = false
          and title = "Warning!"
    notify(title, msg)
      with sticky = not transitory
  }
}
```

When this action is applied, the notification will be sticky by default and use the title "Warning!" as before. However, the developer can call it with the optional parameter `transitory` to change that default behavior:

```
if error_level > 12 && error_level < 15 then
  send_warning("Abnormal error levels")
    with transitory = true
```

A defined action, like a function, can have declarations before the action to compute intermediate values:

```
global {
  send_warning = defaction(msg) {
    configure using transitory = false
              and error_code = 0
    title = error_code < 5 => "Warning!" |
            error_code < 10 => "Error!" |
            error_code < 15 => "Critical!" |
                               "Danger!"
    notify(title, msg)
      with sticky = not transitory
  }
}
```

This example computes the `title` given an optional error code that defaults to 0. This makes the default title "Warning!" but bases the title of the notification on the value the user supplies for `error_code`.

A defined action can use more than one action; compound actions (see Chapter 6, "Live Web Rules") can be used in a defined action as well. For example, the following user-defined action will place the notification box and append a warning banner to the `<div/>` element named `warning_box` on the page:

```
global {
  send_warning = defaction(msg) {
    configure using transitory = false
              and error_code = 0
    title = error_code < 5 => "Warning!" |
            error_code < 10 => "Error!" |
            error_code < 15 => "Critical!" |
                               "Danger!"
    every {
      notify(title, msg)
        with sticky = not transitory;
      append("#warning_box", "A #{title} alert is active")
```

```
    }
  }
}
```

Because defined actions are expressions (they appear on the right side of declarations), they can be treated like values and passed and returned from functions. They can also be passed into and returned from user-defined actions.

User-Defined Modules

KRL integrates several cloud services and provides built-in libraries to access them. But there are thousands of cloud services and no way for those who maintain KRL to integrate all of them into the core language. The answer is to allow developers to create their own modules that integrate these services.

Note

We use the term *library* to refer to built-in modules and *modules* to refer to user-defined modules.

In KRL, any rule set can be a module. Only declarations in the `global` block are available to another rule set that uses the module. You may not want everything in the `global` block to be exported, however. Consequently, there are mechanisms for declaring what is exported, which also allows for private definitions. Modules can be parameterized and aliased.

Note

To keep things straight, when I say "module" in this section, I'll be referring to the rule set acting as a module. When I say "rule set," I'll be referring to the rule set using the module. At present, any rules in the module are not available for use by the rule set using the module. They can be used to test the module, however.

I'll introduce the use of modules with a simple example. The following rule set defines a module that defines a function and two actions to interact with a data service called StringBin (a simple cloud-based key-value pair storage system). StringBin requires a developer pin.

```
ruleset a369x115 {
  meta {
    name "StringBin Module"
    provide read, write, destroy
    configure using pin = "nopin"
  }
  global {
```

```
    datasource sb_data <- "http://api.stringbin.com/1/read?";
    defaction write(k, v) {
     http:get("http://api.stringbin.com/1/write")
       with params = {"pin": pin,
                      "key": k,
                      "value": v}
    };
    defaction destroy(k) {
     http:get("http://api.stringbin.com/1/write")
       with params = {"pin": pin,
                      "key": k,
                      "value": ""}
    };
    read = function(k) {
     datasource:sb_data({"pin":pin,"key":k}).pick("$.string");
    }
  }
}
```

Two important things to note in this module definition are the `provide` and `configure` clauses. The `provide` keyword is followed by a list of names that will be available *outside* the module. Note that the `datasource` declaration `sb_data` is not provided to rule sets using the module and thus the implementation details are hidden. The only way to reach the data source is using the provided function named `read`.

The `configure` keyword indicates the module parameters and their default values. In this case, there is one parameter: the value of the developer pin. Any rule set using this module must supply a pin or it won't work because the default value is "nopin".

You use a module by declaring its use in the `meta` section, giving any configuration parameters using a `with` clause. The `use module` pragma requires a rule set name and an optional alias (`StringBin` in this case).

```
meta {
 use module a369x115 alias StringBin
     with pin = "Xad09da098daZ2N1M"
}
```

Later, you can use one of the module's actions in a rule like so:

```
rule write_to_stringbin {
 select when pageview ".*"
 StringBin:write("yellow", "mellow")
}
```

This rule writes the value `"mellow"` to the StringBin store using the key `"yellow"`. Note that when you declared the module's use, you gave it an alias, and the alias is used to namespace the action (`StringBin:write()` in this case). If no alias is given, the module's name is used.

Because modules are parameterized and can be aliased, you can use a given module multiple times in a single rule set with different parameters. For example, suppose you had two `StringBins` and you wanted to copy a value out of one into the other. First, you declare the module's use twice with different aliases and configurations:

```
meta {
  use module a369x115 alias BinA
      with pin = "Xad09da098daZ2N1M"
  use module a369x115 alias BinB
      with pin = "adaad9d0a9dadffKK"
}
```

You can then write a rule that copies data from `BinA` into `BinB`:

```
rule copy_stringbin {
  select when pageview ".*"
  pre {
    stuffToCopy = BinA:read("yellow");
  }
  BinB:write("yellow", stuffToCopy);
}
```

In this rule, you've read data from `BinA` and then written it to `BinB`. Of course, to accomplish this in a real rule, the key (`"yellow"`) would likely be computed from event parameters in some way.

A Calendar Module

Sam Curren has created a module for interacting with Google Calendar and using the dates in those calendars to control other rule sets. The calendar module is configured by providing the URL of a Google calendar to use and provides two primary functions:

- **onnow(<title>).** This function takes the title of an event as its sole argument and returns true if an event with that title is currently happening in the subject calendar.

- **next(<title>).** This function returns the next event with a title matching the one given as an argument.

Steve Nay, my teaching assistant at Brigham Young University in 2011, used the calendar module in a rule set to post whether office hours were currently happening. If the TA was currently having office hours according to a Google calendar, then the rule set placed a banner at the top of the class wiki as shown in Figure 8.5.

Figure 8.5
Banner on the class wiki indicating whether the TA is having office hours.

Steve's rule set is simple with the Google calendar module. First, Steve uses the module, supplying a calendar URL as part of the configuration:

```
use module a8x114 alias officehours
  with url = "http://www.google.com/calendar/feeds/..."
```

The rule creates a banner and displays it if "Office Hours" is the current event in the calendar:

```
rule ta_is_in {
  select when web pageview
   url #classes.windley.com/462/wiki#
  pre {
   message = <<
    <div class="ta-hours">
      The TA is in!| Office: Cubicle 13 | ...
    </div>
   >>;
  }
  if officehours:onnow("Office Hours") then {
   prepend('.firstHeading', message);
  }
}
```

Just as interesting is the way Sam wrote it for testability. Recall that only the global definitions in a module are available when the module is used. But a module's rules can be used to exercise the module's functions when it's run as a standalone rule set.

Sam ensured that the configuration variable was tested and, if empty, set a test calendar URL in the global declarations:

```
rawurl = url => url
                | "http://www.google.com/calendar/feeds...";
```

Note

Configuration variable default values are only available when the rule set is used as a module.

Rules in the rule set exercise the function in the `global` block so they can be tested. For example, this rule tests the `onnow()` function:

```
rule onnow {
  select when web click "#onnow"
  pre {
   message = onnow("Test") => "On Now!" | "Not on now.";
  }
  notify("onnow test", message);
}
```

Sam's module contains its own regression and integration tests.

Modules provide a convenient way to encapsulate complex code and behavior, making it easy to create rules like the one Steve wrote for the class wiki.

USING THE CLOUD

In this chapter, you've seen numerous KRL features for making use of cloud-based services to create contextualized Live Web experiences. The Live Web is predicated on taking data from various services (each with its own context), linking that data using the user's current context, and then creating a more useful, purposeful, and effective experience for the user.

Creating modules that interact with these cloud services and abstract them for use in KRL provides important building blocks for developers creating Live Web experiences. Putting data together from multiple services across multiple event domains greatly increases the value of an application.

ENDNOTES

1. As of November 2011.
2. See the KRL documentation for details.
3. Stefan Goessner developed JSONPath. Details of JSONPath expression construction can be found in Appendix E, "The KRL Expression Language."
4. See Appendix E for more information on jQuery selectors.

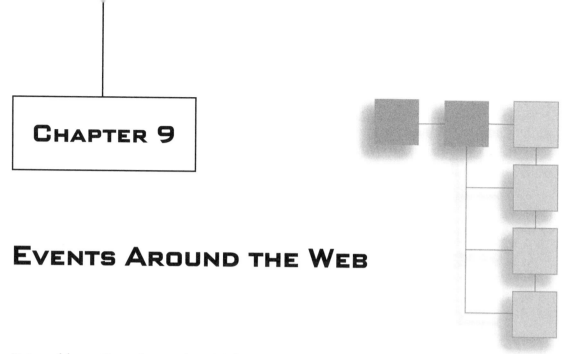

CHAPTER 9

EVENTS AROUND THE WEB

Being able to fire rules against Web sites in people's browsers is a powerful idea that has numerous applications, but the Live Web is bigger than just rearranging HTML in the browser. The Live Web encompasses the whole of the Internet.

Events happen all the time on the Internet, but for them to be visible, something has to notice the event and signal it. You make the Live Web relevant to people outside of browsers with KEA endpoints. The Live Web exists wherever programs working on behalf of users can raise events so that rules can run and respond.

In this chapter, you'll explore endpoints that work with PubSubHubbub, with Web hooks, with email, with IRC, and in a microcontroller. Of course, this isn't the extent of what KRL can be applied to—it is merely a sampling of what's possible. Literally any occurrence on the Internet can be turned into a KEA event for processing by KRL.

ENDPOINTS

In Chapter 5, "Architecting the Live Web," you saw that the primary functions of an endpoint are as follows:

- To raise relevant events to the event processor

- To respond to directives from the event processor

- To maintain state to link separate interactions with the event processor together in meaningful ways to create context

Given this modest list of requirements, endpoints are remarkably easy to create. Almost every programming language has libraries for making HTTP calls—and that is all that is necessary for raising events. Likewise, almost every programming language has libraries for processing JSON—the primary requirement for understanding and reacting to directives.

Maintaining state mostly comes down to managing tokens. Often, these are in the form of HTTP cookies and thus will be automatically managed by the HTTP library. Multi-tenant endpoints (like a cloud-based email endpoint) will require the same techniques for account and state management as in any multi-tenant Web application.

As you've seen, the Web endpoint is a sophisticated JavaScript runtime that raises multiple event types and responds to dozens of JavaScript-based directives. Other endpoints are much simpler. One of the key distinctions between endpoints is whether they are scriptable. The Web endpoint implemented by the Web Runtime is scriptable. A rule set can send JavaScript to the Web endpoint to be run on the browser. This makes the Web endpoint extremely capable and flexible. Like the browser it runs in, the Web endpoint can be made to serve almost any purpose.

In contrast, directive-based endpoints are not scriptable. Instead, they have a set menu of actions they can support. If the endpoint doesn't support an action, then the only option is to change the endpoint. Updating some endpoints, like the email endpoint discussed later in this chapter, is relatively easy because they live in the cloud. These endpoints can be updated for everyone by changing the code on the server. For endpoints that are downloaded and installed in the user environment, scriptability increases their flexibility and reduces the need for reinstallation when they change.

Open-source endpoint code is available on GitHub (see http://github.com/kynetx). As the libraries and endpoints built on them become more capable, more and more endpoints will be scriptable. Eventually, all endpoints will likely support scripting of some kind unless they are severely resource constrained (like those running in microcontrollers).

USING WEB HOOKS AND PUBSUBHUBBUB

As discussed in Chapter 1, "The Live Web," the Live Web already exists. It is exemplified by emerging technologies and concepts such as PubSubHubbub and Web hooks. PubSubHubbub (PuSH) is a method for augmenting RSS and Atom feeds that turns the formerly request-response-style interaction of RSS into one that makes calls to subscribers when relevant updates are posted. Web hooks are a simple way to use HTTP for creating callbacks between Web services.[1]

Both of these technologies are raising events, although not in a form directly usable by KEA. One approach to using them with KRL would be to write a custom endpoint. For special projects, however, it's often just as effective to put together pieces from existing Web services to do the transformation from one kind of event to another. In this section, you'll explore an example that uses both PuSH and Web hooks with KRL that doesn't require writing a custom endpoint.

On the Prowl

Prowl is an iPhone application that raises Growl-style notifications on your phone. Those notifications can come from your computer, from the Web, or through the Prowl API. In this example, you'll send notifications to a phone when a Blogger Web site is updated. Blogger RSS feeds are PuSH enabled, so when the blog is updated, services that have subscribed to the feed are notified immediately.

Notify.io is a service for mapping various real-time happenings on the Web (called sources) into one or more output formats. For example, you can configure notify.io to listen to PuSH-enabled RSS feeds and publish the pushed items to a Web hook. Kynetx provides a Web service[2] that translates events raised via a Web hook into KEA-style events that KRL understands. Using these two services together, you can create a translating endpoint that raises events whenever a blog is updated. The wiring diagram is shown in Figure 9.1. You could use this endpoint to watch any number of PuSH-enabled feeds and raise an event. In this case, you're only watching a few blogs for new posts, so you'll configure the Kynetx Web hook service to raise a KEA event with type newpost whenever it sees a new post.

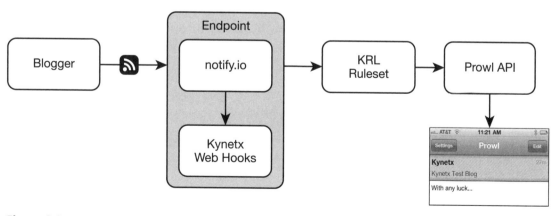

Figure 9.1
Configuring a virtual PuSH endpoint.

The Prowl API can be easily encapsulated in a KRL module. The `meta` section sets some configuration parameters and provides a single definition, `send`, as shown here:

```
meta {
  name "Prowl Module"
  configure using apikeys = {} and
            application = "Kynetx"
  provides send
 }
```

The `global` section defines `send` as an action that uses the Prowl API to post the notification to the user's cell phone. Notice that the action uses the module parameters defined previously and declares an optional parameter called `priority` for the new action:

```
global {
  send = defaction(title, description) {
    configure using priority = 0
    http:post("https://api.prowlapp.com/publicapi/add")
      with params = {
        "apikey": apikeys.pick("$.apikey"),
        "providerkey": apikeys.pick("$.providerkey"),
        "application":application,
        "priority": priority,
        "event": title,
        "description" : description
    }
  }
}
```

Writing a rule to listen for the event from the endpoint and call the `send` action is simple. You need API and provider keys from the Prowl Web site. You declare keys and use the module in the `meta` section of the rule set:

```
key prowl {"apikey":"API KEY GOES HERE",
        "providerkey": "PROVIDER KEY GOES HERE"}
use module a16x83 alias prowl
    with apikeys = keys:prowl()
```

Remember, you declare the keys using the key pragma so that they can be automatically redacted if the rule set is shared. You use an alias to name the module `prowl` for convenience.

The rule to listen for the Web hook event and send the notification to Prowl is simple:

```
rule send_to_prowl is active {
  select when webhook newpost
  prowl:send(event:param("title"), event:param("text"));
}
```

When an event is raised with a type that matches newpost, the rule sends the event's title and text parameters to Prowl. The result is a notification on the iPhone like the one shown in Figure 9.1.

Using a few RESTful Web services and a simple module, you can create a system for notifying users of real-time events online. Amber alerts and other services could use similar techniques to create special-purpose phone apps for their constituencies.

BUILDING ENDPOINTS

You can build endpoints in almost any language, because almost every language has access to libraries for HTTP and JSON that provide the building blocks for raising events and responding to directives. This section will build a simple endpoint using an open-source Ruby gem called kns_endpoint—a library for building KEA endpoints in Ruby. If you have Ruby on your computer, you can install the gem by entering the following on the command line:

```
gem install kns_endpoint
```

Endpoint functionality is controlled by a user-defined class that inherits from Kynetx::Endpoint. For example, the following Ruby class defines a simple echo endpoint that will be used in the examples that follow:

```
class TestEndpoint < Kynetx::Endpoint
 rule set :a18x26
 domain :test_endpoint
 event :echo
 event :echo_hello do |p|
  p[:message] = "Hello #{p[:message]}"
 end
 event :write_entity_var
 event :read_entity_var
 directive :say do |d|
  d[:message]
 end
end
```

The class declares the rule set to which it raises events (a18x26), specifies four events using the keyword event, and defines what to do when it receives a directive named say using the directive keyword.

Any event declaration can specify code for pre-processing event parameters. All the events in the preceding code are simply declared except for the echo_hello event. The code associated with it pre-processes the parameters that accompany the event by prepending "Hello" to any event parameter named message.

You can use this endpoint class in a Ruby program with the following code:

```
TestEndpoint.echo({:message => "Hello World"})
```

The preceding line of code would raise the event echo with an event parameter called message. You can raise any of the events declared in the class with any parameters you like.

Suppose you created the following rule in rule set a18x26 (the rule set declared in the preceding class):

```
rule first_rule {
  select when test_endpoint echo
  pre {
    m = event:param("message");
  }
  send_directive("say") with message = m;
}
```

This rule would fire when an echo event is raised, returning a directive named say with a directive parameter named message whose value is equal to the message that came in with the event. Note that there's nothing in the rule about the endpoint. Any endpoint that raises the echo event in the event domain test_endpoint would fire this rule. A single rule can service multiple endpoints, each implemented in a different way, as long as they raise the same events and understand the same directives.

The directive from the preceding rule would be returned to the test endpoint, and would be processed using the code associated with the directive say as declared in the class. ·

The Ruby endpoint gem manages entity state automatically. Suppose rule set a18x26 contained the following rules:

```
rule write_rule {
  select when test_endpoint write_entity_var
  pre {
    m = event:param("message");
  }
  always {
    mark ent:message with m;
  }
```

```
}
rule read_rule {
  select when test_endpoint read_entity_var
  pre {
    m = current ent:message;
  }
  send_directive("say") with message = m;
}
```

Notice that when `write_rule` is fired, it puts the value of the event parameter `message` into an entity variable named `ent:message` but takes no action. When the rule `read_rule` is fired, it retrieves the value from the entity variable and sends the results back in the directive. Consequently, the following event would store the value "Hey!" in the entity variable:

```
@endpoint = TestEndpoint.new()
@endpoint.signal(:write_entity_var, :message => "Hey!")
```

Later, the endpoint could send the following event and get the value back:

```
puts @endpoint.signal(:read_entity_var)
```

Note

We've created an instance of the class to signal the session because the session ID is stored in the instance and not the class (by design). If you use the class directly, the session ID will be lost between calls.

Clearly, the idea is not to use the rule set as a storage location for the endpoint (although that would work), but to demonstrate the ability of the Ruby endpoint to maintain entity state across events. As you've seen, every entity would have a different entity session as the rule set executed.

Using the Ruby gem, building a custom endpoint to raise events and respond to directives is easy and quick. As a gem, it is perfect for embedding endpoint behavior into Ruby programs. The email endpoint explored next was written using this Ruby gem.

EMAIL

Email is still one of the most popular ways of interacting online, despite the rise of more modern social networking tools. Email is in many ways the least common denominator of online interaction. Almost everyone has an email account (or three), and automating interactions with those email accounts—and processing events between email and other Internet services like the Web—can provide significant value for users.

Email processing is an important component of the Live Web. Automatically processing email and attachments represents a fertile area for providing customer value. Several online businesses, like TripIt and Posterous, have created significant value for their customers using systems that recognize and process email attachments and place the results in cloud-based services that users can access. Visa's RightCliq service (now defunct) used a KRL-powered email processing rule set to automatically parse and store receipts that customers emailed to it.

Likewise, email automation can help in a customer-support situation. Suppose your company's support email address, `support@mycompany.com`, is listed on your Web site. An event-processing system can watch for "email received" events and process the email according to flexible rules. The message might automatically create a case in the company's CRM system and assign it to an appropriate skillset queue. Alternatively, the message might be compared against an API of frequently asked questions, prompting an automated response. In fact, both could happen, or the choice could be made based on membership in a customer-loyalty program, time of day, or even the number or content of previous emails received from the customer.

The real power, however, comes from combining the email event with other events using eventexes. You could treat the email differently if the sender had previously called in, giving it priority. Or, you could show the customer the status of his or her query on the Web site.

In this section, you'll explore the use of a simple email endpoint that has been used successfully in automating email processing for Fortune 500 companies.

Watching IMAP

There are many ways you might envision building a KEA endpoint for email. Perhaps the simplest is a daemon that speaks the IMAP and POP protocols and simply acts like an email client.[3] The KEA open-source project contains a Ruby gem for creating email client endpoints.[4] This section will use its design as a basis for discussing email endpoints, but recognize that nothing about email events is built into KRL.

The email endpoint is configured to connect, as a client, to one or more email accounts using IMAP or POP. Once connected, the endpoint watches the account for specific kinds of activity and raises appropriate events. The endpoint also manipulates the account according to directives it receives. Each connection can specify a different KRL rule set to receive the events raised, optional event arguments to be sent, and authentication information for the inbound and outbound components of the connection.

The email endpoint, at present, only raises one event: `received`. (Of course, because it's open source, you can update it to look for the email events that matter to you.)

The `received` event is raised when an email has been received by the account being watched. Raised events include the following parameters:

- **msg.** The entire message envelope, including the headers
- **body.** The body from the message envelope
- **from.** The sender of the message
- **to.** The addressees of the messages
- **subject.** The subject of the message
- **label.** The label from the message
- **unique_id.** The unique ID string for the message

The email endpoint understands the following directives:

- **forward.** Forward an email. This directive takes the following parameters:
  - **to.** The addressees of the email
  - **body.** The body of the email
  - **subject.** The subject of the email
  - **unique_id.** The ID of the message. (You usually don't have to specify the `unique_id` parameter because the email endpoint is stateful and will forward the message that caused the event to be raised if a forward directive is returned in response.)
  - **delete.** A Boolean value specifying whether to delete the email after it has been forwarded
- **reply.** Reply to an email. The parameters are the same as for `forward`.
- **delete.** Delete an email. The only parameter is `unique_id`. Again, if `unique_id` is missing, the message that raised the event will be deleted.
- **move.** Move a message to a folder. This directive will only work with IMAP accounts. The parameters are as follows:
  - **unique_id.** The ID of the message to move
  - **folder.** The name of the folder to which the message was moved. The folder must exist in the IMAP account.

KRL provides an `email` module that automatically translates actions to the proper directives. For example, the following action:

```
email:forward() with
  to = "cookies@windley.org"
```

becomes the directive shown here:

```
send_directive("forward") with
  to = "cookies@windley.org"
```

The examples that follow will use the action form rather than the directive form.

Cloud-Based Email Rules

Using the email endpoint and some simple KRL rules, you can create a cloud-based rule set to perform many of the functions you would normally do inside your mail client's rule-processing system. For example, in Apple's Mail client, I can create a rule like the one shown in Figure 9.2. This rule puts any email addressed to me in the Archive folder.

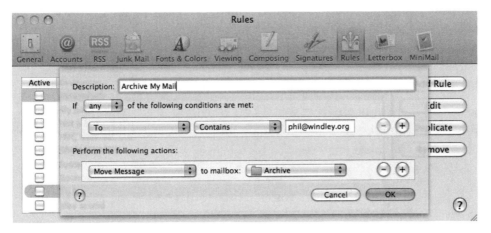

Figure 9.2
A rule to move a message to me to the archive folder.

You can create the same rule in KRL as shown here:

```
rule archive_my_mail {
  select when email received to re#phil@windley.org#
  pre {
    id = event:param("unique_id");
  }
  email:move() with
    unique-id = id and
    folder = "Archive"
}
```

Note

A menu system could generate the preceding rule in response to user input if this system were meant to be user-configurable. KEA defines an API for interacting with rule repositories programmatically so that programs that write rules for users can create rule sets in response to user actions.

The advantage of using KRL over using the rule system in my mail client is that this rule lives in the cloud and consequently can be applied to any email account that you access through IMAP. In fact, it can apply to all of them so that a single change to your cloud-based email rule set updates the behavior for all of your email accounts.

Email Articles to a Blog

The true power of using KRL to interact with your email comes from combining email processing with other online actions. For example, I like to post a periodic article on my blog that lists the things I've read recently. The easiest thing for me to do from within a browser on my desktop or the RSS reader on my iPad is to simply mail the link to the article to an email address.

Suppose I've set up an email address for that purpose and attached an email endpoint to the IMAP account associated with the email address. The following rule would fire whenever that email address received a message. When the rule fires, it formats the appropriate HTML from the contents of the message, appends the HTML to a Google spreadsheet for later use, and replies to the message (for testing) with the resulting HTML. The email is deleted as well.

```
rule process_readings {
  select when email received
  pre {
    subject = event:attr("subject");
    textbody = event:attr("msg");
    url = textbody.extract(re#^(http:\/\/.*)$#);
    item = << <li><a href="#{url}">#{subject}</a></li> >>;
  }
  {
    spreadsheet:submitsingle(item);
    email:reply() with
      message = item and
      delete = true;
  }
}
```

This rule is fairly straightforward, getting the URL from the body of the message and formatting an HTML list item in an extended quote. The `submitsingle()` action puts the HTML in a Google spreadsheet using Steve Nay's Google Docs module (a163 × 73). The module must be properly configured by giving it the spreadsheet key and form key when it is used.

This simple rule automates a part of my life that formerly consumed between 30 and 45 minutes of my week. Once I've emailed the link, the properly formatted text gets accumulated in a Google spreadsheet. I simply open the spreadsheet once a week, cut out the HTML, and paste it into a blog article. (You might be wondering why I don't just have a rule update the blog as well. That's next on my list.)

Node.js and the Live Web

A number of languages support event frameworks that use events to create online services. Node.js (JavaScript), Twisted (Python), POE (Perl), and EventMachine (Ruby) are all event frameworks. In general, that means they provide an easy way to create a network listener for a given protocol (TCP, UDP, HTTP, etc.) and to call a user-supplied callback script when something happens on that port. In the case of HTTP, the event might be a GET or POST request, for example.

KRL, of course, is also a system for dealing with events. The key differences between a system like Node.js and KRL are as follows:

- KRL events are higher level. KEA operates a layer or two up the protocol stack. KRL isn't concerned with responding to protocols like TCP, UDP, or HTTP, but rather works on an abstract notion of events embodied in the Evented API specification (see Appendix F, "The Evented API Specification," for more details).

- KRL event expressions can easily look for complex event scenarios, whereas event frameworks typically only handle primitive (single) events.

You wouldn't use KRL to write an HTTP server. Similarly, while you can use Node.js to write many applications that can be done with KRL, you'll often end up writing more code. This is particularly true of applications that require complex event scenarios and user identity. Programming language event frameworks are complementary to KRL because they can easily be used to create endpoints for KEA.

Building an IRC Bot

Internet Relay Chat (IRC) is the granddaddy of chat systems. Before instant messaging and Google Chat, there was IRC. One of the long-standing features of IRC is bots—automatic programs that administer a channel, offer help, and interact with users for mundane needs. IRC bots are snarky and irreverent, but an absolute necessity on a popular IRC channel. You can use Node.js to create an IRC endpoint for KEA. Once that's done, creating an IRC bot in KRL is relatively straightforward.

An IRC Endpoint

The Node.js `kns` library[5] provides the necessary operations for creating a KEA endpoint using Node.js. You enable it by requiring the library and then creating a Node.js object that links to a particular KRL rule set (by rule set ID):

```
var knsevents = require('kns');
var myapp = new knsevents('a16x485');
```

Once you've created the object, there are two primary methods:

- **signal.** This raises an event to the rule set associated with the object. `signal` takes two arguments: the event type to raise and a map of event parameters. The following would raise an event with type `hello` and the event parameter `eventarg`:

  ```
  myapp.signal("hello", {"eventarg":"world"});
  ```

- **on.** This responds to a directive. `on` is given the directive name to which it responds and a JavaScript function that will be executed when the directive is received. The following would write the contents of the directive parameter `text` to the console when a `say` directive is received:

  ```
  myapp.on("say",function(responseParams){
      console.log(responseParams['text'];
      });
  ```

Using the `kns` library along with the Node.js `irc` library, you can create an endpoint that bridges the IRC protocol to KEA. The following declares an object named `kns` that you create using the `knsevents` object you declared earlier and an IRC client named `client`:

```
kns = new knsevents('a16x485', {
  'eventdomain': 'irc'
});
var client = new irc.Client('chat.freenode.net', 6667);
client.connect('PhilsIRCBot');
```

The client is connecting to the IRC port on `chat.freenode.net` and creating a user named PhilsIRCBot. There are several Node.js callbacks for managing various IRC events, including joining a channel, leaving a channel, and getting disconnected.[6] The following defines callback functions for when a user joins a channel and for the client receiving a message:

```
client.addListener('JOIN', function(prefix, channel, text){
  var user = irc.user(prefix);
  kns.signal("joined", {"user":user, "channel":channel});
```

```
});
client.addListener('PRIVMSG',
            function(prefix, channel, text) {
  var user = irc.user(prefix);
  kns.signal("received",
        {'text':text,'channel':channel,'user':user});
});
```

Notice that the primary function in both is to signal an event to KEA using the `kns` object (joined and received respectively). The rule set associated with this Node.js object will see the events, and rules can respond to them as appropriate.

A tilde prepends IRC "commands." Bots can listen for these commands and respond. You can create an `~insult` command by writing a KRL rule. Suppose you've made the following global declarations:

```
global {
   // datasource which has the insults
   datasource shakespeare:HTML <- "http://www.pangloss.com/seidel/Shaker/";
   getChannel = function(parameters){
    parameters.pick("$.channel").match(re/^#/) =>
        parameters.pick("$.channel") |
        parameters.pick("$.user");
   };
  }
```

The following rule uses these declarations and listens for a received event that has the string `~insult` in the message text and returns a random insult from the Shakespearian insult Web site:[7]

```
  rule irc_insult {
   select when irc received
      text re#.*?~insult\s+(\w+).*?# setting (username)
    pre {
     eventAttrs = event:attrs();
     channel = getChannel(eventAttrs);
     page = datasource:shakespeare({});
     insult = page.query("font[size=+2]", true);
    }
    send_directive("say") with
      text = "#{username}: #{insult[0]}" and
      to = channel;
  }
```

The rule works by grabbing the username to insult from the event text and then queries the Shakespearean insult `datasource` declaration. The site doesn't have an

API, so the rule gets the HTML from the page and screen-scrapes it using the HTML query operator built into KRL. The directive returns the insult to the channel.

There are dozens of rules in the sample code; adding new behavior is as simple as adding a new rule. KRL has several advantages over doing this in straight Node.js:

- Built-in support for various data types and little languages (like Query and JPexes) make getting various data feeds for bot functionality quick and easy. Less code means fewer errors.

- Complex eventexes are easy to write. For example, suppose you wanted to refuse help to users who've used the ~insult command to send someone a random insult within the last 10 minutes. You could write an eventex like the following:

```
select when irc received text re#~help#
    after irc received text re#~insult#
    within 10 minutes
```

Node.js and KRL are a good combination. Node.js excels at easily creating endpoints that translate actions in one protocol into the KEA domain. KRL provides an easy way to dynamically respond.

An Evented World

In this chapter, you've explored events that go beyond the Web and encompass other domains such as email and IRC. There's no need to stop there, however. Endpoints can be part of almost everything. In this section, you'll explore the use of an Arduino open-source prototyping platform as an endpoint.

An Arduino[8] (see Figure 9.3) is a prototyping system for making computers that can sense and control things in the physical world. The Arduino is an open-source physical computing platform based on a simple microcontroller board. Using the development environment, you can write software for the board.

Figure 9.3
An Arduino open-source prototyping platform. Image printed under Creative Commons License (CC-SA-BY).

Jessie Morris wrote a simple endpoint for the Arduino platform that allows it to raise KEA events and respond to a simple KRL directive. The Arduino endpoint raises the following events:

- **checkin.** This is called automatically every *n* seconds. The periodicity is set using the set_delay directive.
- **button.** This indicates that the on-board button was pushed.

The endpoint responds to several directives. To aid in easily parsing the directives on the device, the directives are encoded one per line with the directive first and the parameters following separated using a pipe character (|). The directives are as follows:

- **set_delay.** Sets the time until the next checkin. This directive takes a single parameter, param1, that sets the number of seconds in between checkin events.

- **fade.** Fades the tri-color LED between two colors. This directive takes the following parameters:
  - **param1.** Red value (between 0–255) of color 1
  - **param2.** Green value (between 0–255) of color 1
  - **param3.** Blue value (between 0–255) of color 1
  - **param4.** Red value (between 0–255) of color 2
  - **param5.** Green value (between 0–255) of color 2
  - **param6.** Blue value (between 0–255) of color 2

- **fade_delay.** How long the fade cycle should be (in milliseconds). This directive takes the following parameters:
  - **param1.** Red value (between 0–255)
  - **param2.** Green value (between 0–255)
  - **param3.** Blue value (between 0–255)

- **color.** Set the LED to a specific color. This directive takes the following parameters:
  - **param1.** Red value (between 0–255)
  - **param2.** Green value (between 0–255)
  - **param3.** Blue value (between 0–255)

Using this endpoint, you can create a simple rule set that fades the on-board LED between two randomly selected RGB values whenever someone pushes the button on the Arduino board. The following rule set makes this happen:

```
rule set_up is active {
  select when webhook button
  pre {
    fr = [math:random(256), math:random(256), math:random(256)];
    to = [math:random(256), math:random(256),math:random(256)];
    fadeTime = math:random(5);
    delay = 2;
    message = <<
|fade|#{fr[0]}|#{fr[1]}|#{fr[2]}|#{to[0]}|#{to[1]}|#{to[2]}|#{fadeTime}|
|set_delay|#{delay}|
    >>;
  }
  send_directive("text") with body = "#{message}"
}
```

The Arduino endpoint is a demonstration of what is possible in an evented world. Using cheap, networked microcontrollers, almost everything can become part of the Live Web, raising events and responding to directives.

AN ARDUINO-POWERED SPRINKLER CONTROLLER

Setting a sprinkler controller's configuration via knobs and buttons while trying to make sense of small markings on a tiny screen can be a frustrating experience. The solution (of course!) is a sprinkler controller that is powered by KRL. Placing the logic and programmability in the cloud makes it easy to program, update, and monitor.

This section explores an Arduino-powered sprinkler controller built by Sam Curren and Randall Bohn. You program the watering zones by changing settings in a Google Calendar. The logic is on written in KRL, making the controller itself quite simple.

The hardware portion of the sprinkler controller is an Arduino Mega, with a Wifly shield and relay control boards to switch the sprinkler valves (see Figure 9.4). Simple status is displayed on a small screen from a Nokia cellphone, and there are two buttons and two switches. One switch is for power to the system, and the other switch disables turning zones on.

The hardware described here is a prototype system. Still, the overall cost was only about $200. Mass produced, this system would be as affordable as many sprinkler controllers available at hardware stores today.

Figure 9.4
An Arduino-powered sprinkler controller.

The hardware is configured via USB, to set credentials for the WiFi access point as well as the URL that is used to raise events. The sprinkler raises several events that can be seen by KRL. These events are as follows:

- **reset.** Sent when device is first powered-on.
- **status.** Sent when the controller is checking in.
- **complete.** Sent when a zone has completed its watering.
- **ButtonPress.** Sent when one of the buttons on the device is pressed.

The controller responds to the following directives:

- **SetMessage.** Used to set either of the two display lines on the device's display.
- **SetCallback.** Used to tell the controller when to check in next.
- **RunZone.** Runs a zone for a certain number of minutes.

The set of events and directives is simple by design, so the controller doesn't need much processing logic. Placing the logical components of this system in the cloud enables the operation to be easily updated without making modifications to the controller itself.

The KRL rule set used in conjunction with the controller provides the control logic for watering. The rule set pulls data from a Google Calendar that records the desired watering schedule. Setting appointments on the calendar with a title matching the zone number turns the zone on at the scheduled time. The length of the appointment controls the watering length. Repeat events cause the watering to happen on a schedule.

Using a calendar for scheduling the watering allows for arbitrarily complex watering scenarios that can be easily set and modified using a familiar interface. You can also look at the watering schedule in conjunction with other calendars to avoid conflicts, such as the sprinklers coming on during your backyard BBQ. Of course, as you've seen, data from the calendar could be augmented with other API-based information such as weather forecasts or seasons.

The controller rule set declares two functions in the global section that are used to look up information about the next scheduled zone and the currently scheduled zone (if any). The following declaration gives the nextzone function:

```
nextzone = function(){
  calzone = cal:next("Zone");
  title = calzone.pick("title");
  zone = title.extract(re/Zone (\d+)/).head();
  start = calzone.pick("$..when[0].start");
  end = calzone.pick("$..when[0].end");
  minutes = (time:strftime(end, "%s")-time:strftime(start, "%s")) / 60;
  till = math:int((time:strftime(start, "%s")-time:strftime(time:now(), "%s")) / 60);
  start_str = time:strftime(start, " %m/%d %I:%M %P").replace(re/ 0/g, " ").replace(re/
0/g, " ");
  nextmessage = "Zone #{zone} at#{start_str} for #{minutes} min";
  nz = {
    "message":nextmessage,
    "zone":zone,
    "minutestill":till
  };
  nz;
};
```

The currentzone function is similar. These functions make use of the Google Calendar module (aliased as cal here) described in Chapter 8, "Using the Cloud." The global section defines several other convenience functions. The global section of the rule set also declares several custom actions for the directives to be sent to the controller:

```
text = defaction(textstring){
  configure using mode = null
```

```
  send_directive("text") with body = textstring and mode = mode;
};
SetMessage = defaction(line, message){
 text("M#{line}#{message}|") with mode = "append";
};
SetCallback = defaction(minutes){
 text("CB#{pad(minutes, 3)}|") with mode = "append";
};
RunZone = defaction(zone, minutes){
 text("RZ#{pad(zone, 2)}#{pad(minutes, 3)}|") with mode = "append";
};
```

The SetMessage, SetCallback, and RunZone actions make use of the text action to send directives named text to the controller. The controller parses these text directives and determine what to do.

The currentzone and nextzone rules control the regular watering behavior. The currentzone rule fires if a zone is currently active, and sends directives that set the message on the controller display, set a callback time based on the minutes in the current schedule, and run the desired zone:

```
rule currentzone {
  select when webhook reset or webhook status or explicit status
  pre {
    cz = currentzone();
    message = cz.pick("message");
    zone = cz.pick("zone");
    minutes = cz.pick("minutes");
  }
  if zone then {
    SetMessage("A", message);
    SetMessage("B", "");
    SetCallback(minutes+5);
    RunZone(zone, minutes);
  }
  fired {
    last
  }
}
```

If the currentzone rule does not fire, the nextzone rule will run, displaying an appropriate message and setting the callback time so that the next status event will be signaled when the zone should start watering. The SetCallBack action is defined so that the callback time is the shorter of the time given or a default callback time to enable the system to detect changes to the schedule within a reasonable amount of time.

```
rule nextzone {
  select when webhook reset or webhook status or explicit status
  pre {
    nz = nextzone();
    nextmessage = nz.pick("message");
    till = min_num(nz.pick("minutestill"), 60);
  }
  {
    SetMessage("A","Next: #{nextmessage}");
    SetMessage("B","");
    SetCallback(till);
  }
}
```

The remainder of the rules, which won't be shown for the sake of brevity, mostly focus on a special test mode that becomes active when the B button is pressed. This test mode cycles through the zones, running each for one minute. This enables a quick test of the system. The system also logs its operation using rules, actions, and functions that aren't shown. For example, a rule, triggered by a timed Web hook, emails the recent history of the system to the owner. You can set the rule to email only when the watering history falls below a pre-determined threshold. This is helpful in ensuring that the lawn doesn't go too long if the system has been disabled or if an error has prevented it from operating correctly.

With the power of an evented system and KRL, you can easily adjust the controller to include additional logic or connect it to additional systems. Adding voice or SMS control to the system using a telephony API like Twilio (See Chapter 10, "Mobile and the Live Web" for details) would provide for remote control and monitoring. And, of course, none of these changes would require changing the actual hardware or firmware in the controller.

BUILDING THE LIVE WEB

As you've seen, the Live Web isn't just about the World Wide Web and HTTP. The Live Web encompasses everything that can talk to the network—and even things that can't. Events are everywhere, and raising them allows you to create loosely coupled networks of interacting devices, components, and services that flexibly respond to user needs and purpose.

Endpoints are the key to making this a reality. This chapter has merely scratched the surface of the kinds of endpoints that can be created and the applications that can be enabled when more of our world is networked and participating in the Live Web.

ENDNOTES

1. The term *Web hook* was introduced by Jeff Lindsay (@progrium).
2. Documentation for the Kynetx Web hook service is at http://docs.kynetx.com/docs/Webhook_Endpoint.
3. An email endpoint that is part of a mail transfer agent like Sendmail or Postfix is also possible, but not covered here.
4. The email gem is based on the KEA Ruby gem discussed in the previous section. For more information, see `kns_email_endpoint` on GitHub (https://github.com/kynetx/kns_email_endpoint).
5. Available on GitHub (https://github.com/kynetx/kynetx-node). The library is also available from the Node package manager via the command `npm install kns`.
6. The entire sample IRC endpoint along with a sample rule set can be found on GitHub (https://github.com/kynetx/scottphillips).
7. See http://www.pangloss.com/seidel/Shaker/.
8. See http://arduino.cc/en/Guide/HomePage.

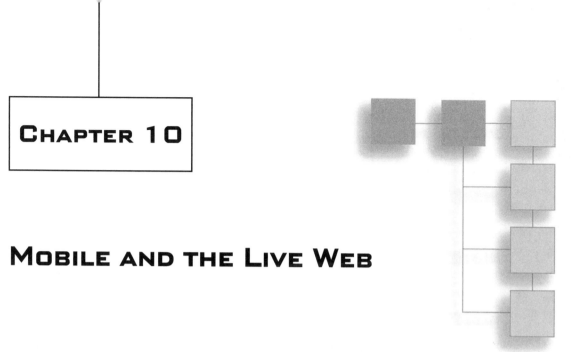

CHAPTER 10

MOBILE AND THE LIVE WEB

Any Live Web strategy that doesn't make use of mobile technology is giving up a huge advantage: People carry their mobile phones with them everywhere they go. The significance of mobile is that people are *always connected*. Being able to work with mobile phones makes a Live Web application more useful by making it more accessible and more ubiquitous.

Smartphones have taken the computing world by storm since the iPhone, and then the Android, were introduced several years ago. But despite the amazing advances in smartphones—connecting to the Web and running apps that use Web-based APIs—sometimes the best way to interact with someone is using voice or SMS. While many people do not have mobile phones that are capable of running apps, every phone has voice and nearly every phone uses SMS. Fortunately, incorporating voice and SMS into Live Web applications has never been easier.

In this chapter, you'll explore how to build mobile Live Web applications. You'll start with voice, move onto SMS, and finally show how KEA endpoints can be built into smartphone apps.

A PBX IN THE CLOUD

In the old days, if you wanted to build a system that took calls or sent SMS messages, you'd have to learn some strange telecom programming language or set up a PBX using software like Asterisk. Now there are several virtual PBX companies that provide telephone services, including voice and SMS text messages, as cloud services. These include Tropo, Orange, Ribbit, and Twilio.

Note

PBX, short for "private branch exchange," refers to a telephone system owned and operated outside of the companies that use them that act as common carriers. Asterisk is an open-source software system for creating IP-based PBXs.

Any of these cloud-based telephony API companies can be used with KRL. The examples that follow use the Twilio service because its Web hook–based API makes it a near-perfect fit for KRL and Live Web applications.

Anyone can create an account and provision phone numbers using the Twilio service. When someone calls or sends a text message to one of these numbers, Twilio uses a Web hook to call a RESTful Web service that the account owner has set up. The response from the service should be an XML file that tells Twilio what to do next (see Figure 10.1).

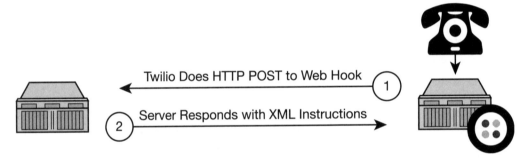

Figure 10.1
Twilio works using Web hooks that call out to servers for instruction files written in XML.

For example, the instruction file sent back from the Web service to Twilio might look like this:

```xml
<?xml version="1.0" encoding="UTF-8"?>
<Response>
    <Gather method="POST" numDigits="5"
            action="http://example.com/getzip.cgi">
        <Play>greeting.wav</Play>
        <Say>Please enter your 5 digit zipcode.</Say>
    </Gather>
</Response>
```

These instructions tell Twilio to gather information in the form of keypad input from the user. As part of that task, the Twilio server will play the greeting in the named WAV file and then say the phrase asking for the ZIP code. Once the user enters his or her ZIP code, the Twilio server will call the URL given in the `action` attribute with the ZIP code and expect another XML instruction file to tell it what to do next.

In addition to playing audio, verbalizing text, and gathering user input, Twilio can record audio from the user, dial out to numbers, connect callers, create conference calls, and send and receive SMS messages. Twilio charges on a pay-as-you-use basis.

Events from Voice

Once you've signed up for a Twilio account, you can provision phone numbers and associate them with callback URLs, or Web hooks. When one of your phone numbers is called, the Twilio service will `POST` to the Web hook associated with that number. (The number actually has two URLs—one for voice and one for SMS. This section talks about voice, but almost everything you do is applicable to SMS interactions as well.)

The beauty of the Twilio architecture is that its use of Web hooks means that it's already part of the evented Web. You can use the Kynetx Web hook service to cause Twilio's Web hook calls to raise events in KEA. When the event selects a KRL rule, the rule's response is sent back as the response to the Web hook.

The following shows the Web hook format to use with Twilio when raising KEA events:

```
http://webhooks.kynetxapps.net/t/{appid}/{eventtype}
```

To raise an event with type `inbound_call` to rule set `a16x33` from Twilio, you'd configure Twilio with the following URL:

```
http://webhooks.kynetxapps.net/t/a16x33/inbound_call
```

Because the Web hook endpoint is used, this event would normally have an event domain of `webhook`, but the endpoint has been constructed to use the domain `twilio` when the first part of the URL path is `t`. Any parameters that Twilio sends with the Web hook are passed on to the rule set as event parameters. For example, Twilio sends the parameter `From` with the caller ID of the inbound caller when calling a Web hook after a call.

The `twilio` Library

One of the built-in libraries in Kynetx supports Twilio directly. This makes sending Twilio directives easier. As mentioned, you can control Twilio by sending back XML files that instruct the Twilio engine on what to do next. The Twilio XML format is called TwilML.

The KRL `twilio` library defines actions that send back TwilML. For example, if a rule set returned the following TwilML, the Twilio engine would respond by saying "Hello Monkey" to the caller:

```
<Response>
  <Say>Hello Monkey</Say>
</Response>
```

The following action in KRL does the same thing:

```
twilio:say("Hello Monkey")
```

Some TwilML directives take optional arguments that can be passed to the action using a `with` clause:

```
twilio:say("Hello Monkey")
 with voice = "woman"
```

Table 10.1 shows the actions associated with the various TwilML directives. The `twilio:raw()` action has no corresponding Twilio verb. You can use it to send any XML you like to Twilio in case the preceding actions don't provide what you need.

Table 10.1 Kynetx Twilio Module Actions for TwilML Directives

Twilio Verb	Kynetx Action
`<Say>`	`twilio:say("text")`
`<Play>`	`twilio:play(url)`
`<Gather>`	`twilio:gather_start() twilio:gather_stop()`
`<Record>`	`twilio:record()`
`<Sms>`	`twilio:sms(message)`
`<Dial>`	`twilio:dial(number)`
`<Conference>`	`twilio:dial_conference(name)`
`<Dial>`	`twilio:dial_start() twilio:number(number) twilio:dial_stop()`
`<Hangup>`	`twilio:hangup()`
`<Redirect>`	`twilio:redirect(url)`
`<Reject>`	`twilio:reject()`
`<Pause>`	`twilio:pause(length)`
	`twilio:raw_response(xml)`

To see how all this works, let's build a Hello Monkey demo[1] by writing a KRL rule to say hello to callers by name (in this example, pretend the callers are monkeys) for numbers that it recognizes:

```
rule answer is active {
   select when twilio inbound_call
   pre {
      callerid = event:attr("From");
      dir = {"+14158675309":"Curious George",
             "+14158675310":"Boots",
             "+14158675311":"Virgil",
             "+14158675312":"Marcel"};
      dir_match = dir.pick("$.#{callerid}");
      name = dir_match.length() != 0 => dir_match
                                      | "Monkey"
   }
   {
     twilio:say("Hello #{name}");
     twilio:hangup();
   }
}
```

This simple rule uses the `From` event attribute to get the caller's phone number and looks up an associated name in a directory. In this example, you just list the monkeys in the `dir` map, but you could easily consult an outside data source to find people from a company directory or other list using an API call. The action tells Twilio to so "Hello" followed by the name and then hang up.

You can expand this example to ask the monkey for his or her favorite number. You gather input from the caller using the dial pad by adding the `twilio:gather()` action to the `answer` rule and add another rule to process the caller's response.

First, the updated `answer` rule:

```
rule answer is active {
   select when twilio inbound_call
   pre {
      callerid = event:attr("From");
      dir = {"+14158675309":"Curious George",
             "+14158675310":"Boots",
             "+14158675311":"Virgil",
             "+14158675312":"Marcel"};
      dir_match = dir.pick("$.#{callerid}");
      name = dir_match.length() != 0 => dir_match
                                      | "Monkey"
```

```
  }
  {
    twilio:say("Hello #{name}");
    twilio:gather_start("monkey_handle")
        with numDigits="1";
      twilio:say("What is your favorite number?");
    twilio:gather_stop();
  }
}
```

You've replaced the hangup() action with three actions that together start to gather the user input, prompt the user to enter his or her favorite number, and end the user input. Once Twilio has gathered the caller input, it will call the Web hook that is constructed by the KRL twilio module using the parameter passed to the twilio:gather_start() action as the event type monkey_handle.

You can respond to that event using another rule:

```
rule picked is active {
    select when twilio monkey_handle
    pre {
      favorite = event:attr("Digits");
    }
    {
      twilio:say("Your favorite number is #{favorite}.");
      twilio:hangup();
    }
}
```

Any response from a gather action will have an event attribute called Digits that contains the user input. The rule simply says it back to the monkey, but you could store it in an entity variable for later use and, for example, display it on a Web page for the monkey to see.

Together, these rules create a simple phone application that greets callers, takes input, and responds. Let's put your newfound knowledge to work.

EXTENDING THE TA RULE SET

Chapter 8, "Using the Cloud," introduced a module for communicating with Google Calendar and used it to place a banner on the CS462 Web site wiki when the teaching assistant was in office hours, as shown in Figure 10.2.

Figure 10.2
Banner on the CS462 class wiki, indicating whether the TA is having office hours.

Recall that the `ta_is_in` rule used a function called `onnow()` from the module aliased as `officehours` to check whether the calendar showed a current event with a specific name:

```
if officehours:onnow("Office hours") then {
  prepend('.firstHeading', message);
}
```

Now that you know how to respond to phone calls from a rule set, you can easily add the following rule to respond to users who call in and give them the status of office hours:

```
rule call {
  select when twilio inbound_call
  pre {
    resp = officehours:onnow("Office hours") =>
            "The TA is in. Stop by Cubicle 13." |
            "The TA is not in right now.";
  }
  twilio:say(resp)
}
```

This rule assumes that you've already configured a number at Twilio to call a Web hook with the event type `inbound_call`.

Using SMS

There's no reason to stop with voice. Using Twilio to add SMS message capabilities to the TA rule set is simple. Every Twilio number has an associated Web hook for voice calls and one for SMS messages. Let's assume you've configured that Web hook to raise the event `sms`. You can send an SMS message in a similar manner to how you handled voice:

```
rule sms {
  select when twilio sms
  pre {
    resp = officehours:onnow("Office hours")  =>
            "The TA is in. Stop by Cubicle 13." |
            "The TA is not in right now.";
  }
  twilio:sms(resp)
}
```

The only difference is that you're looking for the `sms` event in the eventex and using the `twilio:sms()` action. (Naturally, you could factor out the common bits into a function to avoid repeating them.) Note that you don't care what text message gets sent to the SMS number; you always reply with the current status.

You can extend this rule to report back, via SMS, the next time office hours will be held. The Google Calendar module has a `next()` function that returns a `datetime` object. Using that object, you can create a string that gives the next office-hour time and text it back:

```
rule sms {
  select when twilio sms
  pre {
    smsdate = function(d){
```

```
            datestringA =
                time:strftime(d, "on %A (%B %d) at %I %M %p")
            datestringA.replace(re/ 0/g," ");
        };
        nexttime = officehours:next("Office hours");
        ohtime = nexttime =>
            "Office hours scheduled" +
                smsdate(nexttime.pick("$.when[0].start")) |
            "No office hours scheduled";
        resp = officehours:onnow("Office hours") => "The TA is in Cubicle 13 now."
                                                | ohtime;
    }
    twilio:sms(resp)
}
```

This rule defines a function that creates a properly formatted string from the date-time object, gets the next time office hours will be held, and formats it. The response indicates that office hours are being held now or gives the time they will next be held.

The text of the SMS message is contained in the Body event attribute. You can use the Body attribute to always return the next time office hours will be held when the body of the incoming text message contains the word "next," as follows:

```
rule sms {
    select when twilio sms Body #/\bnext\b/#
    pre {
        smsdate = function(d){
            datestringA =
                time:strftime(d, "on %A (%B %d) at %I %M %p")
            datestringA.replace(re/ 0/g," ");
        };
        nexttime = officehours:next("Office hours");
        resp = nexttime => smsdate(nexttime.pick("$.when[0].start"))
                        | "No office hours scheduled";
    }
    twilio:sms(resp)
}
```

This rule checks the body of the incoming text for the word "next" in the eventex and only fires if that condition is true. Of course, if you were going to have both of these rules in the same rule set, you'd want to factor out the common definitions and put them in the global block.

AN INTERACTIVE VOICE RESPONSE SYSTEM

Building a flexible, advanced interactive voice response (IVR) system typically requires spending lots of money on a commercial system and learning a strange telecom language or installing an open-source platform like Asterisk and figuring out how to script the desired behavior. But that needn't be the case. Twilio and KRL offer a convenient, inexpensive, and flexible way to create sophisticated IVR features.

If you call the Kynetx main number, you'll reach an IVR system that Sam Curren wrote using KRL and Twilio. Sam's IVR features include the following:

- Contextual menus that change based on outside data and events. For example, the Kynetx IVR watches a Google calendar and changes the menu options based on what's happening right now.

- A conference-call feature that enables up to 20 people to schedule and join calls.

- An office-hours system that allows callers to join an "office hours" conference call when it is scheduled (and doesn't present the option when it isn't). If someone calls and no one from Kynetx is on the call, the IVR dials out to a hunt group of numbers to find someone to answer the call.

- A fall-through for people who seem to be stuck in the office-hours menu that automatically connects them to a person.

The entire IVR system is too complex (and uses features I won't introduce until the next chapter), so a simplified version is presented here.

Handling the Call and Giving the Menu

Suppose you've configured Twilio to raise the event `callstart` when someone calls your phone number. To get started, you define an action to play a recorded greeting and gather the user input after saying the menu:

```
play_menu = defection(text) {
   twilio:play(".../thank_you_for_calling_kynetx.mp3");
   twilio:gather_start("menuchoice") with numDigits = 1;
     twilio:say(text);
   twilio:gather_stop();
}
```

The following rule handles the `callstart` event, defines the text of the menu, and calls the `play_menu()` action:

```
rule newcall {
```

```
select when twilio callstart or twilio givemenu
pre {
  saythis = "Press 1 to speak to Kynetx" +
            "Press 2 to join a meeting";
}
{
  play_menu(saythis);
  twilio:redirect("givemenu");
}
}
```

An interesting feature of this rule is that it is recursive. If the caller responds to the gather action, a new event, menuchoice, will be raised. But if the user doesn't respond within a certain amount of time after Twilio presents the menu, the gather action times out and falls through to the redirect. Notice that it raises the event givemenu and will run this rule again because of the disjunction in the eventex.

What if the caller never responds? Twilio and KRL would be engaged in an endless dance, repeatedly going back and forth until the caller hung up. To avoid this, you can count the number of times through the menu in an entity variable and only take action for a set number of iterations:

```
rule newcall {
  select when twilio callstart or twilio givemenu
  pre {
    saythis = "Press 1 to speak to Kynetx" +
              "Press 2 to join a meeting";
  }
  if(ent:menucount < 3 then {
    play_menu(saythis);
    twilio:redirect("givemenu");
  }
  fired {
    ent:menucount += 1 from 1;
  }
}
```

Now the rule will only fire three times and then stop. You want to hang up when that condition is met, however, so you add the hangup rule:

```
rule newcall {
  select when twilio givemenu
  if(ent:menucount >= 3) then {
    twilio:say("Goodbye");
    twilio:hangup();
```

```
  }
  fired {
    clear ent:menucount
  }
}
```

This rule hangs up and clears the menu counter when the counter is greater than 3. This is a KRL pattern you've not encountered to date. Often, you will have more than one rule fire on the same event (in this case, the givemenu event from Twilio) and take action that is accretive or, as in this case, conditional. This style is common to rule languages, but unusual in procedural languages where a programmer would use an else clause to take an alternative action. (Of course, you could alternatively define an action that uses a choose compound action to either redirect or hang up, depending on the value of an argument sent to the action and avoid two rules.)

Handling the Menu Choices

When the caller makes a choice in the preceding menu, Twilio will issue a menu-choice event with an event parameter named Digits that contains the choice. You can handle this event with a rule for each menu choice by carefully writing the select statement to look for the menu item. In the following, the speak rule handles the menu item:

```
rule speak {
    select when twilio menuchoice Digits re#1#
    {
        twilio:dial(mainofficenumber);
        twilio:hangup();
    }
}
```

The first rule is straightforward, just connecting the caller to the main office number. If the dial action falls through (for example, because no one answered the main office number), the rule hangs up.

The chooseconf rule handles the second menu item:

```
rule chooseconf {
    select when twilio menuchoice Digits re#2#
    {
        twilio:gather_start("joinconf") with numDigits = 2;
        twilio:say("Please enter the two digit number of the conference you wish to
join.");
        twilio:gather_stop();
```

```
        twilio:redirect("givemenu");
    }
}
```

The second rule gathers more input from the user about the conference he or she wishes to join, raising the `joinconf` event with the results. Again, if the caller doesn't reply, the `gather` action falls through and the caller is taken back to the main menu.

Handling the `joinconf` event is equally easy. You grab the conference number from the event parameter `Digits` and issue actions that join that conference number:

```
rule joinconf {
    select when twilio joinconf Digits re#(.*)#
        setting (confnum)
    {
        twilio:say("Joining meeting #{confnum}");
        twilio:dial_conference("conf#{confnum}")
            with hangupOnStar = "true";
        twilio:redirect("givemenu");
    }
}
```

When the caller exits a conference call, you send him or her back to the menu.

Handling Bad Choices and Cleaning Up

You need to handle bad input from the caller and ensure that you clean up after yourself. If the caller enters a digit you don't handle in a `menu` rule, you need to redirect the caller back to the main menu:

```
rule badmenu {
    select when twilio menuchoice Digits re#([34567890])#
        setting (invalidchoice)
    twilio:say("#{invalidchoice} is not a valid option");
    twilio:redirect("givemenu");
}
```

When the caller chooses a good menu item, you want to clear the entity variable so the caller isn't unfairly penalized and doesn't remain stuck in the menu:

```
rule menurepeat {
    select when twilio menuchoice Digits re#[12]#
    always {
        clear ent:menucount;
    }
}
```

With seven simple KRL rules, you've created an IVR system. Adding new menu choices and handling them is as easy as adding a rule. Just as you did in the TA example, you could also handle SMS queries to the main number with a few more rules.

Beyond Voice: Mobile Live Web Applications

Being able to integrate voice and SMS into a Live Web application is important, but there is more to mobile than just voice and SMS. In fact, smartphone applications should participate on the Live Web as first-class citizens for several important reasons.

Perhaps the most compelling reason is that smartphones have become the computing device of convenience for most people. There's an old saying: "The best camera is the one you've got with you." That's doubly true for computers. Most people have their smartphones with them all the time. Thus, smartphones represent a perfect platform for Live Web applications.

Because of the ubiquity of smartphones, life logging has gone from an obscure hobby by a few fanatics to something almost everyone does in one form or another. Companies like FitBit, Endomondo, Foursquare, and others provide apps that help you accumulate pieces of your life in digital format. At present, most of these life-logging apps are silos that keep their data in their format in the cloud, but there is great pressure to give people more direct access to the data and control of its use. In other words, rather than just showing people where they've checked in, users want to use these apps to correlate their location stream with other data, such as what purchases they've made or the photos they've taken.

Another important factor is that smartphones are equipped with an increasingly wide variety of sensors that make them ideal for understanding and reacting to user context. Combined with their always-present nature, smartphones are becoming continuous sensing platforms that understand important data about the owner's current environment and, often, their intent. Moreover, phones are networked in several ways, making them an ideal local connection point for other sensors.

Microelectromechanical systems (MEMSes) that are integrated into modern smartphones include accelerometers, compasses, gyroscopes, pressure sensors, dual microphones, proximity sensors, and light sensors. MEMSes take analog data from the environment and translate it into digital data that is available to applications on the phone.

In addition to MEMSes, the phone is also a perfect device for sensing location. Smartphones provide both cell-tower triangulation and integrated GPS systems for determining location and provide ample data about where the phone is located. Combined with MEMSes, the smartphone becomes a powerful tool for determining owner context and inferring intent.

Using KRL in Mobile Apps

The primary short-term opportunity for mobile on the Live Web is apps that function as endpoints in KEA. Mobile apps can raise events based on their reading of the smartphone sensors. Mobile apps can also receive directives from rules that react to those events. Mobile endpoints have access to contextual data from sensors that allow them to manage the state of the owner in ways not possible on other devices.

Many apps allow users to view Web pages without leaving the app by using the smartphone's browser engine inside the application. Consequently, one easy way to run rules in a smartphone app is to plant KEA script tags on Web pages that the in-app Web browser opens. When tags are planted on those pages in the same way as browser extension endpoints, rules can annotate the page content in all the ways discussed in Chapter 7, "Creating Contextual Web Experiences."

More generally, mobile apps can use a library to raise events directly. Kynetx has developed open-source libraries for both the iPhone and Android platforms.[2] While still simple, these libraries provide a good start for anyone developing mobile endpoints for KRL.

The libraries provide the means to signal an event to a specified RID in a specified event domain. The signal method takes a name and a map of name-value pairs as arguments, formats the KEA event URL, and raises the event. The response directive is parsed and placed in a data structure that the program can use.

You'll recall the Best Buy example I used in Chapter 3, "Event Expressions: Filtering the Event Stream," to motivate compound eventexes:

> As you drive through town, your phone notifies you that the DVD you added to your Amazon wish list this morning is available and on sale at the Best Buy you're passing.

Using the libraries for the iPhone and Android platforms, you can make this scenario real. As it happens, Best Buy has a great API for determining whether particular stores have a specific product. To keep the example simple, assume the wish list is stored in persistent entity variables instead of being accessed from the Amazon API.

The sample endpoints for both the iPhone and Android libraries subscribe to location change notifications from the underlying operating system. These libraries support a `raise_kea_event()` function for raising events and a `show_notification()` function for notifying the user of the result. The endpoint executes the following algorithm to raise a KEA event when the OS notices a location change:

```
on location_change(function(lat, long) {
    directive = raise_kea_event
                 ("mobile",
                  "location_update",
                  {"newLocation": [lat, long]});
    if(directive.name eq "notify") {
      show_notification(directive);
      }
  })
```

Given the latitude and longitude of the new location, the endpoint raises a KEA event with the event domain `mobile`, the event type `location_update`, and an event attribute `newLocation` that contains the latitude and longitude. The endpoint processes the directive that is returned to show a notification as shown in Figure 10.3.

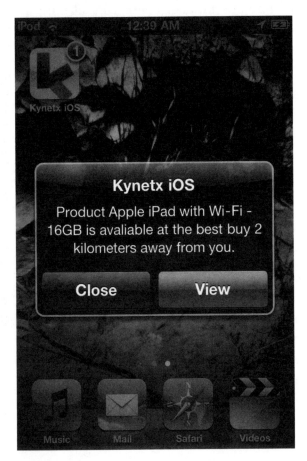

Figure 10.3
Notification of Best Buy product discovery on an iPhone.

The endpoint is a fairly simple program. The real work is being done by the KRL rule set in the cloud. The rule set makes use of a Best Buy API for finding products and a wish list stored in the user's entity variable space. (Ignore the rules for adding products to the wish list in this example.)

The Best Buy API is accessed using a KRL function called get_product_data() that takes a SKU, latitude, and longitude, and constructs an API for the Best Buy API. Notice that you're only getting products that are on sale and are available at stores in a particular geographic area:[3]

```
get_product_data = function(sku, lat, long) {
  datasource:bby_open_api(
    "products(onSale=true&sku=#{sku})+" +
    "stores(area(#{lat},#{long}))" +
    "?apiKey=#{keys:bby_open()}&format=json"
  ).pick("$.products", true);
}
```

The function makes use of API keys and a previously defined data source to make an API request to Best Buy and retrieve a JSON-formatted product record. You will get back the product data for stores within a 10-mile radius (the default) of the latitude and longitude you supply.

The check_stores rule uses this function and is selected when the endpoint raises a location_update event:

```
rule check_stores {
  select when mobile location_update
  foreach ent:wishlist_items setting (wishlist_item)
  pre {
    best_buy_prod_data = get_product_data(wishlist_item);
    product_name = get_product_name(best_buy_prod_data);
    distance = calcDistToBestBuy(best_buy_prod_data,
                                  event:attr("newLocation"));
  }
  if (not ent:shownProduct within 5 hours &&
      distance < 2 &&
      best_buy_prod_data.length()) then
    send_directive("notify") with
    text = "Product #{product_name} is available at the Best Buy #{distance}
kilometers away from you."
    fired {
      set ent:shownProduct true;
    }
}
```

The rule loops through the items in the wish list, looking for them in the Best Buy catalog. It sends back a `notify` directive with the offer text and distance if:

- It hasn't shown an offer in the last five hours.

- The distance to the nearest store is within two kilometers.

- There is a product on the user's wish list to show.

Note

> The rule makes use of several straightforward functions that are not shown to get the name from the product map and to calculate the distance between where you are and the store.

If the rule fires, you set the `showProduct` entity variable so that the user isn't bombarded with reminders.

Because the logic for this product notification system is in the cloud, it can be easily updated without waiting for smartphone users to update their apps. A production rule would probably display the product and store data on a map rather than use a text notification.

Going Mobile

In this chapter, you've seen how KRL applications can be written that use voice, SMS, and mobile endpoints to bring people onto the Live Web when they're not sitting at their computer. The real power of the Live Web is only apparent, however, when you combine events from multiple domains. In coming chapters, you'll explore techniques that allow multiple rule sets to work together and then see how you can use those techniques to create larger Live Web applications.

Endnotes

1. The Hello Monkey demo in PHP appears on the Twilio "Getting Started" documentation page. The rules here are adapted from that demo. See http://www.twilio.com/docs/quickstart/twiml/hello-monkey.

2. You can access the code at https://github.com/kynetx. Alex Olsen developed the Objective C library for the iPhone and Jessie Morris developed the library for the Android.

3. See the Best Buy API documentation (https://developer.bestbuy.com/bbopen-apis) for more details about how the API works.

CHAPTER 11

BUILDING EVENT NETWORKS

The preceding chapters have focused on how rules respond to events. But there's another way that rules and events interact: Rules can raise events. The power of KRL expands significantly when rules raise events because rules can be used to build event networks. Events that are raised by a rule are called *explicit events*.

One of the key design goals for KRL is to enable developers to create rule sets that are loosely coupled. Rules should add behavior in an accretive manner so that rules can be added or deleted without affecting the behavior of other rules.

This chapter explores explicit events and how they can be used to create event networks. You will see that explicit events provide an important means of abstraction in KRL through event synthesis and rule chaining. A number of event intermediary patterns present themselves when you can raise explicit events.

UNDERSTANDING EVENT TYPES

There are two ways to raise an explicit event: in the rule postlude using the `raise` statement or as an action using the `raise_event()` action. Figure 11.1 shows the difference between these two kinds of explicit events.

An explicit event in the postlude handles the event in the same processing episode as the original event and results in a possibly increased set of directives being sent back to the endpoint. The explicit event causes further processing to happen on the rules engine without further involvement by the endpoint.

In contrast, the `raise_event()` action sends instructions back to the endpoint that cause it to raise another event. The disadvantage is that there is a second round trip

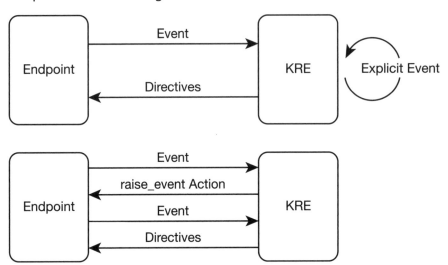

Figure 11.1
Explicit event types.

from the endpoint to KRE made in response to the action. The advantage is that additional information on the endpoint can be sent along with the new event and is thus available for processing on the rules engine.

When an event is raised in the postlude, the event will have the event domain explicit, so you would use an eventex like the following to write a rule that is selected when this event is raised:

```
select when explicit <event_type>
```

When an event is raised by the endpoint in response to a raise_event() action, the new event will have the event domain of the endpoint raising the event. The following eventex would select a rule based on an explicit event raised from the Web endpoint:

```
select when web <event_type>
```

RAISING EXPLICIT EVENTS IN THE POSTLUDE

Explicit events are raised in the rule postlude with a raise statement:

```
raise explicit event foo for "a16x48"
    with a = "hello"
    and b = 4 + x;
```

The for clause is optional. If it's missing, the event will be raised within the current rule set. The for clause is followed by an expression that is evaluated to determine which rule sets should see the event. The result of the expression should be either a string or an array of strings. The strings should contain a single rule set IDs.

The `with` clause allows the developer to add event parameters to the explicit event. The right side of the individual bindings in the `with` clause can be any KRL expression.

Like any other postlude statement, explicit events can be guarded:

```
raise explicit event foo
    with a = "hello"
     and b = 4 + x
  if (flipper eq "two");
```

The event in the preceding example will only be raised if the variable flipper has the value "two".

Explicit events allow KRL programmers to chain rules together. Rule chaining is good for modularization, error handling, preprocessing, and abstraction, as you'll see in the following sections.

Automatically Raising Events

Sometimes, it's useful to explicitly raise an event to handle responses from an action. (This is different from the `raise_event()` action discussed in the next section.) For example, when you use `http:post()` as an action, you might want to respond to status codes indicating an error. Explicit events can be used to cause another rule to handle that response. While you can simply use the `raise` statement in the postlude as was just discussed, this happens often enough for certain actions that they support shorthand for raising explicit events from the action.

Certain actions automatically raise events using the optional `autoraise` parameter. (Currently, only the `post` action in the `http` module supports `autoraise`.) The `autoraise` parameter is given with a string as its value. When the explicit event is automatically raised, one of the event attributes will be `label`, and it will have the value of the `autoraise` string.

Each action defines its own event domain and type. For the `http:post()` action, the event that is raised will have an event domain of `http` and an event type of `post`. Similarly, each action will include relevant data from the action. The response values given previously are sent as event attributes and can thus be checked as part of the event selection. The `http:post()` action includes response information from the `POST`.

The following simple example shows a rule that has an `http:post()` action with an event `autoraise`:

```
rule r1 is active {
  select when pageview "/archives/(\d+)/" setting(year)
  http:post("http://www.example.com/go")
    with params = {"answer": "x"} and
        autoraise = "ex";
}
```

This is roughly equivalent to the following rule:

```
rule r1 is active {
  select when pageview "/archives/(\d+)/" setting(year)
  http:post("http://www.example.com/go") setting (response)
    with params = {"answer": "x"};
  always {
   raise explicit event post with resp = response
  }
}
```

The only difference is that the `autoraise` creates an event with the event domain `http`, while the `raise` statement creates an event with the event type `explicit`.

Note

At present, the `raise` statement does not allow the developer to choose the domain. That restriction may be relaxed in future versions of KRL.

Assuming you automatically raised an event in the first rule, you could chain additional rules for subsequent processing of the response. The following two rules check the status code of the response and present a notification of the result:

```
rule r2 is active {
  select when http post label re #ex# status_code re#(2\d\d)#
    setting (status)
  notify("Status", "Success! The status is " + status);
}
rule r3 is active {
  select when http post label re#ex# status_code re#([45]\d\d)#
    setting (status)
  fired {
   log <<Error: #{status}: #{event:attr("status_line")}>>
   last;
  }
}
```

The second rule fires when the status code in the response indicates an error, logs the error, and uses the `last` control statement in the postlude to stop subsequent processing of rules in the rule set.

You can also process responses based on other event attributes, such as `content_type`. The following rule shows the content of the response if its `content_type` is `"text"`.

```
rule r4 is active {
  select when http post label re#ex#
  if(event:attr("content_type") like "^text") then
    notify("Page says…", event:attr("content"));
}
```

Rule chaining from an `autoraise` on an `http:post()` action provides a convenient, event-driven way of dealing with the results of an action.

THE EXPLICIT EVENT ACTION

The Web endpoint supports a `raise_event()` action that causes the runtime to raise an event. The `raise_event()` action causes control to be passed back to the rules engine from the Web endpoint for further processing. (While only the Web endpoint currently supports the `raise_event()` action, future endpoints in other domains will also support it since it provides an important control flow mechanism.)

The `raise_event()` action takes a string argument that declares the event name and two optional parameters: `app_id` and `parameters`. The `app_id` identifies the rule set for which the event will be raised. If the `app_id` is missing, the event is raised to the current rule set. `parameters` is a map of name value pairs.

```
raise_event(<event_type>)
   with app_id = <rid> and
       parameters = {"name_0": value_0,
               …
               "name_n": value_n
               };
```

You can see how this works with an example. Suppose rule set A has the following rule:

```
rule Raise_Event_Action {
  select when pageview ".*"
  {
  notify("Kynetx Event Walkabout",
      "Raise_Event_To_Remote_Ruleset");
```

```
raise_event("event_remote_ruleset")
  with app_id = "B";
 }
}
```

And rule set B contains the following code:

```
rule Catch_Remote_Event {
  select when web event_remote_ruleset
  notify("Catch_Remote_Event",
      "Received from remote Ruleset!")
}
```

When `Raise_Event_Action` is selected, the notification boxes shown in Figure 11.2 will appear in the user's browser.

Figure 11.2
Simple `raise_event()` action interplay.

You can make this simple example more interesting by making rule set B callback to the rule set that raises the event it processes. First, add the following rule to rule set A:

```
rule Catch_Event_Callback {
  select when web event_callback
  notify("Catch_Event_Callback",
      "Received Callback Event!")
}
```

You also add some parameters to the `raise_event()` action in the `Raise_Event_ Action` rule in rule set A:

```
rule Raise_Event_Action {
  select when pageview ".*"
  {
    notify("Kynetx Event Walkabout",
        "Raise_Event_To_Remote_Ruleset");
    raise_event("event_remote_ruleset")
      with app_id = "B"
```

```
    and parameters = {
          "callback_rid" : "A",
          "callback_evt" : "event_callback"
          }
  }
}
```

Now you change the rule in rule set B to look for and process the callback:

```
rule Catch_Remote_Event {
 select when web event_remote_ruleset
 pre {
  callback_rid = event:attr("callback_rid");
  callback_evt = event:attr("callback_evt");
 }
 {
  notify("Catch_Remote_Callback",
       "Received from remote Ruleset!");
  notify("Now Raise Callback",
       "rid: #{callback_rid} name: #{callback_evt}");
  raise_event(event_callback)
    with app_id = callback_rid;
 }
}
```

Note that `Catch_Remote_Event` uses the event type and rule set ID that are set in `Raise_Event_Action` to determine which event to raise and specify the rule set that will process it. The `Catch_Event_Callback` rule you added to rule set A catches the callback, causing the notification boxes in Figure 11.3 to appear.

Figure 11.3
Explicit event action with callback.

EXPLICIT EVENTS AS RULE ABSTRACTIONS

In Chapter 7, "Creating Contextual Web Experiences," you created a rule set that greeted people by name if an entity variable with the person's name was present. Otherwise, the rule set placed a form on a page asking for the person's name and then responded by showing the name submitted in place of the form. Recall that the rule that responded to the submit event looked like this:

```
rule respond_submit {
  select when web submit "#my_form"
  pre {
   name = event:attr("first")+" "+event:attr("last")};
  }
  replace_inner("#my_div", "Hello #{name}");
  fired {
    mark ent:name with name;
  }
}
```

The rule that used the data and replaced the form with the name looked like this:

```
rule replace_with_name {
 select when web pageview ".*"
 pre {
  name = current ent:name;
 }
 replace_inner("#my_div", "Hello #{name}");
}
```

The problem with this design is that you're using replace_inner() in two different places to paint the greeting on the page. Experienced programmers try to avoid doing the same thing in two places because it leads to maintenance problems. For example, if you change the greeting to "Howdy #{name}!" you have to remember to change it in two places.

The answer to problems like this is almost always some kind of abstraction. You saw one possible solution, changing the eventex of the second rule, in Chapter 7. Since Chapter 7, you've learned about user-defined actions, which are another important kind of abstraction in KRL. That would be a second way to solve the problem. You could define an action called send_greeting() that abstracts the greeting like so:

```
send_greeting = defaction(name) {
 replace_inner("#my_div", "Hello #{name}")
}
```

Replacing the action in both rules with send_greeting() would abstract away the details of the greeting and put them in one place. Now you have one place to change the greeting, but you are still taking the same action in two places.

Another way to deal with this problem is to use an explicit event to chain the rules, letting just one rule send the greeting. The first rule would now look like this:

```
rule respond_submit {
  select when web submit "#my_form"
  pre {
    name = event:attr("first")+" "+event:attr("last")};
  }
  always {
    mark ent:name with name;
    raise explicit event name_stored
  }
}
```

The only purpose of this rule is to record the response to the Web form submission.

The second rule is changed to select when there is an appropriate pageview event or an explicit event of the right type:

```
rule replace_with_name {
  select when web pageview ".*" or explicit name_stored
  pre {
    name = current ent:name;
  }
  replace_inner("#my_div", "Hello #{name}");
}
```

With this change, you have separated the functionality of each rule so that each does one thing. The first rule stores the value of the submission, and the second rule sends the greeting. This creates a clean separation of concerns among rules in the rule set.

EVENTS AND LOOSE COUPLING

The rules in the previous section create the desired functionality accretively—a key design goal in rule-based programming. Note that the name of the explicit event, name_stored, describes a state rather than giving a command. This is a subtle but important distinction. If the event had been named send_greeting, it would have worked as well for this purpose, but the state (i.e., that the name has been stored) had been given a specific semantics (i.e., send the greeting). By describing the state instead, the door is opened for other rules that care about that state change to respond. For example, you might later add a rule that stores the visitor names in a database.

One of the dangers of explicit events is that you can use them to introduce a form of tightly coupled rule calling in your rule sets that I call *rule chaining*. Rule chaining occurs when one rule raises a narrowly focused event that is designed for a single purpose: forcing another rule to fire.

Rule chaining can be useful in certain circumstances, but you should be aware that creating lots of narrowly focused, specific events as a way of calling certain rules runs the danger of introducing tight coupling into your application. In Chapter 12, "Advanced KRL Programming," you'll see that refactoring a rule set to remove rule chaining and replace it with broad-interest events can lead to new opportunities for easily expanding the application.

Remember that the purpose of raising an event is to send a notification, not call a rule. If the event name you choose belies your intention of making a request or issuing a command rather than merely issuing a notification, then you should consider rethinking the event name so that it describes a new condition instead. In fact, if you find yourself thinking about calling rules, then you're probably doing it wrong.

EXPLICIT EVENTS FOR ERROR HANDLING

Now that you have an understanding of explicit events in KRL, you're prepared to explore how KRL provides for error handling. Events are a natural way to handle errors.

Raising Errors

KRE will raise errors for various system-level errors that happen during the execution of a KRL rule set. For example, KRL will raise an error when a rule attempts to take an undefined action or for a type mismatch on an operator—for example, applying the `length()` operator to an integer. (For a complete list of the error types raised by the system, see the KRL documentation.)

When KRE raises an `error` event, it uses the event domain `system` and the event type `error`. The following event attributes are attached to the event:

- **level.** The level of the event: `error`, `warn`, `info`, or `debug`. Processing continues for all levels except `error` where execution is terminated.
- **msg.** A string giving details about the error.
- **rid.** The rule set ID of the offending rule set.
- **rule_name.** The name of the offending rule.
- **genus.** A token from the top level of the error taxonomy (described momentarily), indicating the first-level classification of the error.

- **species.** A token from the second level of the error taxonomy, indicating the classification of the error within the genus.

The KRL error taxonomy provides a two-level classification of errors. For example, if the genus of the error is `expression`, the species can be one of `invalid opera-tor, type mismatch, recursion threshold exceeded, array reference undefined,` or `function undefined.` See the KRL documentation for a complete list.

In addition to system errors, KRL programs can also raise errors explicitly in the rule postlude. The syntax of an explicit error statement is as follows:

```
error <level> <expr>
```

In this statement, `<level>` is one of `error, warn, info` or `debug`, and `<expr>` is any valid KRL expression that results in a string (or something that can be cast as a string, such as a number).

The following example would raise an event with domain `system` and type `error` with level `info` and a message with the value of a variable named `query` if the rule were to fire:

```
fired {
  error info "query:"+query
}
```

The following would only raise the event if the query variable were empty:

```
fired {
  error info "Empty query" if(query like "^$")
}
```

Explicit errors set the `rid` and `rule_name` attributes from the current rule set ID and rule name. The genus is set to "user".

Handling Errors

Handling errors is as easy as creating a rule with the right `select` statement. For example, the following rule will use the `send_error()` action from an `errorstack` module (aliased as `es`) to record an error using the Error Stack service:

```
rule process_error {
  select when system error
  pre{
    genus = event:attr("genus");
    species = event:attr("species");
```

```
  }
  es:send_error("(#{genus}:#{species}) " + event:param("msg"))
     with rule_name = event:param("rule_name")
      and rid = event:param("rid");
}
```

Like any other event, if an error event is raised and no rule is selected for it, nothing happens.

Because developers often want to process all errors from several rule sets in a consistent way, KRL provides a way of routing error events from one rule set to another. In the meta section of a rule set, developers can declare another rule set that is the designated error handler. For example, if the preceding process_error rule were defined inside rule set a16x88, then the following declaration would automatically route error events from the current rule set to a16x88 for processing:

```
meta {
  errors to a16x88
}
```

Raising events for errors and then handling them with rule sets gives developers a great deal of flexibility in dealing with exceptional situations in their code.

EVENT INTERMEDIARIES

One of the key ideas of distributed systems is using intermediaries to filter, augment, route, and process data between its origin and ultimate destination. Intermediaries can reduce the volume of data that the processor handles as well as improve its quality. Intermediaries make use of the age-old computer idea that a level of indirection can cure many ills. Intermediaries go by different names in different systems: middleware, routers, proxies, gateways, and so on.

As shown in Figure 11.4, event intermediaries sit between the endpoint and the rules that ultimately service them. They provide an improved stream of events to subsequent rules and make their implementation simpler by pre-processing the events.

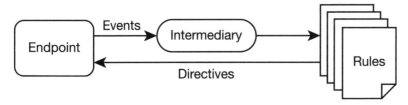

Figure 11.4
Event intermediaries sit between the endpoint and the rules that process the events.

The general idea behind all event intermediaries is event synthesis: creating new, meaningful events from the originals. Synthesized events appear to be simple events, but are the result of a planned computational process that uses complex streams of events as input, processes them in some way, and creates a new event that contains the relevant data from the originals.

In KRL, event intermediaries are rules. Intermediary rules are just like normal KRL rules. They can be in the same rule set as the other rules in an application or kept separate. One thing most event intermediary rules have in common is that they take no action. The rule consists of an event expression, some data manipulation in the prelude, and a postlude that raises the new event.

EVENT INTERMEDIARY PATTERNS

Intermediaries can take many forms, so you will explore them by looking at some common intermediary patterns.

Event Logging

One of the simplest intermediary patterns is the event-logging pattern. The intermediary rule looks for the expected event scenario, calls a logging statement (either using the built-in log command in KRL or making an HTTP POST) and then passes the event on using an explicit event.

The following rule illustrates this by using http:post() to create a log:

```
rule logger_rule is active {
  select when phone outboundconnected
  http:post("http://example.com/mylogger.cgi") with
    with number = event:attr("phonenumber")
  always {
   raise explicit event outboundconnected with
     phonenumber = event:attr("phonenumber") and
     time = event:attr("time");
  }
}
rule use_phone {
  select when explicit outboundconnected

  ...
}
```

In this example, the rule is logging the event and some data from it before passing the event on as an explicit event. Event logging might be used for debugging, billing, rule set analytics, and so on.

Abstract Event Expressions

Because of the nature of rule languages, you may often write several rules that have the same eventex. This goes against the grain of programmers used to traditional programming languages, where repeating yourself is not only wasteful but leads to code-maintenance problems.

The right response is to abstract the portions of those multiple rules that are repetitive and that are apt to be changed frequently. You've seen how functions, user-defined actions, and modules can help with that. But none of these can help with a repeated complex eventex. Explicit events solve that problem. In addition to increasing maintainability, using explicit events to abstract a complex eventex by giving it a name can facilitate program readability.

The following example names a complex eventex. The first rule contains the complex eventex and names it `called_first`:

```
rule abstract_called_first is active {
  select when phone outboundconnected
     before email received to re#@apple.com#
  always {
    raise explicit event called_first
     with msg = event:param("msg");
  }
}
rule use_called_first_1 is active {
  select when explicit called_first

  ...
}
rule use_called_first_2 is active {
  select when explicit called_first

  ...
}
```

Notice that the first rule raises an explicit event with the name `called_first` whenever it sees a particular event pattern. Two later rules use the `called_first` event. If the complex event expression is changed or updated, the two rules will both respond appropriately. When the event expression is used in this manner, you call `called_first` an abstract or named event expression.

Event Preprocessing

Sometimes, event parameters need to be preprocessed before they are used. Based on the results of the preprocessing, you may want to do different things. Preprocessing is a way of enriching the event by using the event parameters in some way—for example, looking up relevant data from online data sources and then sending along the results.

Preprocessing is an important form of event abstraction because when you enrich an event or preprocess the event parameters, you avoid doing the same calculations multiple times in other rules.

The following rule pre-processes an email event to look up data from an online data source, making the data in the message body more relevant:

```
rule pinentered is active {
  select when email received
  pre {
    msg = event:attr("msg");
    from = event:attr("from");
    item = datasource:pds({"key":from});
    relevant_data = msg.query("li[type=#{item}]");
  }
  always {
    raise explicit event mail_received with
      from = event:attr("from") and
      to = event:attr("to") and
      msg = relevant_data
  }
}
```

In this example, the message from an email that's been received is preprocessed using the `query` operator to retrieve just those portions of the message that are HTML `<li>` elements with an attribute named `type` equal to a value that is retrieved from a data source named `pds` using the email's "from" address.

Often, it's helpful to perform a complex mapping step once. Using explicit events, you can put the preprocessing in a single place, where it can be more easily maintained and tested.

Event Stream Splitting

Related to the idea of event preprocessing is the notion of event stream splitting. The previous example shows how to perform event-parameter preprocessing. You can use the event parameters to split the event stream and send it in two different directions. Often, preprocessing will be done in support of splitting the event stream.

The following rule preprocesses the event data and then uses a rule condition to raise one of two possible explicit events, depending on the result of the condition:

```
rule pinentered is active {
  select when webhook pinentered
```

```
pre {
  pinattempt = event:param("Digits");
  phone = datasource:pds({"key":"phone"});
  pin = phone.pick("$..value.pin");
}
if pinattempt == pin then
  noop();
fired {
  raise explicit event correct_pin
} else {
  raise explicit event bad_pin
}
}
```

In this example, the data in the event attribute `Digits` is compared with data retrieved from another data source (`pds`). If they're equal, the rule raises the explicit event `correct_pin`; otherwise, the rule raises the explicit event `bad_pin`. Subsequent rules continue processing as necessary. In this case, none of the original event's data is passed on with the new events, but that need not be the case.

Semantic Translation

Suppose you have an expense report rule set that automatically enters information from your travel in an expense report. The rule set wants to know when you've arrived at your destination or when you've arrived home so it can book those transactions.

The problem is that your smartphone probably isn't signaling an `arriving` event; more likely, it's sending a `location` event. The idea of *arriving* is specific to the context of traveling from one airport to another. So, a `location` event only equals an `arriving` event if you were just on a plane. For example, if your travel itinerary shows that you were scheduled to be on a flight from Salt Lake City to San Francisco, it's a pretty good bet that you're arriving at San Francisco, not departing or merely dropping someone off.

The expense report app needs to work in concert with a travel app that knows the context of what you're doing and translates events like `location` to `arriving` when you've just gotten off a plane or to `departing` when you're scheduled to board a plane shortly. Here's how you might express this in KRL:

```
rule arriving {
  select when mobile location airport re#(\w+)# setting current_airport
      after mobile location where airport ne current_airport
    within 24 hours
```

```
  noop();
  fired {
    raise explicit event arriving with attrs = event:attrs()
  }
}
```

There are a few holes in the preceding code. Production code would need to be more complicated in calculating if this event is really an arrival, taking into account things like arriving and departing on the same day, late flights, and so on. The idea of *departing* is slightly more complicated. Nevertheless, the preceding example should make clear the idea of using rules for semantic translation.

App Controller Rule Set

Complex apps will often be based on more than one rule set. In Chapter 14, "Designing Event Systems," you'll see an example that uses a dozen or so. I expect to see apps that use many more than that. One of the problems when building complex applications with multiple rule sets is keeping track of the control points in the app—which events are causing which behavior. Developers often want a single place in the code where they manage control flow.

Using the patterns outlined previously, you can create a controller rule set that is the main entry point for the app and controls the rules that get executed in other rule sets. Here are a few of the advantages of using a controller rule set in your app:

- **Routing.** Each complex event pattern to which the app responds is represented in the controller rule set. Each of these event patterns raises an explicit event to which the other rules in the app respond (event abstraction).

- **Authentication.** When you have an app that needs to be authenticated, you typically will also need a single place to control the authentication. An event controller solves this problem by being the one point of control, and thus serving as the place where authentication can be controlled as well.

- **Normalization.** Preprocessing event parameters in the controller app provides a normalized version of data and can serve to insulate the rest of the app from changes in outside event sources and endpoints.

As an example of how a rule set can play a controller role, the following shows how one rule set can cause a dynamic list of rule sets to be evaluated. For simplicity, the example is limited to the Web domain.

In the `global` section, you define a data source that uses the KRE `dispatch` API. You can query this API by RID to determine which sites a rule set should run on. You also define a list of rule set IDs. In a production rule set, you'd probably store this in an entity variable and let the user manage the list using a form so that it was truly dynamic.

```
global {
  datasource dispatchHash <- "https://init.kobj.net/js/dispatch/";
  ruleset_list = ["a1x56", "a16x44", "a8x32"];
}
```

The `fire_schedule` rule is a simple rule that watches for `pageview` events and raises `scheduler` events. You might wonder about this indirection. By having a rule translate the event, you're performing a bit of semantic translation like you saw in the last section, making the RulesetController_Scheduler rule that we discuss next useful in other situations.

```
rule fire_schedule {
  select when pageview url re#.*#
  noop();
  always {
    raise explicit event scheduler with rulesets = ruleset_list
  }
}
```

The `RulesetController_Scheduler` rule loops through the rule set IDs in the `rulesets` attribute. For each one, it queries the `dispatch` API. If the hostname of the current page matches one of the hostnames returned from the API, then the rule uses the `raise_event` action to tell the Web Runtime that it should raise an event for that rule set.

```
rule RulesetController_Scheduler {
  select when explicit scheduler
  foreach (event:attr("rulesets")) setting (appRID)
  pre {
    hostname = page:url("hostname");
    resultHash = datasource:dispatchHash(appRID);
    appDispatch = resultHash{appRID}.head();
  }
  if (appDispatch.has(hostname)) then {
    raise_event("pageview") with app_id = appRID;
  }
}
```

This simple example shows one rule set being used to dispatch others—as if events had been raised specifically for them. With more work, you could imagine this rule set being enabled by a browser extension, enabling it to manage any number of rule sets. One rule set to rule them all, as it were.

COMPLEX EVENT SCENARIOS

Chapter 3, "Event Expressions: Filtering the Event Stream," explored KRL event expressions and the multitude of scenarios that can be described with them. Because eventexes are roughly equivalent in computing power to regular expressions, there will always be scenarios that are too complex to express using eventexes alone. Explicit events allow rules to be chained together to create scenario detectors that are as complex as they need to be.

The answer to this problem is to create an intermediate rule that implements a recognition engine for the scenario. To understand this, consider one of the complex eventex examples introduced in Chapter 3. The eventex is designed to select when an RSS feed contains a story that includes a stock ticker symbol, and the price of that same stock goes up by more than 2% within 10 minutes:

```
select when rss item content re#Stock Symbol: (\w+)#
        setting (symbol)
   before stocks direction eq "up" && ticker eq symbol && percent > 2
 within 10 minutes
```

Suppose, however, that you want to be more sophisticated and vary the percentage gain and the time frame according to the levels shown in Table 11.1. There's no good way to do that from a single eventex.

Table 11.1   Urgency Levels for Stock-Price Rises

Percent	Time (Min)	Level
2	10	Urgent
1.5	30	High
1	60	Medium
0.5	360	Low

You can, however, write rules that abstract the percent gain and time as shown in the table and raise another event with the result. The first rule merely captures the timestamp of the stock mention and passes it on:

```
rule stock_mention {
  select when rss item content #Stock Symbol: (\w+)#
        setting (sym)
  always {
```

```
  raise explicit event "stock_rise" with
    rise_timestamp = event:attr("timestamp") and
    symbol = sym;
}
```

The second rule does all the work, calculating the elapsed time and then setting the urgency according to Table 11.1. The result is an explicit event that has parameters for the relevant information. Other rules can then key off this explicit event.

```
rule stock_rise {
  select when explicit stock_rise symbol re#.*# setting(symbol)
      before stocks direction eq "up" && ticker eq symbol && percent > 0.5
      within 360 minutes
 pre {
  elapsed = time:diff(event:attr("rise_timestamp"),
              time:now(), "minutes");
  percent = event:attr("percent");
  urgency = (elapsed < 10 && percent > 2)   => "urgent" |
            (elapsed < 30 && percent > 1.5) => "high" |
            (elapsed < 60 && percent > 1)   => "medium" |
                                    "low";
  }
 always {
  raise explicit event stock_rise with
    symbol = symbol and
    percent = percent and
    urgency = urgency and
    elapsed = elapsed
  }
}
```

Together, these two rules serve to create a detector for a complex event scenario that is difficult, if not impossible, to express in a single eventex.

EXPLICIT EVENTS

Along with functions, user-defined actions, and parameterized modules, explicit events represent one of the *key* abstraction mechanisms in KRL. Explicit events allow rule chaining and event synthesis, both a key to abstraction.

Explicit events open up the use of event intermediaries in KRL and significantly expand the viability of complex apps built from multiple rule sets. Explicit intermediary rule sets like an app controller greatly reduce the cognitive complexity of large applications.

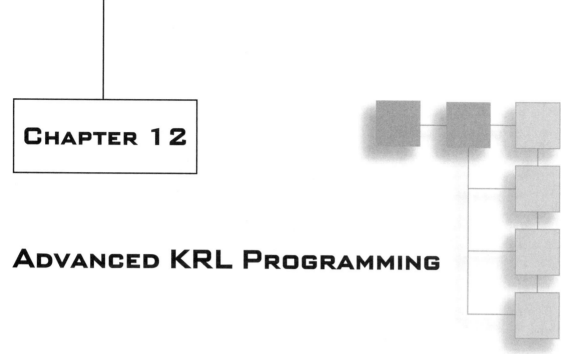

CHAPTER 12

ADVANCED KRL PROGRAMMING

So far, you've seen rule sets that work in a variety of domains and in a variety of circumstances. All the examples have been small, however, involving just a single rule set of a few rules. In addition, the event interactions have been simple. In this chapter, you'll tackle applications that require multiple rule sets and more complicated event interactions. This chapter also introduces a tool called an *event hierarchy* for exploring complicated event interactions.

Knowing how to build applications in KRL using multiple rule sets opens up the possibilities of what you can build on the Live Web. Along the way, you'll come to understand event normalization as well as some programming principles that support loosely coupled applications where functionality can be added without significant changes to the underlying parts.

In this chapter, you'll build a blogging tool using KRL. Building a blog with KRL is easier than you'd think, and departs in several significant ways from the examples you've explored previously in this book.

A BLOG IN KRL

The blog application uses four rule sets:

- **KBlog Configuration.** This is a module used to configure the application and hold common definitions.

- **KBlog.** This is the main rule set that controls the HTML assets and presentation. This rule set functions like the presentation layer of a traditional Web application, responding to user input and displaying results.

- **KBlog Data.** This rule set manages the blog data assets and provides access rules. The rule set uses application variables to store the blog data as a simple way of getting started.

- **KBlog Post.** You separate posting from the other parts of the application so that only people who had access to this rule set can post. This is not a good solution to controlling access to blog posting, but it is sufficient for demonstration purposes.

The following sections explore each of these rule sets in turn. Later, this chapter covers a fifth rule set to show how loose coupling supports application extension.

Configuring the Blog with the `KBlog Configuration` Rule Set

`KBlog Configuration` provides several common definitions for variables, functions, and actions that are used in the other rule sets. `KBlog Configuration` is built as a module because other rule sets will access the definitions it contains.

The variables declared in the module include `blogtitle`, which holds the string that will be used as the blog's title. The various rule sets use `blogtitle` to construct page titles. The right column of each blog page contains some text describing the blog. `KBlog Configuration` provides a variable called `about_text` to store this text, even though it's only used in one place. Having it in the configuration module allows you to go to just one rule set to change the various fixed textual elements of the blog.

`KBlog Configuration` also defines two actions: `paint_container` and `place_ button`. I will describe their function later. The `provides` pragma in the `meta` section of the rule set makes each of these available to the other rule sets in the KBlog application:

```
provides blogtitle, about_text, paint_container, place_button
```

The other rule sets in the application use the configuration module with the `use module` pragma in their `meta` section:

```
use module a16x93 alias config
```

Building the Blog with the `KBlog` Rule Set

The primary job of the `KBlog` rule set is presenting the blog. `KBlog` does this by preparing the container for the blog articles and then filling it with the articles.

The blog is built in a style called single page interface, or SPI. (See http://en.wikipedia.org/wiki/Single-page_application for a complete description of the principles behind single page interface Web applications.) In SPI-style Web applications, the basic framework of the application—the HTML, CSS, and JavaScript libraries—are loaded in an initial call. Partial changes to the page are then made incrementally via JavaScript AJAX calls.

Sites like Google, Twitter, Gawker, and others made this style of Web site construction popular. The chief advantage is a faster user experience due to reduced bandwidth, because the HTML and CSS need not be downloaded each time. KRL is a natural way to build sites that use this style of construction.

The DOM

Figure 12.1 shows the basic layout of the site. A navigation bar at the top contains links that can be used to navigate between different parts of the site—the Home page and About page.

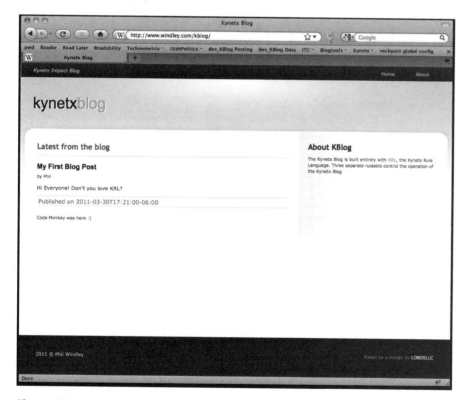

Figure 12.1
A blog written in KRL.

The DOM for the navigation bar is initially empty:

```
<nav id="sitenav">
 <ul id="navlist">
 </ul>
</nav>
```

You'll use rules to place buttons in the navigation bar as appropriate.

The primary section of the blog—the left container—is where page content is written. Initially, it is empty, and has the following structure:

```
<div id="leftcontainer"></div>
```

The information section of the blog—the About section on the right—is also initially empty:

```
<div id="sidebarwarp">
  <h2>About KBlog</h2>
  <p id="about"></p>
</div>
```

Unlike other KRL applications you've built in previous chapters, the blog application isn't triggered by an event from the endpoint. Instead, you'll plant tags in the DOM that trigger the event and cause the blog application to execute. That way, anyone—not just people with an endpoint installed—can see the blog. Here are the JavaScript `<script/>` tags that you place in the page:

```
<script type="text/javascript">
  KOBJ_config= {"rids":["a16x88"],
               "a16x88:kinetic_app_version":"dev",};
</script>
<script src="http://init.kobj.net/js/shared/kobj-static.js" />
```

The first JavaScript tag sets the configuration variable to identify the rule set IDs (RIDs) for the KBlog rule set (a16x88 in this case). The configuration also sets the `kinetic_app_version` configuration variable to `"dev"`, indicating that the development (most recent) version and not the production (last deployed) version of the rule set should be executed. This ensures that you don't have to continually deploy the rule set as you are testing. Later, when the application is finished, you'll either change the value of this variable to `"prod"` or simply delete it because `"prod"` is the default. Note that the variable is namespaced using the RID.

The second `<script/>` tag loads the Web endpoint. The endpoint will read the configuration you set up and initiate a `pageview` event for this page. Normally, this is all done by a browser extension, but it works just as well to put the `<script/>` tags in place directly for an SPI Web application.

Even though you're placing the tags directly in the page's HTML, that doesn't change the method you'll use to construct KRL rule sets. The structure and functionality of the application follow from the desired behavior, not the method that is used to raise events.

The Rules

The rules in the KBlog rule set handle the content of the page. As noted earlier, the overall structure of the page and the CSS style sheet are loaded when the user goes to the URL for the blog. The `<script/>` tags discussed in the previous section initiate a pageview event.

The init_html rule is selected when the pageview event is raised. This rule is responsible for painting the About text on the right side and setting up the navigation buttons. init_html is the only rule in the entire application that is selected on a pageview event. The selector is very general because it should fire whenever the blog is viewed.

```
rule init_html {
  select when pageview ".*" setting ()
  {
    replace_html("#about", config:about_text);
    config:place_button("Home");
    config:place_button("Contact");
  }
  always {
    raise explicit event blog_ready
  }
}
```

init_html places the buttons using an action, place_button(), from the configuration module. place_button() takes a name as its only parameter, creates the correct HTML for the button using the name, places it in the navigation bar, and attaches a watcher to the button so that any clicks will raise events:

```
place_button = defaction(button_name) {
      id = "siteNav" + button_name;
      label = button_name;
      button = <<
<li><a href="javascript:void(0);" id="#{id}">#{label}</a></li>
    >>;
    {
      prepend("#navlist", button);
      watch("#" + id, "click");
    }
  }
```

init_html raises the explicit event blog_ready to indicate that the blog is ready to be populated with the page content. There are two pages in this example: the Home page showing the blog articles and the Contact page that has contact information.

show_home is selected when one of two events occurs: Someone clicks the home link on the navigation bar or there is an explicit blog_ready event. (This makes the Home page the default). The show_home rule sets up the container to receive blog posts and sets the title:

```
rule show_home {
  select when web click "#siteNavHome"
          or explicit blog_ready
  pre {
    container = <<
<h2 class="mainheading">Latest from the blog</h2>
<div id="blogarticles">Code Monkey was here :)</div>
    >>;
    title = config:blogtitle;
  }
  config:paint_container(title, container);
  always {
    raise explicit event container_ready;
    raise explicit event need_blog_data for a16x89
  }
}
```

The show_home rule makes use of a user-defined action, paint_container(), from KBlog configuration:

```
paint_container = defaction(title, container) {
  {replace_inner("title", title);
   replace_inner("#leftcontainer", container);
  }
}
```

paint_container is also used by the show_contact rule, which displays the Contact page when someone clicks that link. A user-defined action ensures that you do this the same way both times.

show_home raises two explicit events: one that indicates that the container is ready and another that says that data is needed. The rules that respond to the latter event are discussed in the next section. Ultimately, the result of that process is that the explicit blog_data_ready event is raised.

Putting the actual blog articles in the container is the job of a rule named show_articles. This rule fires when the container_ready and blog_data_ready events are raised. Both events must occur before you place the articles on the blog, but the order is unimportant. The rule loops over each member of the hash representing the blog data, formats the correct HTML, and inserts it into the page:

```
rule show_articles {
  select when explicit container_ready
         and explicit blog_data_ready
   foreach event:param("blogdata") setting (postKey, postHash)
    pre {
      postArticle = <<
<article class="post">
 <header>
  <h3>#{ postHash.pick("$.title") }</h3>
  <span class="author">by #{ postHash.pick("$.author") }</span>
 </header>
 <p>#{ postHash.pick("$.body") }</p>
 <footer>
  <p class="postinfo">
  Published on <time>#{ postHash.pick("$.time") }</time></p>
 </footer>
</article>
    >>;
    }
   prepend("div#blogarticles", postArticle);
}
```

Note

Note that the HTML in the preceding rule isn't HTML at all, but rather well-formed XML. Modern browsers will happily display it using any relevant CSS style sheet declarations. You could use `<div class="article post"/>` instead of `<article/>`, for example, if making up HTML tags offends your sensibilities as long as you update the CSS definitions as well.

By initializing the blog, placing the page container, and then filling it in with separate rules, you build the blog in pieces. Navigation actions simply update the portion of the structure that is changing, leaving the rest unchanged. In high-volume Web sites, this can amount to a considerable savings in bandwidth and increase the user's perception of application responsiveness.

Handling Data with the KBlog Data Rule Set

One of the goals in creating the demonstration blog was to separate the handling of data from the rules that perform presentation. Certainly, that's good design—even if all the rules are in the same rule set. But, the event hierarchy is more interesting and the application better demonstrates loose coupling if the data-handling rules are in a separate rule set.

For this example, you'll make use of KRL's built-in persistent storage to keep the blog post data. In a production blog, of course, you'd use a database, not persistent variables. Using persistents as a substitute for a database can speed prototyping, but persistents are not designed for the kind of heavy-duty data operations that databases are.

Because you're using persistent variables, application variables are the right construct because every visitor will see the same set of blog posts. If you used entity variables, every visitor to the blog would see their own posts and no others.

The structure of the application variable will be a map of maps with each entry in the map representing a blog post. Each blog post has an author, title, body, and time-stamp. The following function formats the map representing a single blog post:

```
mk_article = function (author, title, body) {
  postTime = time:now({"tz":"America/Denver"});
  { postTime : {"author" : author,
                "title"  : title,
                "body"   : body,
                "time"   : postTime
               }}
}
```

The function calculates the timestamp and uses it as a key for the map as well as placing it in the blog entry map.

The only place where you can mutate a persistent variable is in the rule postlude. That means if you are going to use persistents to store blog article data, you have to use a rule to process the data. add_article watches for articles, formats the data with the mk_article function, and adds it to the app variable BlogArticles:

```
rule add_article {
  select when explicit new_article_available
  pre {
    post = event:param("post");
    postHash = mk_article(post.pick("$..postauthor"),
                          post.pick("$..posttitle"),
                          post.pick("$..postbody"));
    articles = app:BlogArticles || {};
  }
  always {
    set app:BlogArticles articles.put(postHash);
    raise explicit event new_article_added for a16x88;
  }
}
```

Note that this rule takes no action. The benefit is all in the effects. Whenever a new article is available, `add_article` will use the `post` data from the `event` parameter to format a new entry and put it in the application variable `BlogArticles`. The disjunction operator in the declaration of `articles` ensures that `articles` will be defined as an empty map if `BlogArticles` is undefined. Otherwise, the `put` operator won't function correctly.

When `add_article` fires, it raises an explicit event to indicate a new article has been added. The `KBlog` rule set contains an intermediary rule, `show_new_article`, that transforms this event into a `blog_ready` event. As you saw earlier, the `show_home` rule is listening for the `blog_ready` event and this causes the screen to be repainted.

```
rule show_new_article {
  select when explicit new_article_added
  noop();
  always {
   raise explicit event blog_ready
  }
}
```

You saw in the preceding discussion that the `show_home` rule raises an explicit event, `need_blog_data`. This is about as close to a request as you get in this example. A request would direct a specific function to return the data. The event merely says that data is needed. The `show_home` rule doesn't know who will respond.

The `retrieve_data` rule selects on the explicit event `need_blog_data` and raises the explicit event `blog_data_ready`, attaching the blog data from the application variable as an event attribute:

```
rule retrieve_data {
  select when explicit need_blog_data
  noop();
  always {
   raise explicit event blog_data_ready for a16x88
   with blogdata = app:BlogArticles || []
  }
}
```

Posting with the `KBlog Post` Rule Set

All that's left to complete the application is adding the ability to post. The KBlog Post rule set provides that functionality. As explained earlier, this functionality is in a separate rule set and layered on top of the basic functionality of the blog. Most users will never need the functionality and won't see it. Only posters need access to the rules that enable posting. This could be accomplished by providing posters with a browser extension that has access to this rule set or by using a bookmarklet.

The first order of business is to add a navigation button to the bar at the top of the page exposing the functionality. The `place_button` rule fires on a `pageview` event, puts the button in place, and makes it active by attaching a watcher to it using the `place_button()` action you defined earlier:

```
rule place_button {
  select when pageview "kblog"
  config:place_button("Post");
}
```

Note that, as before, you've aliased the configuration module as `config`.

When someone clicks on the Post button, the Web endpoint will raise a `click` event and the `place_form` rule will fire. `place_form` creates a form, places it on the page by replacing the left container, and attaches a watcher to the Submit button. (Note that some of the HTML in the form has been removed for brevity.)

```
rule place_form {
  select when web click "#siteNavPost"
  pre {
    form = <<
<h2 class="mainheading">Post</h2>
<article class="post">
 <form method="post" class="form" id="blogform">
  <p class="textfield">
   <label for="postauthor"><small>Name</small></label>
   <input name="postauthor" tabindex="1" type="text"></p>

  ...
  <p><input name="submit" type="image" src="submit.png"></p>
  <div class="clear"></div>
 </form>
</article>
    >>;
    title = config:blogtitle + "- Post";
  }
  {
   config:paint_container(title, form);
   watch("#blogform", "submit");
  }
}
```

Figure 12.2 shows the result of this rule firing: The form is painted on the page so the user can fill it out.

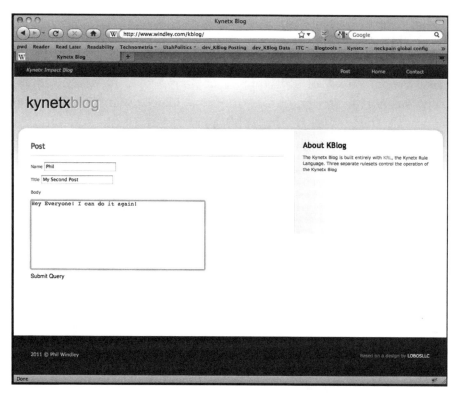

Figure 12.2
The blog posting form is painted on the blog in place of the blog articles.

When the user clicks on the Submit Query link on the form in Figure 12.2, the Web endpoint raises a submit event. The handle_submit rule handles that event:

```
rule handle_submit {
  select when submit "#blogform"
  always {
    raise explicit event new_article_available
    for ["a16x89", "a16x91"]
    with post = event:attrs();
  }
}
```

handle_submit raises the new_article_available event with the data from the form. As you've seen, the new_article_event is handled by add_article from the KBlog Data rule set.

With the addition of the KBlog Post rule set, you now have a complete—albeit simple—blog application. The blog owner can post articles and control the content on other pages. Visitors to the blog see the articles that the owner has posted.

EVENT HIERARCHIES

Building an application with three rule sets is quite a bit more complicated than other examples you've seen. Keeping track of everything that's happening in your head can be difficult, especially because the programming model is likely unfamiliar. One tool you can use to help with the design of the application is an event hierarchy. An event hierarchy traces the events through the rules to see the causal relationships. Figure 12.3 shows the event hierarchy for the blog application. In the graph, rectangular boxes are rules. They are named as verbs. The ovals represent events. They are nouns.

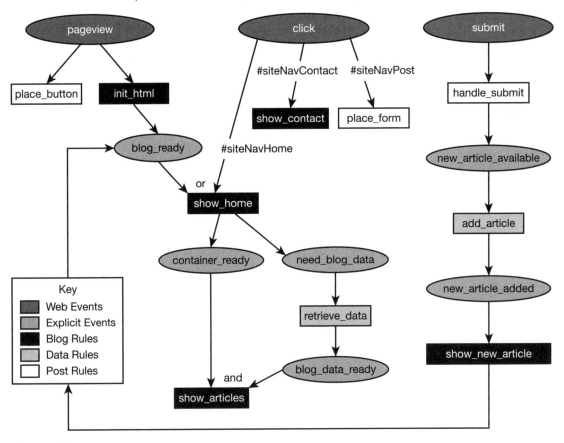

Figure 12.3
The event hierarchy for the blog application.

Getting the right names and the meanings for events is important. This is called *event normalization*. Thinking of events as nouns and rules as verbs is a useful way to keep your design straight. If you find yourself naming events with verbs, you're probably not really creating an event-driven application. Rather, you're using events to make a request.

In Figure 12.3, the Web events are the entry point for any path through the graph. There are three Web events: `pageview`, `click`, and `submit`. The `click` events are differentiated by the name of the element that was clicked.

Once the event causal chain is initiated from a Web event, the rest of the event hierarchy consists of explicit events raised in the rules as indicated in the graph. Rules that don't produce events are terminals in the graph.

Understanding which rules were listening for which events and how they interact is the key design space. The event hierarchy plays an important role in understanding these interactions. Once that is done, writing the rules is relatively simple.

Looking at the longest chain, from the Web `submit` event, you see that submitting a blog post results in seven events being raised and six rules firing. This might seem inefficient at first, but you could say the same thing about control flow in a traditional programming model that uses multiple objects or functions.

You might be tempted to think of the event hierarchy as a kind of state diagram, but that's not quite right—the transitions don't happen because of an input. The events themselves are the input. Events are most useful when they are moving, so there's no notion of stopping at some point in the diagram. Once you enter at the top, you flow through to one of the terminal rules.

Design Considerations

One of the objectives of the blog application was to create a design where new functionality can be layered on to the base. The `KBlog Post` rule set shows how this works. People who aren't posting never use that rule set. Rules in `KBlog Post` affect the rest of the application through the use of events.

You'll discover later in this chapter that you haven't gone far enough in raising explicit events. Good rule design might dictate that every rule raise an event when it's done—no terminal rules. Remember, events that don't have a listener are simply ignored. For example, the `show_articles` rule is terminal in the event hierarchy in Figure 12.3. At that point, the blog articles are showing, but there is no event to notify other interested parties of that change in status of the blog.

Nothing in the preceding rule sets uses such an event, but what if someone else wants to layer functionality onto this application later in a loosely coupled way? They might want to know when the articles are ready so they can take the next step, whatever that is. Any given rule, terminal now, may not always be so as new functionality is envisioned.

One objection to the design might be that the controller logic is not clearly delineated in some kind of controller module. For this application, the controller is in the various `select` statements. Using more intermediary rules in a controller rule set could bring the controller logic for the application together, but finding and understanding the `select` statements is easy.

MAKING THE BACK BUTTON WORK

One issue with the current implementation of the blog application is that the Back and Forward buttons in the browser don't work. That's a big problem because many people use them to navigate.

Browser Back and Forward buttons operate by moving the user around in the browser's history. The browser doesn't know there's a new page or put it on the history unless the URL changes. SPI Web applications get around this by writing URL fragments (the stuff after the # symbol) to the URL of the page as the application state changes. Adding a fragment doesn't cause the browser to reload the page because fragments are designed for inter-page navigation.

Not only does the application have to rewrite the URL when the application state changes, but it also has to change the application state when the fragment changes. Otherwise, the Back button will change the URL, but not the page. The following sections handle both of these problems in turn.

Change the URL Fragment

There's currently no action in KRL to rewrite the URL. Fortunately, KRL rules can emit JavaScript as an action, giving them the ability to flexibly adapt to situations that were not anticipated in the language.

The rules that rewrite the container (`show_home` and `show_contact`) cause a change to the application state and should therefore rewrite the URL. By deliberately not including `place_form`, the rule that displays the form, you keep it out of the history, avoiding the problem of Back buttons and form posting.

You'll add a user-defined action to the `KBlog Configuration` module to emit JavaScript that modifies the fragment:

```
update_frag = defaction(name) {
  emit <|
    self.document.location.hash='!#{name}';
  |>;
};
```

Note

The JavaScript `location.hash` variable has an inconsistent interface. When you set it, you don't include the `#`. But when you read it, the string you get back has the `#` prepended.

Remember that you also need to update the `provides` pragma or this definition won't be visible outside the module.

Next, you modify the appropriate rules to use the new action. Here's the `show_contact` rule that controls the Contact page:

```
rule show_contact {
  select when web click "#siteNavContact"
          or web hash_change newhash "/contact$"
  pre {
   contact_html = <<
    <h2 class="mainheading">Contact</h2>
     <article class="post">
      <p>Contact information here</p>
     </article>
   >>;
   title = config:blogtitle + " - Contact";
  }
  {
  config:paint_container(title, contact_html);
  config:update_frag("/contact");
  }
 }
```

This ensures that whenever the Contact page is displayed, the URL will have `#!/contact` appended:

```
http://www.windley.com/kblog/#!/contact
```

You make similar changes to the Home page so that it has `#!/` appended to the URL whenever you visit that page.

Note

Technically, I shouldn't be putting the `!` in the fragment because that indicates to search engines that the page is available at the non-fragmented URL for search-engine crawlers. While I won't enable this functionality in this tutorial, it's a good idea to make SPI pages crawlable. More information, including techniques for building this functionality, can be found here: http://code.google.com/web/ajaxcrawling/docs/getting-started.html.

Updating the Page When the Fragment Changes

Now that you've modified each of the rules that control a page, they will all be identified with the right fragment as you navigate from page to page using the links in the navigation bar at the top of the blog. But that's just half the problem. The Back and Forward buttons are still broken. If you use them, the URL will change, but the content displayed on the page will remain the same. As I said before, the browser does not alert the server when the fragment changes.

To remedy this problem, you'll use a jQuery plug-in called `hashchange`. Because the KRL Web endpoint has jQuery built in, using jQuery plug-ins is easy. The first step is to put the code for the plug-in on your server and change the jQuery variable in the final line of the plug-in to use `$KOBJ` instead of `jQuery`:

```
...
// was --> })(jQuery);
})($KOBJ);
```

The plug-in must call the KRL jQuery library, named `$KOBJ`, because the Web endpoint uses jQuery in extreme compatibility mode to ensure that it doesn't interfere with Web pages that have already loaded jQuery.

The second step is to load the plug-in in your rule set. KRL provides a facility for loading external JavaScript resources as a pragma in the `meta` section of the rule set:

```
use javascript resource "http:/.../jquery.hashchange.js"
```

This loads the library in the browser once (and only once) when the rule set is executed.

Third, you need to deploy the `hashchange` watcher so that it monitors the fragment and raises an event to KRE when it changes. The `hashchange` watcher is designed so that it runs a function. You might be tempted to put the call to `hashchange` in the `global` block. Programmers are used to `global` blocks being evaluated once. That's true for KRL as well, but in KRL, it's once per event. Any given interaction with the blog causes multiple events, however. Putting `hashchange` in the global block would result in the watcher being added to the page every time someone clicked a button, submitted a form, or viewed the page. Because the watcher is not idempotent, the effect would compound—which is not what you want.

What you should do instead is place the fragment watcher once when you initialize the blog. The `init_html` rule is responsible for initialization and is only run once per blog interaction—on the initial pageview. In fact, recall that `init_html` uses `place_button()` to put the buttons in the navigation bar and place watchers on them to monitor when they're clicked. Here's `init_html` modified to emit the correct JavaScript to watch for fragment changes:

```
rule init_html {
 select when pageview ".*" setting ()
 {
  replace_inner("#about", blogconfig:about_text);
  blogconfig:place_button("Home");
  blogconfig:place_button("Contact");
  emit <|
    self.document.location.hash='!/';
    $KOBJ(window).hashchange(function() {
      if(KOBJ.a16x88.previous == undefined ||
        KOBJ.a16x88.previous != self.document.location.hash) {
      var app = KOBJ.get_application("a16x88");
      app.raise_event("hash_change",
        {"newhash": self.document.location.hash});
      KOBJ.a16x88.previous = self.document.location.hash;}});
  |>;
 }
 always {
  raise explicit event blog_ready
 }
}
```

The only thing new is the `emit` action. The JavaScript in that action sets the hash in the page URL to the default page fragment (`!/`) and attaches a `hashchange` JavaScript watcher to the window. The function that it calls uses the Web endpoint runtime to get the app object associated with the current rule set and raise an event called `hash_change` to the KRL engine with the new fragment as a parameter. The whole thing is wrapped in an `if` statement to ensure it only runs once per fragment change.

Note that you are making use of the `KOBJ` object that is defined in the Web runtime to store values. The preceding code uses the rule set ID as a namespace in `KOBJ` to avoid variable name collisions with other rule sets the user may running.

The built-in `raise_event()` method allows you to pass event attributes to KRE. These attributes will be used by any rules that respond to the `hash_change` event.

The last step is to modify the rules that present the pages, `show_home` and `show_contact`, to respond to the `hash_change` event. There are two changes you need to make:

■ You must add another clause to the `select` statement that looks for a `hash_change` event that has a parameter named `newhash` with the value matched by the appropriate regular expression to ensure you're looking at the right page (/contact for the contact page and / for the home page).

■ You must set the previous variable in the browser to ensure that this event only happens once. This is most conveniently done in the update_frag() action.

Here's the select statement from the show_contact rule showing how it has been changed:

```
select when web click "#siteNavContact"
          or web hash_change newhash "/contact$"
```

The result of the rule is unchanged.

Here is the new definition for update_frag() showing the changes to the Java-Script that is emitted:

```
update_frag = defaction(name) {
  emit <|
    KOBJ.a16x88.previous = '#!#{name}';
    self.document.location.hash='!#{name}';
  |>;
};
```

Changes to the Event Hierarchy

Making the changes outlined previously has created a new event, hash_change. You've also modified rules to watch for that new event. This modifies the event hierarchy as shown in Figure 12.4. This event hierarchy diagram is only slightly more complicated than the one in Figure 12.3. Specifically, Figure 12.4 shows the new event at the top and its interaction with the show_home and show_contact rules. These rules are selected for specific values of the event attributes.

With these changes, navigating the blog causes the URL to update. Conversely, changing the URL changes the blog. Now the Back and Forward buttons function correctly.

AN EXPERIMENT IN LOOSE COUPLING

You've created an application that uses multiple rule sets and has a more complicated event hierarchy than the KRL rule sets you've seen in previous chapters. You've used JavaScript to make the Back button work. You even added a new event type (web: hash_change) using JavaScript.

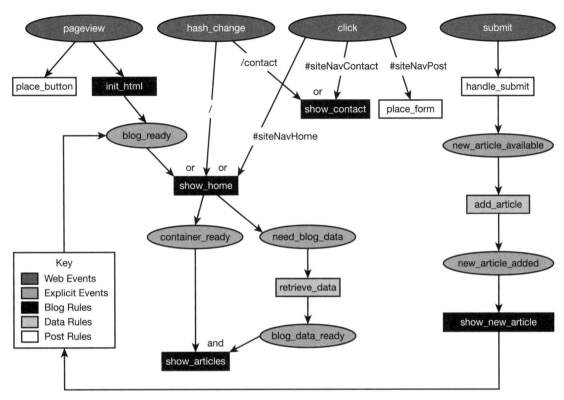

Figure 12.4
Event hierarchy for blog application after fixing the Back button.

A blog is an interesting laboratory for exploring how event-driven applications can be extended in a loosely coupled way. I've argued in previous chapters that because event-driven applications don't rely on request-response interactions, they can be more loosely coupled. Functionality can be layered onto event-driven applications in ways that are difficult to imagine in more tightly coupled architectural styles.

Unlike a typical program, where control flow is made explicit through the use of procedure calls, or a Web program, where control flow occurs through the request-response interactions, the event consumers themselves specify control flow in event-driven applications. Traditionally, programming languages have used hooks to make control flow more flexible. Hooks are not events, but rather are places in the control flow where other programs can insert themselves. One key difference is that events provide a level of indirection so that what runs can be determined dynamically.

Tweeting a Post

In this section, you'll expand the blog application by layering on functionality that gives the author of a post the option of automatically tweeting the blog post title.

The goal is to use what's already in the application to add the functionality with minimal changes to the existing application.

If you recall, the rule that listens for the event raised when a form is submitted, handle_submit, raises the event new_article_available. You can post the title of the blog article to Twitter by listening for that event and doing what's necessary to format and send the information to Twitter:

```
rule send_tweet {
  select when explicit new_article_available
  pre {
    post = event:attr("post");
    tweet = <<
New blog post from #{ post.pick("$..postauthor")}:
#{ post.pick("$..posttitle")} http://www.windley.com/kblog
>>;
  }
  if (twitter:authorized()) then {
   twitter:update(tweet);
  }
}
```

send_tweet listens for the new_article_available event and uses the built-in KRL twitter library to check the keys (stored in the key pragma of the rule set's meta section) and update the associated Twitter stream. Adding this functionality is easy because the event was already being raised; the twitter library does the heavy lifting.

Making Tweeting Optional

You can take some satisfaction in your ability to easily add new functionality to the original application. The next step, however—making tweeting the post optional—reveals some mistakes in the previous design that get in the way of modifying it by simply adding new rules without modifying the original ones.

To give the author the option of tweeting or not, you want to add a checkbox to the blog post form. Adding the checkbox is relatively easy if an event reveals when the form is available. In the current design, the place_form rule is terminal in the event hierarchy, meaning that it raises no events. Without an event, there's nothing for the rule that adds the checkbox to watch. To resolve this, modify the place_form rule to raise the explicit event post_form_ready. Now the place_checkbox rule can listen for that event and add a checkbox to the form:

```
rule place_checkbox {
  select when explicit post_form_ready
```

```
pre {
  form_id = event:attr("form_id");
  checkbox_html = <<
<p class="checkbox">
 <label for="posttitle">Post to Twitter?</label>
 <input id="tweet" type="checkbox" checked="checked"></p>
  >>;
 }
 after(".text-area", checkbox_html);
}
```

This rule adds a checkbox to the form without modifying the original rule set beyond the fix to raise the event. Other changes to the form for other features could also be added. The form now becomes a canvas that rules can paint as they modify the functionality of the underlying application. Figure 12.5 shows the change to the form when the rule fires.

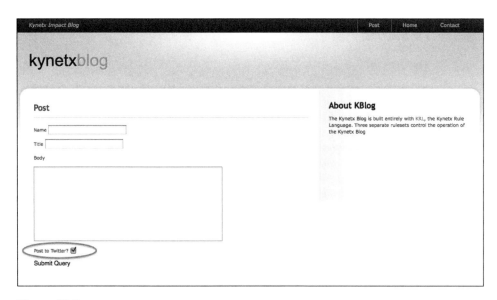

Figure 12.5
Form with Post to Twitter? checkbox added before the Submit Query link.

Now that there's a checkbox on the form, the `handle_submit` rule will include it in the event attributes for the `new_article_available` event because of how they are passed:

```
raise explicit event new_article_available
  for ["a16x89", "a16x91"]
    with post = event:attrs();
```

The function `event:attrs()` passes all attributes along even as they change based on other rules. However, when I first wrote `handle_submit`, the `raise` statement looked like this:

```
raise explicit event new_article_available for a16x89 with
  postauthor = event:attr("postauthor") and
  posttitle = event:attr("posttitle") and
  postbody = event:attr("postbody");
```

The design of this explicit event worked fine for the original blog functionality, but obviously, it won't pass new attributes, like the value of the Post to Twitter? checkbox. Loose coupling demands that you make accommodation for the uses you don't envision. This sounds hard, but there are rules of thumb that help. The next section explores some of them.

The `send_tweet` rule can be modified to use the Post to Twitter? checkbox value by adding an additional Boolean test to the rule condition as follows:

```
if (post.pick("$..tweet", true).length() &&
    twitter:authorized()) then {…
```

The optional second parameter to `pick` causes it to always return an array if true. Otherwise, the `pick` operator will return individual values. In HTML, the checkbox input has a value if it's checked, but is just not sent otherwise. By forcing the result to be an array, you can use length to determine whether it's empty. A length of 0 means the check is missing, in which case you don't want to update Twitter.

LESSONS LEARNED

The new rule set consists of two rules: `place_checkbox` for putting the checkbox in the form and `send_tweet` for composing and sending the tweet if the checkbox is checked. The new rules overlay the existing application to add the functionality without interrupting the existing features. If they're not present, then the functionality isn't either. The application keeps on working just as it did before. Adding the functionality requires no configuration of the original application or wiring the new functionality in place. Everything fits nicely together and comes apart just as easily because of events.

But as you saw, there were design decisions made in the original application that made it more tightly coupled than you'd like. You ran into two problems:

- Terminal rules
- Over-specified attributes

Let's explore the rules that arise from solving these problems in turn.

Avoid Terminal Rules

Terminal rules reduce opportunities for loose coupling. Because the `place_form` rule was terminal—it didn't raise any events to indicate what it had done—there was no way for another rule set to extend its functionality. The lesson here is that terminal rules should be avoided if your goal is to create extensible, loosely coupled applications that don't require code modifications. That said, as long as you have access to the code, adding explicit events to rules when you need them isn't difficult and is unlikely to break anything, so it's a low-cost, low-risk code modification.

Generalize Attribute Passing

Specificity in event attributes leads to tight coupling. When events have attributes, you should send them on as a map. Picking out individual attributes and sending them on by name means that only those attributes will ever be available to other rules. That doesn't mean you can't filter attribute maps to remove data you don't want available downstream. But the result ought to be everything but the data you filter, not just the data you choose to pass on. Pass attributes as a structure rather than by name for the greatest flexibility.

Supporting Extensibility

The problems highlighted in this section are easy to find. A simple test application showed where they existed. Writing applications as collections of rule sets in such a way that they support extending functionality through accretion in a loosely coupled manner is practical, but it does require some planning and design effort.

CHANGING THE EVENT HIERARCHY AGAIN

The modification to the event hierarchy is fairly modest because only two new rules were added. This reflects the loosely coupled nature of the application. Figure 12.6 shows the changes.

There is a new rule set for the tweet rules. The `place_form` rule now raises the `post_form_ready` event for which the `place_checkbox` rule is listening. The `send_tweet` rule listens for the `new_article_available` event. As they should be, the new rules are accretive to the overall event hierarchy, not requiring changes to it but merely adding to it.

BUILDING LOOSELY COUPLED APPLICATIONS

This chapter has focused on an application built from multiple rule sets. The example, a blog application, isn't the first kind of application that one thinks about when

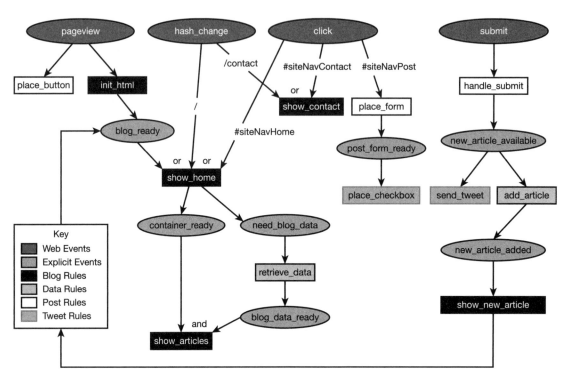

Figure 12.6
Event hierarchy for the blog with the ability to tweet blog posts.

building event-driven systems, but you've seen that events are actually a reasonable way to build a blog.

As mentioned, there are several improvements you could make to the application if you wanted to use it in a production system, including using a database instead of application variables and adding some kind of authentication method to the posting subsystem. These changes would also allow for the application to be multi-tenanted—enabling multiple users to install and use it to manage their own blog.

The ideas of event normalization and even hierarchies provide tools for understanding large event systems. Combined with the rules you discovered for making event systems more loosely coupled, you're equipped to build and understand large event-driven applications.

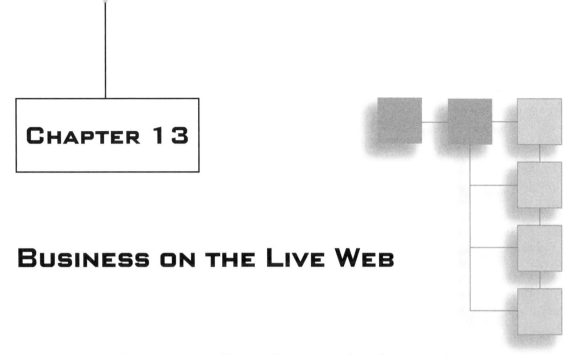

CHAPTER 13

BUSINESS ON THE LIVE WEB

In 1994, I started a company called iMall with my friend Ross Jardine. Our intention was to use the Internet to sell things. At the time, commercial use of the Internet was discouraged, and the things we take for granted today—like shopping carts and online credit-card payments—didn't exist.

We believed that Internet retailing—what came to be called *ecommerce* by 1998— would be very different from brick-and-mortar retail experiences. Some of what we envisioned early on, like product recommendations and online shopping carts, came quickly; other things did not. The truth is that ecommerce in 2011 isn't much different from the standard brick-and-mortar or catalogue experience. Merchants still market products with ads, select the products they offer, place them in a catalogue (albeit online), process the transaction, and deliver the goods. Web 2.0 merely gave us better catalogues, not a completely new experience.

The result isn't just a lost opportunity for better commerce. Because the Internet just made the old retail model more efficient, it also increased the demand for the drug that feeds retail: advertising. The effects have been devastating to personal privacy. Data about you and your online activities is for sale to the highest bidder. Web sites track us across the Net to better target us with ads. Companies use words like *capture, lock in*, and *own* to describe their interactions with customers—words more akin to the slave trade than commerce.

In 2006, I attended the O'Reilly Media Emerging Technology Conference. The theme was something that seemed to be on everyone's lips in those days: the attention economy. Attention economies are a natural way to look at how the Web has evolved in such a way that sites care as much about your attention as your wallet. Of course, sites care about your attention because they're being paid from advertisers.

At that same conference, a friend of mine, Doc Searls, had an epiphany: *Intention is more valuable than attention.* Consequently, the current economy of the Web notwithstanding, intention will eventually be the predominant currency of the Web. Doc felt strongly enough about that inspiration to devote the next five years of his life bringing it to fruition, doing research and promoting the ideas around the intention economy as a member of Harvard University's Berkman Center for Internet and Society. He has recently published a book, *The Intention Economy: When Customers Take Charge*, that clearly and convincingly describes his ideas.

The most concrete example of the intention economy is something Doc calls *vendor relationship management,* or VRM—a play on the more well known *customer* relationship management systems that companies use to manage interactions with their customers. In Doc's words:[1]

> In a narrow sense, VRM is the reciprocal—the customer side—of CRM (or Customer Relationship Management). VRM tools provide customers with the means to bear their side of the relationship burden. They relieve CRM of the perceived need to "capture," "acquire," "lock in," "manage," and otherwise employ the language and thinking of slave-owners when dealing with customers. With VRM operating on the customer's side, CRM systems will no longer be alone in trying to improve the ways companies relate to customers. Customers will also be involved, as fully empowered participants, rather than as captive followers.

In some cases, such cooperation would be through standards and APIs. On the Live Web, the CRM vendor might provide an app that installs and runs on client systems to provide custom interaction or simply raise appropriate events to the user's personal event network.

Ignoring the Attention Economy

The attention economy is based on the idea of broadcast—a few voices sending information to the masses. As Tim Wu sets forth in his book *The Master Switch*, this wasn't necessarily ordained by the technology of radio, TV, and so on, but was the work of people like David Sarnoff who explicitly jiggered regulations to favor fewer powerful, long-range stations to make radio a fit medium for advertisers—at the expense of mass participation. TV followed suit, again with the explicit help of people who saw it as better medium for advertising and worked to make it so.

While the Web seems to be anything but broadcast, underneath the surface a few large companies essentially broadcast ads across the Web regardless of what sites you visit. These ad networks thread ads through the search results, blog articles, and news you read in a way that would make Sarnoff proud.

Over the last decade, the marketing landscape has changed rapidly, with channels and devices proliferating, mobile connectivity increasing, and consumers who are more and more willing—even demanding—to interact with companies on social platforms. Although all of these have provided even more places for the attention economy—based on ads—to flourish, they have also made it easier than ever for people to simply ignore ads. Take TiVo, for example. As more and more people time-shift video content, they simply skip over the ads. I have a number of ad-supported apps on my phone, but I find it quite easy to simply ignore them. The content continues to vie for our attention, but people are better and better at paying attention to the content rather than the marketing messages.

Purveyors of the attention economy have fought back in ways that are sometimes clever and sometimes pathetic. On the clever side are product placements in which the products are seamlessly worked into the stories themselves. More pathetic are the ways that Web properties are making ads bigger and bigger—even overlaying or obscuring the content that people have come to find—forcing users to close or move the ad to get to the story.

PRIVACY MATTERS

The caption of Peter Steiner's legendary 1993 *New Yorker* cartoon reads, "On the Internet, nobody knows you're a dog." But as a recent *New York Times* article, "Upending Anonymity: These Days the Web Unmasks Everyone," points out, that's not really true anymore:[2]

> This erosion of anonymity is a product of pervasive social media services, cheap cellphone cameras, free photo and video Web hosts, and perhaps most important of all, a change in people's views about what ought to be public and what ought to be private. Experts say that Web sites like Facebook, which require real identities and encourage the sharing of photographs and videos, have hastened this change.
>
> "Humans want nothing more than to connect, and the companies that are connecting us electronically want to know who's saying what, where," said Susan Crawford, a professor at the Benjamin N. Cardozo School of Law. "As a result, we're more known than ever before."

This loss of anonymity is sometimes voluntary—say, when I post something on Twitter. Often, however, it's a side effect of our online activities. People call this *exhaust data*. This chapter demonstrates an architecture for ecommerce that minimizes the traceable exhaust data from the activities associated with shopping for a product and trying to find the best deal.

Marketers use this exhaust data to try to make ads more personal. The problem with personal ads, of course, is that they're still ads. No one wants more ads, even if they're more relevant and more personal. Even more insidious is the fact that marketers track customers and share their personal data behind their backs to create personalization.

People are increasingly uncomfortable with the amount of information companies know about them and suspicious that it's being used to manipulate them. More and more laws regulating customer tracking are being proposed, making life increasingly difficult for companies that make their living doing it.

Turning the Tables

On the other hand, customers are using the social Web—Twitter, Facebook, and the rest—to change the vendor-customer dynamic. In the book *Pre-Commerce*, author Bob Pearson notes that companies have often thought their job is to build a community for their customers to interact in when, in fact, customers already have their own communities. Instead, the company's job is to become a *relevant peer* in the communities that their customers already use.

Your customers are talking about you, and they don't care if you're part of the conversation or not. Your customers are happy to search the Internet to find information. If you happen to show up and provide useful information, they'll use it and be grateful for it, but they won't wait. Moreover, they won't sit still while you pepper them with ads, surveys, and product promotions. People frequently turn to search engines to make a buying decision, even when they intend to shop offline. The information they find enables them to make buying decisions before they show up in a store.

These facts point to an important shift in the balance of power that has taken place over the last few years. More than ever, the customer is in charge. Customers have more information at their fingertips than ever before, and they want companies to engage in real-life conversations. People are increasingly unwilling to be managed by the companies with whom they do business. Companies are also discovering that paying attention to the places their customers hang out online means they don't have to build the community—an expensive proposition.

The downside of using existing communities is that this tactic works only when companies engage in real conversations, are helpful and friendly, and can present an authentic, human face. Notice how different that is from targeting people with relevant ads based on demographic data. Companies that can't do these things are at a disadvantage and are quickly "outed" by community members. Of course, this is why people prefer these interactions.

That doesn't mean all is well on the social Web. Social networks—Facebook in particular—are all too willing to encourage users to overshare personal information with potential advertisers and partners and even sell people's data.

BUSINESS ON THE LIVE WEB

The Live Web facilitates a different kind of interaction from what exists today. Doc Searls often uses the example of a car rental to illustrate how:[3]

> In The Intention Economy, a car rental customer should be able to say to the car rental market, "I'll be skiing in Park City from March 20–25. I want to rent a 4-wheel drive SUV. I belong to Avis Wizard, Budget FastBreak and Hertz 1 Club. I don't want to pay up front for gas or get any insurance. What can any of you companies do for me?"—and have the sellers compete for the buyer's business.

You might recognize this as similar to a request for quotes (RFQ). Big companies and governments use them all the time to ensure they get a good deal. Why don't people use RFQs? Well, historically, they were a lot of work. Before now, only large organizations had the resources necessary to write and issue RFQs, not to mention sufficient buying power to force vendors to respond. But as you've seen in the preceding chapters, automating routine interactions is all in a day's work on the Live Web.

The Live Web reduces transaction costs. In the scenario Doc describes, you get the rental car you need with less searching and researching. We're all the beneficiaries of the reduced transaction costs that ecommerce produces, but now we can move beyond early gains.

CREATING PERSONAL RFQs

Let's envision how what you know about KRE and KRL could change the way retail transactions occur online. As you've seen, the key to making a personal RFQ work is to automate the interaction on the buyer and seller side as much as possible. In a Live Web retail interaction, *buyer intent* is the signal that drives the transaction. Someone or something must register that intent and take action on it. In the parlance of VRM, that something is called the *fourth party*. Doc Searls explains:[4]

> Among numbered parties, the best-known one today is the third party. Wikipedia currently defines a third party this way (at least for the computer industry):
>
>> Third-party developer, hardware or software developer not directly tied to the primary product that a consumer is using.
>
>> Third-party software component, reusable software component developed to be either freely distributed or sold by an entity other than the original vendor of the development platform.
>
> In general, a third party works on the vendor's side of the marketplace. However, the vendor is not generally called the "first party" (except in the game business).

So, if third-party services are merchant driven, it stands to reason that the customer-driven services that represent them would be the fourth party. Figure 13.1 shows the four parties and how they are arrayed in a Live Web interaction. The merchant and customer do not necessarily interact directly, but through software agents called the third and fourth party.

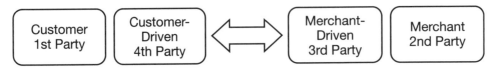

Figure 13.1
The four parties in a Live Web transaction.

Fourth-party services, be they simple or sophisticated, act as brokers that work on the customer's behalf to manage their interaction with the vendors of various products and services. Without such automated agents, no one would willingly take on the work that would be necessary to manage the hundreds of relationships each of us has with vendors. But with them, magic happens.

Fourth-party services built as apps in KRL are a natural because, as you've seen, the system is designed for creating client-side applications that help users achieve a purpose. What's more, using data in context is easy to do in KRL.

If you unpack Figure 13.1 in terms of KRE, you might come up with something like Figure 13.2. The system includes not only KRE, but also numerous sources of personal data for the customer to which KRE has access. Merchants have supplied rule sets that represent the third party, acting on their behalf. Customers have installed various applications that represent the fourth party.

A typical scenario in this system would flow as follows:

1. The customer visits a merchant. This could be online or in person (e.g., the app could be running on the customer's phone and using location in context).

2. At the same time, any fourth-party apps that the customer has installed are invoked as long as they are relevant to the current activity.

3. KRE executes the rules associated with the presented apps. (Assume for the sake of this example that those apps need personal data to work on the user's behalf and access to that data has not been previously granted.)

4. KRE requests the required user information from the personal data store (PDS).

5. The customer is asked to authorize access and grants it.

6. The PDS requests the data from various sources as necessary and returns it to KRE. As envisioned here, the PDS acts more like a virtual directory than an actual repository, although that's not a strict requirement.

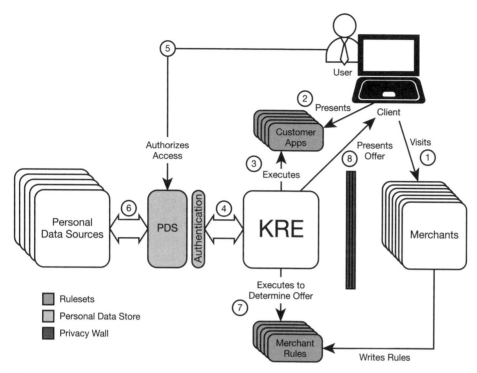

Figure 13.2
Creating personal RFPs with KRE.

7. KRE executes any relevant merchant rules (determined by the app, the current context, and the data retrieved in step 6) to determine how they want to relate. This may be specific offers, discounts, special service levels, and so on. I call this *the offer*.

8. Finally, the results are presented to the customer's client.

A key feature of the scenario as shown is the privacy wall. That's there to illustrate the idea that in this model, the customer's data is never given to the merchant. The merchant's rules act against it, but the merchant never sees it. For fourth-party apps to work, customers will need assurance that their data is being treated in a way that respects privacy. They will also need to trust the agents working on their behalf.

A few other points to note:

- KRE has no access to customer data except as authorized by the customer. The customer is entirely in control of the experience and what data is used.

- The merchant rules could exist as KRE modules or in another rule format such as RuleML and be stored in any repository as long as they were discoverable.

- The same holds for customer data. There's no need for it to be in a single place as long as it's in standard formats, is discoverable, and has a clear, unambiguous meaning as discussed in Chapter 4, "Telling Stories on the Live Web."

- Merchant rules, customer data, and customer apps are all orthogonal to each other. The system shown in Figure 13.2 isn't a single application, but a platform where fourth-party apps can be built using whatever customer data and merchant rules are available.

- Successful fourth-party apps won't just be conduits for merchants to send offers to customers. Rather, these apps will manage the relationship between merchants and customers in sophisticated ways. They could, for example store receipts, initiate and mediate support issues, manage returns, and so on.

This scenario focuses on one interaction where the app and the merchant rules could conduct a complete, complex negotiation. Keep in mind, however, that the key is the relationship—and the relationship is bigger than a single deal or negotiation. Successful fourth-party apps will be seen by users as trusted agents, not merely as a way to get a good deal on a single transaction.

A key difference between this model and a traditional ad network is the idea of *pull*. Ads are not pushed (note that successful pushing requires tracking and targeting users, neither of which is being done here). Rather, more holistic information about what I'm calling *offers* is being pulled to the customer based on the customer's purpose and intent. Thus, the inclusion of intent data in the scenario is important because data that signals user intent or purpose is much more useful in creating compelling fourth-party apps than demographic data (that is, mere facts such as gender or household size that leave the app to infer intent). Guessing will become less necessary because customers will have convenient, privacy-protecting ways to share intent. In this model, attention gives way to intention just as location gives way to purpose.

ANONYMOUS ECOMMERCE: BUILDING A REAL FOURTH-PARTY OFFER APPLICATION

You can use KRL to make the aforementioned scenario real. In this section, you'll build a simple RFQ system based on the architecture of Figure 13.2. In this example, you'll build a fourth-party shopping assistant using several Kynetx rule sets. As discussed, it is possible to imagine a Kynetx rule set acting as a representative of the shopper (the fourth party) and other rule sets acting on behalf of the merchant (the third parties). These rule sets can interact to provide shoppers with the information they need and take into account their personal situation without their personal data being shared with the merchant or the merchant's representatives in a way that is traceable back to the shopper.

The Scenario

One of the benefits of online shopping is the ability to quickly check out the same product from multiple vendors and find the best deal. There are lots of sites that try to do this for you, but they don't really take your individual situation into account, and they rarely give you comparisons between final prices (including discounts, taxes, and shipping).

In this section, you'll build a simple offer application that shows a shopper what offers other merchants will make to him for the product he's currently viewing. The scenario starts when the fourth-party shopping app—I'll call it the *offer app*—notices that the shopper is visiting a relevant product page and places a Want button on the page. Here's what happens:

1. Shopper visits Scott's Microwave Store using his browser.

2. Shopper clicks the Want button next to a product that has caught his eye.

3. Shopper gets personalized offers for the product from some of his favorite merchants.

The offer looks like what's shown in Figure 13.3.

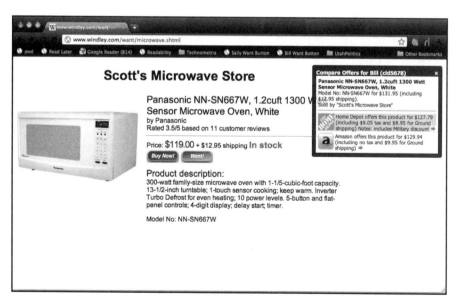

Figure 13.3
Bill's offer from a personal RFQ system in response to a customer-generated intent signal.

Behind the Scenes

Of course, although the preceding customer interaction is simple, the RFQ system is doing the heavy lifting behind the scenes. Figure 13.4 is similar to Figure 13.2, but more specific to this scenario.

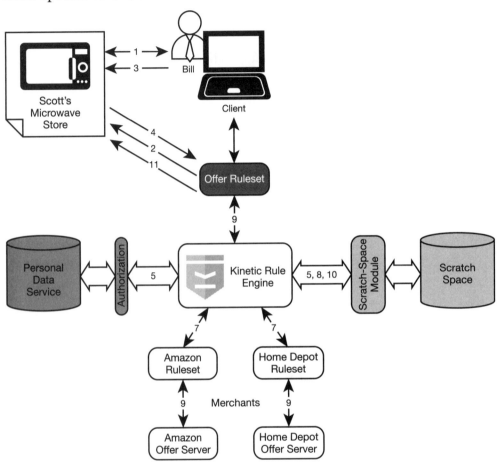

Figure 13.4
Detailed schematic of the RFQ demonstration system.

Assume that the shopper, Bill, already has a PDS that contains important information like his zip code, what discounts he's entitled to, and his list of preferred merchants. Also assume that Bill has previously authorized access to this data for the offer app that represents him in the transaction.

1. The customer, Bill, visits Scott's Microwave Store using his browser.

2. The offer app that Bill has installed to help with online shopping sees the request and places a Want button on the page so Bill can register his interest in this product if he desires.

3. Bill clicks the Want button.

4. The app gathers information about the product from the page, encoded using the Schema.org Product specification.[5]

5. The offer app accesses the personal data store and puts information about both the product and Bill (for example, his ZIP code and discounts for which he is eligible) into a scratch space using a one-time identifier.

6. The app raises an `rfq` event, passing along the one-time identifier so that the merchant rule sets have the required information.

7. Merchant rule sets for Bill's preferred merchants—Home Depot and Amazon— see the event and execute rules to determine what offer they are willing to make for that particular product.

8. As part of their effort to respond, the merchant rule sets get information such as Bill's ZIP code and discounts for which he is eligible from the scratch space.

9. Merchant rule sets contact their own offer systems, passing along information about the product and the relevant personal data.

10. Merchant rule sets write offer information into the scratch space and raise an event to signal they are finished with their offer.

11. The offer app sees the events from the merchant rule sets and uses offer information from the scratch space to present comparison offers for the product to Bill.

There are several features of this interaction:

- A single-use identifier protects the shopper's information from being aggregated and correlated by merchants.

- Merchants are responsible for their own rule sets and the logic that determines how they will respond to the RFQ.

- In this scenario, once Bill decides to purchase the product, he interacts directly with the merchant; the offer app only mediates the RFQ process.

- The system is using Schema.org encoded data from the page to gather information about the product Bill wants, but that's not required.

Using this system, Bill receives personalized offers that take into account what he wants and who he is. During the process, his personally identifying information is shared in a way that can't be directly linked to him. As built, the system only presents offers, but other components—rule sets—could be added to manage a wish-list system that gathers relevant products and their comparison offers from the RFQ for extended shopping sessions.

Of course, the system is designed to take personal attributes and preferences into account. Bill lives in California and is eligible for a military discount. Suppose another shopper—let's call her Sally—lives in Utah and is an Amazon Prime member; she would see different results, as shown in Figure 13.5.

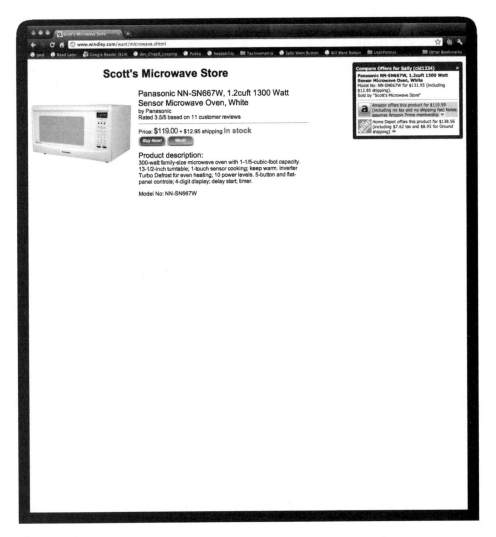

Figure 13.5
Sally's offer from a personal RFQ system.

In the design that follows, watch for the details that enable this personalization of offers.

The Gory Details

Now, let's dig into the details and explore the operations of each of the rule sets and complementary systems that make up the offer system. Before you get into the individual rule sets, however, let's examine the event hierarchy to get a big picture view of what's happening. Figure 13.6 shows the event hierarchy.

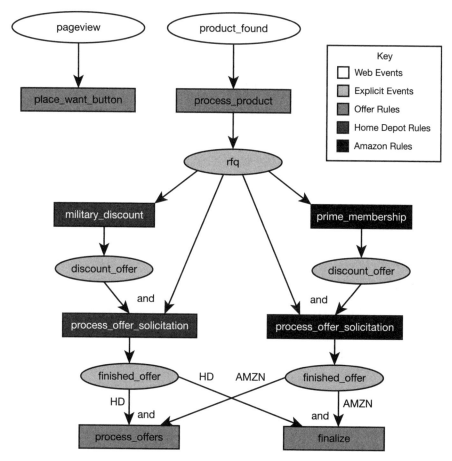

Figure 13.6
The event hierarchy for the offer system.

There are only two Web events in the hierarchy, reflective of the simplicity of the overall user interaction: the pageview event causes the Want button to be placed when a place_want_button event is raised. When the user clicks the Want button, a product_found event is raised that sets off the rest of the interaction.

The product_found event is seen by the process_product rule in the offer rule set. This rule eventually raises the rfq event. Merchant rule sets are watching for that event. The `rfq` event causes the discount rules to fire and eventually, the `process_offer_solicitation` rules wrap everything up. In this simple example, there's only one discounting rule in each merchant rule set, but there could be as many as necessary to accurately reflect the merchant's customer-interaction strategy.

When the `process_offer_solicitation` rules are finished, they raise `finished_offer` events that cause the `process_offers` and `finalize` rules to fire in the offer rule set. The `process_offers` rule is looking for both offers to be returned, but more generally could look for the first two or three in a given period.

The pattern in the event hierarchy shows the overall structure of the system. The rules for the offer rule set are at the top and bottom. The merchant rule sets operate, in parallel, in response to the `rfq` event and raise the `finished_offer` event. While I've built them as near parallels of each other, their internal structure and operation is up to the merchant who owns them.

Now, let's look at the individual rule sets to see the detail of what's happening. You'll start with the scratch space module, move onto one of the merchant rule sets, and finish with the offer rule set.

The Scratch Space Module

The various rule sets in the offer app need a way to share data with each other. They could attach the data as attributes to the events, but that's cumbersome. For this example, I built a simple tag-space store as a scratch space that the apps could use. The scratch space is used to store information about the shopper and the offers that are returned.

The central idea of a tag-space is that objects (in this case, JSON encoded) are stored in a specific namespace and associated with one or more tags. Rule sets use the module to retrieve objects in the tag-space by querying with tags. The tag-space KRL module provides a function for querying the tag-space called `getd()`. `getd()` takes a namespace ID and a set of tags and returns an array (possibly empty) of objects that have been tagged with all the submitted tags. The module also provides an action for storing new JSON objects called `setd()`. `setd()` takes a namespace ID, a set of tags, and a JSON object to store.

You'll use the tag-space by picking a namespace for each shopper and storing relevant personal information such as preferred merchants, ZIP code, and a list of discounts to which the shopper is entitled in the tag-space. In a production system, you'd create a namespace for each interaction, creating a unique, one-time identifier to preserve anonymity. Merchant rule sets retrieve shopper information from the tag-space and store offers into it for the offer rule set to use.

The Merchant Rule Set

For this example, the Amazon and Home Depot rule sets are very similar, so I'll just go over the Amazon rule set. In a real system, of course, that need not be the case. They would simply need to listen for the `rfq` event and raise a `finished_offer` event when they are finished, making appropriate entries in the scratch space along the way.

The Amazon rule set contains a rule called `prime_discount` that is selected on an `rfq` event that determines whether the shopper is a member of Amazon Prime (and thus qualified for free 2nd-day shipping).

```
rule prime_membership {
  select when explicit rfq
  pre {
    customer_id = event:attr("customer_id");
    discounts = tagspace:getd(customer_id, "discounts").head();
  }
  if(discounts.filter(function(x){x eq "AmazonPrime"}).length()>0)
  then noop();
  fired {
    raise explicit event discount_offer with membership="Prime"
  } else {
    raise explicit event discount_offer with membership="Standard"
  }
}
```

The `prime_membership` rule consults the scratch space for the customer with the tag discounts, and tests the list of discounts to see if `"AmazonPrime"` is present. The rule set raises an event `discount_offer` with the `membership` event attribute set to either `"Prime"` or `"Standard"`, depending on the result of the test. Bill, who is not an Amazon Prime member, will see different results from this rule set than what Sally—who is an Amazon Prime member—will see.

I anticipate that rule sets will not do all the work, but will make use of other online systems that the merchant has in place. For the purposes of this demo, I dummied up a system that takes information about the customer and product and returns an offer in JSON format. I declared the API as a data source named `offers` in the `global` section of the rule set:

```
global {
  datasource offers <- "http://.../amazon.cgi";
}
```

The real work of creating the offer is done by the `process_offer_solicitation` rule that is selected when there has been an `rfq` event and a `discount_offer` event:

```
rule process_offer_solicitation {
 select when explicit rfq
       and explicit discount_offer
 pre {
   customer_id = event:attr("customer_id");
   zipcode = tagspace:getd(customer_id, "zipcode").head();
   modelno = event:attr("modelno");
   oid = event:param("offer_id");
   is_prime = event:attr("membership") eq "Prime";
   std_offer = datasource:offers({"modelno":modelno,
                      "zip": zipcode});
   offer = {"price": std_offer.pick("$.price"),
        "shipping": is_prime => 0.00
                   | std_offer.pick("$.shipping"),
        "shipping_type": is_prime => "2nd Day"
                   | std_offer.pick("$.shipping_type"),
     "tax" : std_offer.pick("$.tax"),
     "notes" : is_prime => "assumes Amazon Prime member"
                  | "",
     "url" : std_offer.pick("$.url")
    };
   tags = "offer|#{oid}|Amazon";
 }
 tagspace:setd(customer_id, tags,
          {"offer": offer,
           "zip": zipcode,
           "modelno":modelno,
           "merchant": "Amazon",
           "icon": "http://…/want/amazon_icon.png"});
 always {
   raise explicit event finished_offer for a16x108
    with merchant = "amazon"
 }
}
```

After retrieving customer-specific attributes from the scratch space based on the customer ID that was sent as an event attribute, the rule gets a standard offer from the Amazon offer API (in the `datasource:offers()` call) and then calculates a final offer using information from the discounting rule. The offer, along with other relevant information, is stored in the scratch space using the `setd()` action. Finally, the rule raises the `finished_offer` event to signal it is done.

The merchant rule sets shown here are simple, but the pattern is clear: The rule set responds to an `rfq` event and raises a `finished_offer` event when it's done. In between, the rule set can use as many rules and data sources as necessary to compute the merchant's offer.

The Offer Rule Set

Normally, I'd skip explaining how the Want button is placed on the page because that aspect is fairly rudimentary by now. But because the rule processes Schema.org microdata about the product, it has some new patterns that you should examine. The offer rule set makes use of a slightly modified version of Philip Jagenstedt's jQuery library for processing microdata.[6] The library is loaded as a JavaScript resource in the `meta` section of the rule set like so:

```
use javascript resource "http://.../jquery.microdata.js"
```

The `place_want_button` rule uses the `microdata` library to process the micro-data on the page and send relevant portions along with the `product_found` event:

```
rule place_want_button {
  select when pageview "/want/"
  pre {
    want_button = <<
<span id="want_button"><img src="want%20button.png"/></span>
    >>;
  }
  {
    after("#buy_button", want_button);
    emit <<
$K("#want_button").click(function(){
var jsonText =
    $K.microdata.json("[itemtype='http://schema.org/Product']");
var prodprops = jsonText.items[0].properties;
var offer = prodprops.offers[0].properties;
var seller = offer.seller[0].properties;
app = KOBJ.get_application("a16x108");
app.raise_event("product_found",
    {"prodname":prodprops.name[0],
     "modelno":prodprops.model[0],
     "produrl":prodprops.url[0],
     "price":offer.price[0],
     "shipping":offer.shipping[0],
     "seller":JSON.stringify(seller.name[0], undefined, 2)}});
});
```

```
  >>
 }
}
```

As you can see, JavaScript emitted by the rule does most of the work. The `after()` action places the button and the JavaScript places a listener on the browser `click` event. When the user clicks the button, the callback function processes the microdata on the page and raises the `product_found` event.

This rule would work on any site that uses the `Product` microdata to annotate their HTML, not just the page I dummied up for this example. Whether or not this specific semantic data format is widely adopted, it's a good example of how semantic markup enables common behavior across data with syntactic variability.

The offer rule set makes use of the initialize-then-populate pattern you saw in Chapter 8, "Using the Cloud." The `process_product` rule initializes the response to the user and later, after the merchant rule sets have finished, the `process_offers` rule populates the response.

The `process_product` rule is selected by the `product_found` event. The `process_product` rule is responsible for placing the notification on the page that the shopper will see and initializing it with the correct structure for later rules to write into (the `<div/>` named `offers`). The notification also contains information about the product being quoted, including the calculated final price for the product on the page the shopper is visiting.

```
rule process_product {
  select when web product_found
  pre {
    price = event:attr("price");
    shipping = event:attr("shipping");
    final_price = price+shipping;
    oid = "oid" + math:random(9999);
    a = <<
<div class="prod">
<a href='#{event:attr("produrl")}'>#{event:attr("prodname")}</a>
<br/>Model No: #{event:attr("modelno")} for $#{final_price}
(including $#{shipping} shipping).<br/> Sold by
#{event:attr("seller")}<br/><hr/>
<div id="offers"></div>
</div>
  >>;
  }
  notify("Compare Offers for #{event:attr('who')}", a)
```

```
      with sticky = true and width="300px";
   fired {
     set ent:oid oid;
     raise explicit event rfq for merchants with
       modelno = event:attr("modelno") and
       customer_id = customer_id and
       offer_id = oid;
   }
 }
}
```

The rule postlude stores the offer ID (generated fresh for each interaction) and then raises the `rfq` event with the model number, the customer ID, and the offer ID. For brevity, I've skipped the step where customer attributes are written to the tag space. By changing the customer ID, you change the data that the merchant sees. As you saw, the merchant rules, like `process_offer_solicitation`, use the customer ID as the namespace in the scratch pad and the offer ID to store data relevant to this offer.

The `process_offers` rule is designed to run when all the offers have been calculated by the merchant rule sets. As mentioned, `process_offers` is responsible for populating the notification that the customer sees. The `select` statement in this example is true when offers are complete from Home Depot and Amazon. In a production rule set with many merchants, you might be content with the first two or three offers.

The rule loops over the offers, calculates the final price for each merchant, and displays it in the notification placed on the page by the aforementioned `process_product` rule using the `append` action.

```
rule process_offers {
  select when explicit finished_offer merchant "amazon"
        and explicit finished_offer merchant "homedepot"
    foreach tagspace:getd(customer_id,ent:oid) setting (of)
      pre {
        tax = of.pick("$..tax")>0 => "$"+of.pick("$..tax")+" tax"
                                    | "no tax";
        final_price = of.pick("$..price") +
                of.pick("$..tax") + of.pick("$..shipping");
        shipping =
          of.pick("$..shipping") > 0 =>
                  "$" + of.pick("$..shipping") +
                  " for " + of.pick("$..shipping_type") +
                  " shipping"
                | "no shipping fee";
```

```
      prod_url = of.pick("$..url");
      notes = of.pick("$..notes") neq "" =>
                "Notes: #{of.pick('$..notes')}" | "";
      merchant_id = of.pick("$.merchant").replace(re/ /g,"");
  offer = <<
<div id='#{merchant_id}' class='offer'>
<a href="#{prod_url}" broder="0">
<img height="40px" border="0" align="left"
    src='#{of.pick("$.icon")}'/>
</a>
#{of.pick("$.merchant")} offers this product
for $#{final_price} (including #{tax} and #{shipping}) #{notes}
<a href="#{prod_url}" border="0">
<img src="green_arrow.png" border="0" valign="top" height="13px"/>
</a><br clear="both"/>
</div>
      >>;
    }
    append("#offers", offer);
    always {
      mark ent:prices with {"price": final_price,
                   "merchant": merchant_id}
    }
}
```

There's one more rule in the rule set: The process_offer rule postlude stores a map
with the price and merchant ID in an entity variable for each offer. The finalize
rule uses this information to highlight the offer with the lowest price. The finalize
rule is selected by the same eventex that was used to select the process_offers rule.

```
rule finalize {
  select when explicit finished_offer merchant "amazon"
          and explicit finished_offer merchant "homedepot"
  pre {
    lowest = ent:prices.as("array").sort(
              function(a,b){
                a.pick("$.price")> b.pick("$.price")
              }).head();
    lm_id = "#" + lowest.pick("$.merchant");
  }
  emit <<
$K(lm_id).attr("style","background-color: palegoldenrod");
  >>;
  always {
```

```
  clear ent:prices
 }
}
```

The rule sorts the `prices` entity variable that was created by the `process_offers` rule to find the lowest price and uses the merchant ID to change the background color for that line in the display. Finally, the rule postlude clears the `prices` variable.

A Working Fourth-Party eCommerce System

The system described here is a working example of a system for creating offers in a way that protects customer identity. The system uses a set of merchant rule sets, built and maintained by the merchants themselves, that create offers using data about the product and the customer along with an offer-management rule set that oversees the process for the customer—effectively acting as a fourth party.

The merchant rule sets are not single purpose. In fact, merchants can write them so they can be used by any number of systems that need offers on products for customers. They could respond to any rule set that raises the `rfq` event. Any rule set that listens for the `finished_offer` event could make use of their results. For example, the offer-management rule set described previously used them to present an offer immediately to the customer. Another fourth-party rule set might use them to look for offers for things that the customer has placed on his wish list. Of course, privacy is preserved because these events are being raised on the customer's personal event network and the customer explicitly activated the rule sets raising and listening for events on that network.

By protecting customers' personally identifying information and presenting them with relevant offers, you create a system whereby shoppers feel safe in looking to merchants for information. At the same time, merchants can place highly relevant offers in front of people who have expressed intent to buy.

In this chapter, you've explored the ideas behind the intention economy and personal RFQs. As part of this, you built a personal offer system that uses cooperating rule sets that are, in theory, maintained by separate organizations. The next chapter expands on this to create a more complex scenario of a dozen cooperating rule sets to automate the process of selecting and interacting with service providers.

Endnotes

1. Project VRM main page: http://cyber.law.harvard.edu/projectvrm/Main_Page.
2. See http://www.nytimes.com/2011/06/21/us/21anonymity.html.

3. Searls, Doc. *The Intention Economy*. March 08, 2006. http://www.linuxjournal.com/node/1000035.

4. "VRM and the Four Party System." http://blogs.law.harvard.edu/vrm/2009/04/12/vrm-and-the-four-party-system/.

5. See http://schema.org/Product.

6. See http://plugins.jquery.com/project/microdata.

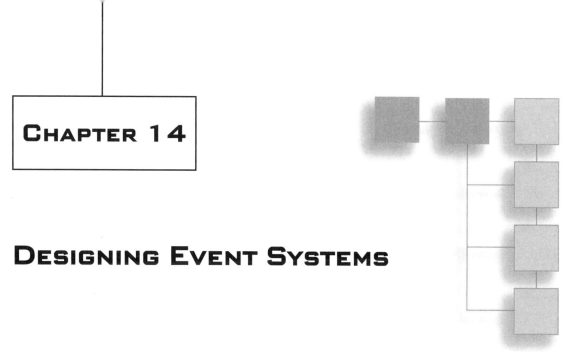

CHAPTER 14

DESIGNING EVENT SYSTEMS

Over the course of the preceding 13 chapters, you've seen various ways in which events and KRL can be used to create single-purpose applications. In this chapter, you will explore an extended example that puts all these various pieces together in a cooperating suite of rule sets to automate a common situation: choosing and contracting with a service provider.

LIFE EVENTS AS INTERACTION SCRIPTS

In 2001, while I was CIO for the State of Utah, we were envisioning how e-government would best work. We came up with a concept called *life events*. The idea was that most people interact with government when something happens in their life that compels them. Further, those events almost never break along departmental lines so that one government agency can handle the entire interaction. A typical life event, like moving to Utah, involves multiple interactions with many different government and non-government entities at all sorts of levels.

At the time, we envisioned building on the Utah.gov portal that would help constituents work through the various tasks associated with a given life event. Only one was built, however: the one-stop business-registration application.[1] Building these cross-cutting applications is hard because a server-side portal is the wrong technology for coordinating interactions across multiple Web sites—especially when they aren't all controlled by a single organization.

One reason server-side solutions don't work is that the server has to make up for the lack of active clients working on behalf of the user—raising events and responding to directives. As a consequence, the server has to simulate this by requiring the user to enter data, click buttons, and select things. In other words, a server turns the user into the active client.

There's another reason the server is the wrong place to build applications that automate life events: Server applications are too tightly coupled. Web services (i.e., SOAP, WSDL, etc.) are a complicated way of trying to create interactions between APIs on the server side. You can make all this work with Web services, but it turns out to be quite brittle. Of course, there are Web-services technologies for creating more loosely coupled systems, but they are less well understood, and they suffer from working on the server, away from the user.

With the Live Web, you can help people with the tasks and activities that matter to them—their purpose for being online at any given time. The example in this chapter shows how that can work. This chapter makes the case that the answer isn't a big, one-size-fits-all, server-side, portal-based application, but a set of loosely coupled, cooperating apps orchestrated using personal data on a personal event network. The overall experience is infinitely customizable because the user can trade any of the components out for something that works better. Further, the experience is incremental, meaning you don't need all the apps at once. You see incremental benefit as you incrementally install apps. The experience grows and changes as you customize your environment to suit your needs. What's more, changing out an app for another one doesn't require upgrading or changing the other apps.

Introducing Scott Phillips

In this scenario, you're going to follow the life of a fictional person named Scott Phillips in a near-term future world where the Live Web is in full swing and Live Web applications that operate on personal event networks are widely available. Scott has an unexplained pain in his neck, and he's had an MRI. A few days later, he receives the report from the radiologist and it's not good. The radiologist recommends that Scott see an orthopedic surgeon and even recommends a few.

Besides the obvious fear and potential disabilities that such news brings, Scott also has to manage the frustration and hassle of finding and scheduling a competent surgeon. The Live Web can't do anything about the surgery itself, but it can help Scott with the secondary hassles.

Three large tasks loom before Scott:

- Selecting a surgeon
- Scheduling the initial consult
- Establishing a patient record with the new doctor

There are other aspects to the relationship—like payments—that this example ignores to keep it manageable.

The various applications in this example were built by my company, Kynetx, in 2010 to show how event-driven systems can enable individual applications to interact in a loosely coupled way. We called it "Project Neck Pain." The events in this example were inspired by the real-life experiences of our CEO, Steve Fulling, who ended up having three vertebrae in his neck fused. You can see the results of his operation in Figure 14.1.

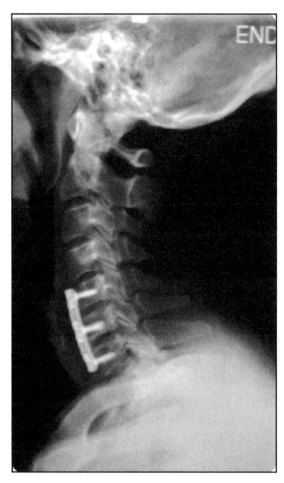

Figure 14.1
Steve's neck following his surgery.

PERSONAL EVENTS

In Scott Phillips' near-future existence, he has a personal event network. As discussed in Chapter 1, "The Live Web," this personal event network where events are raised (in this case, for Scott). Scott has activated a number of rule sets—what he thinks of as Live Web applications—on his personal event network. Scott's personal event network is where his Live Web apps come together with events raised by his endpoints.

A personal computer is *personal* because applications you chose run against data that you own and control. A computer is more than a CPU; it's also input/output devices and storage. Similarly, a personal event network is more than just the rule sets and endpoints. A personal event network needs access to personal data—preferences, traits, attributes, interaction histories, and so on.

In the previous 13 chapters, it was assumed that events were raised on behalf of a particular entity. Entity variables made rule sets respond in personal ways. This is why KRL uses identity as a primary organizational concept for events. The personal event network grows out of that idea, creating the centerpiece of a new kind of Web—one in which individuals see significantly increased utility from the use of their personal data in conjunction with applications that work on their behalf to manage the mundane. The personal event network is a personal cloud.

As a consequence, a personal event network offers increased privacy over the current regime. A personal event network is critical to protecting sensitive information. By segregating events by entity, we ensure that only Scott's rule sets see his events. As the example in this chapter will make clear, there's a lot of sensitive data moving around the Live Web. People will only use Live Web applications if they trust that their personal, private information will be protected and safe. Don't lose sight of the fact that events themselves are a form of personal information that needs to be protected.

In this chapter, you'll see how various endpoints work together as part of Scott's personal event network to raise events related to a large-scale scenario. You'll also see some common rule sets, like those that manage Scott's to-do list and email, that provide foundational components to other rule sets. Scott will use a Live Web desktop to interact with the various rule sets that he has activated in his personal event network. One of the most important components will be Scott's personal data store.

Personal Data

A personal data store (PDS) is a central component of a personal event network. Scott's personal event network also includes a PDS that stores his to-do list, service preferences, health data, and so on. Ideally, the data in the PDS is semantic so that various rule sets can discover its schemas and make links between data elements that are the same despite differences in tagging.

As you discovered in Chapter 4, "Telling Stories on the Live Web," personal data is a key component in creating Live Web experiences. The PDS used in the neck-pain scenario is an extension of the entity variables in KRL, but goes beyond them to provide a stable, cloud-based, data store that is under Scott's control and provides a single interface for data Scott cares about. Scott's PDS is a full participant on his personal event network. Not only can data be stored, queried, and retrieved, but the PDS also raises events about Scott's data. Some of these events are automatic and others are explicit triggers that are set either by Scott or by apps working on his behalf. Because the PDS raises events rather than simply waiting to be queried, it becomes a central player in the scenario that follows.

The PDS isn't Scott's only repository of personal data. He also uses Google Calendar to keep track of his appointments. The Live Web knits together all these various repositories so they work seamlessly for Scott. You shouldn't think of the PDS as a single *place* that stores all the data, but a single *interface* to all of Scott's personal data, regardless of where it is held. The PDS interface is a critical component of his personal event network.

Mary Hodder uses a "bar versus bank" analogy[2] to distinguish between a PDS and other repositories of personal data like Facebook. The analogy holds as well for a personal event network. Facebook is a bar, not a bank. Facebook can change the terms any time it likes and it monetizes your data and transactions around it. (The terms of service that most Web sites foist upon users are called *contracts of adhesion* and are a key feature of the attention economy in which vendors hold most of the power.) There are lots of fun things to do on Facebook, but Facebook has no fiduciary responsibility and isn't required to be interoperable.

Coincidentally, as I was writing this chapter, people were discussing the ongoing security breaches and loss of personal data at Sony. Ed Bott tweeted:[3]

> If Sony were a bank, government regulators would be stepping in right about now to take over operations.

In contrast to current repositories of personal information, a personal event network and its associate PDS have a duty to the user. The terms of service must be such that the user remains in control. A personal event network is based on a completely different philosophy of personal data than the Web 2.0 mentality that creates silos of data, walled off from each other and often at odds with the user's interests.

Principles for Personal Event Networks

Scott's personal event network is the place where all the interactions happen that are necessary for automating scenarios like the one envisioned in this chapter. Without such a service, where Scott's rule sets can interact with his personal data, automating any complex scenario would be difficult.

Here's a list of a principles that describe a personal event network:

- **User-controlled.** Users must control their events and data—who has access and how it is used. Users make decisions about how events and data are used, largely by picking and configuring the rule sets that activated on their personal event network. There are two separate but distinct aspects to user control: permissioning and revocation. Permissioning says that the user determines what apps are installed and who gets access to data. Revocation says that any permission granted can be revoked in the future.

- **Federated.** Personal event networks federate events from various services through the use of endpoints. A PDS doesn't just store your data; rather, it orchestrates the flow of data from various data repositories around the Web.

- **Interoperable.** A personal event network, using standards like the Evented API specification (see Appendix F, "The Evented API Specification"), interoperates with other systems and APIs. Similarly, a PDS must operate with other data sources according to standards if it is to perform its role. When you take money out of your account at Wells Fargo and deposit it at Chase, you don't lose part of the value because Chase doesn't know how to handle some part of the transaction. The monetary system is interoperable with standards and, sometimes, shims that connect it all together. So too will be the Live Web.

- **Semantic.** Events and data have meaning. I've discussed event semantics and semantic translation. Most systems on the Web today are not semantic. Consider Dropbox. You can put all kinds of things in your Dropbox, but it's syntactic, not semantic. For example, you can put healthcare data in Dropbox by creating a folder and putting the data in it with specific permissions. But the fact that there is a folder with a certain name located at a particular place in the folder hierarchy is purely syntactic. In a semantic world, the data itself is tagged (e.g., as healthcare data), and no matter where it's stored, it's protected according to the policies you've put in place.

- **Portable.** A personal event network doesn't trap events or other data. The technology and policies for personal event networks must allow this. Nor will you have to wait until thousands upon thousands of data format specifications get hammered out. Semantic metadata can provide a means of translating from one format to another.

- **Metadata aware.** Information *about* events and data is just as important as the events or data themselves. Semantic information, event-routing data, and access policies are examples of metadata that are critical to a functioning personal event network. Managing this metadata is one of the primary roles of the PDS.

- **Brokered.** A personal event network may be made from multiple rules engines and a federated network of data stores. As an example of why seeing the personal event network as a broker is so important, consider the shortcomings of OAuth. If you use an application that needs access to four OAuth mediated APIs, you have to go through the OAuth ceremony with each API provider separately. Now consider that you might have dozens of apps that use a popular API. You have to go through the OAuth ceremony for each of them separately. In short, a broker saves you from the N×M explosion of permissioning ceremonies.

- **Discoverable.** A personal event network should provide discoverability for its APIs and schemas so that any application you're interested in knows how to interact with it. Discoverability protects users from having to completely specify addresses, mappings, and schemas to every application that comes along.

THE TIMELINE

As mentioned earlier, Scott Phillips has been to the radiologist about a problem with his neck. The results are back, and they're not good. Scott has things to do and choices to make.

The scenario kicks off with Scott getting an email from his radiologist saying that he needs to consult an orthopedic surgeon. The email was created by the patient-management system that the doctor uses. The email contains semantic markup in the form of Schema.org microdata (similar to the Product schema you saw in Chapter 13, "Business on the Live Web"), microformats, or RDFa that identifies the following:

- The linked location of the MRI results. Scott's PDS identifies the link as something related to Scott and places it in his personal data. Whether the MRI results are incorporated into Scott's PDS through reference or copied is beyond the scope of this discussion. Indeed, it might be a preference that Scott can set or a matter of which PDS he is using.

- A task that Scott must complete—specifically, "Choose an orthopedic surgeon."

- A task that Scott must complete—specifically, "Schedule an appointment."

Figure 14.2 shows the timeline for the primary things Scott will do.

Scott has activated rule sets in his personal event network that listen to events from his mailbox. For example, Scott has personal data management rule sets that watch for things like the tagged MRI result and aggregate it into Scott's PDS. Scott has a to-do application that watches his mailbox for things Scott has to do and makes them part of his to-do list.

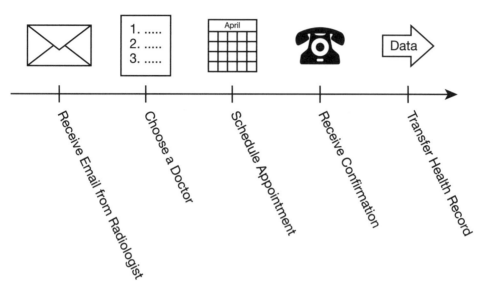

Figure 14.2
Timeline for Scott's interactions.

At some point, Scott picks the "Choose an orthopedic surgeon" item from his to-do list. Scott's insurance provider has given him a rule set that helps him find doctors. The rule set shows Scott three doctors who are in the appropriate specialty, keying off data in the original email. One was recommended by his plan. Two of the selections are in plan and one is not.

Scott visits the first doctor's professional page on the Web. A rule set that Scott got from Angie's List for rating and commenting on service providers overlays the doctor's page with rating and mapping data. The overlay augments the data from the doctor, showing data that the doctor may not normally place on his own page. Not satisfied with the first choice, Scott visits another doctor and is shown the same overlay. Satisfied with what he sees, Scott chooses this doctor. The to-do list item is automatically crossed off the list.

Now that Scott has chosen a doctor, he needs to schedule his initial visit. Clicking on the link activates an "appointment scheduling" rule set, which compares the doctor's free-busy calendar with Scott's and gives him a choice of three different time slots. Scott picks a time, setting the appointment in Google Calendar and sending a scheduling confirmation to the doctor. Because Scott has previously expressed a preference to receive appointment confirmations by phone, the notification comes to his cell phone. He receives a call stating that an appointment has been made and asks him to confirm the appointment time. Scott will receive another reminder call before the appointment.

The doctor's system responds to the scheduling confirmation with a request to send Scott's health record data. This creates a to-do item for Scott. Clicking on it, Scott is presented with a standardized request for data transfer that he's seen many times before when a company needs personal data from his PDS. He selects what he wants to send and the transfer is completed automatically and securely.

With that, Scott's work is done. He has selected a doctor, scheduled an appointment, and completed the preliminary information exchanges. Along the way, he was aided by Live Web applications operating on his personal event network. The following sections discuss the operation of the various pieces that make this timeline real.

Note

You can watch a video screencast of this scenario at http://www.windley.com/pnp.

UNDERSTANDING THE COMPONENTS

Orchestrating the scenario described requires a lot of moving parts: interfaces and devices, endpoints, rule sets, and APIs. Figure 14.3 shows the various components.

As you've seen in earlier chapters, Scott can use a variety of devices and interfaces to interact with the Live Web. Those interfaces use endpoints to raise events on Scott's behalf to his personal event network. Rule sets listen for and respond to events, often using data from APIs provided by various cloud-based services. In the coming sections, you'll explore all these components and understand the details of what they are and how they interact to help Scott with his neck pain.

Live Web Desktop

You're familiar with most of the interfaces and devices that Scott might use—email, a browser, a calendar, and phones—from your own experience. One interface that is specific to Scott's personal event network is the desktop. Various apps that Scott has installed give him management functionality so he can configure them. Scott's desktop serves as a canvas on which various rule sets paint interaction widgets. The prototype desktop used for this example is shown in Figure 14.4. The desktop shows Scott's name, the time, the weather, some pictures from his Flickr account, an agenda from his calendar, and his to-do list.

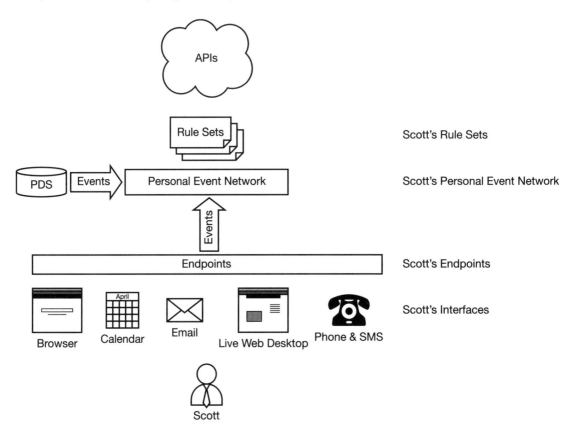

Figure 14.3
Components involved in Scott's scenario.

The Web page representing the desktop is mostly empty. The HTML in the page consists of empty `<div/>` elements that set up the initial structure as shown here:

Note

A production Live Web desktop would likely have less structure than this and would use a configuration application that creates the structure according to the user's wishes.

```
<div id="logo-bar">
 <div id="user-identifier"></div>
 <div id="time"></div>
</div>
<div id="page-wrapper">
 <div id="main-top">
  <div id="calendar"></div>
  <div id="weather"></div>
```

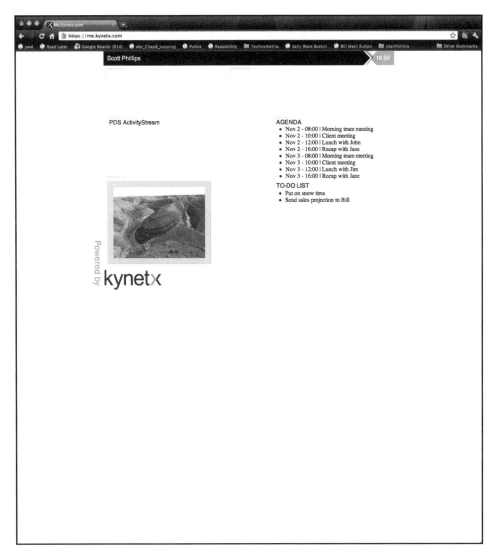

Figure 14.4
Scott's Live Web desktop at the beginning of the scenario.

```
</div><!-- #main-top -->
...
  <div id="right">
   <div id="agenda"></div>
   <div id="to-do"></div>
  </div>
  ...
</div>
```

All the page content is painted by various KRL rule sets. For example, the following rule paints the date in the upper-left corner:

```
rule showdate {
  select when pageview ".*"
  pre {
    msg = <<
      <div id="day">#{dateFormat("dddd")}</div>
      <div id="date">#{dateFormat("mmmm dS, yyyy")}</div>
    >>
  }
  replace_inner("#calendar", msg);
}
```

The rule makes use of a function `dateFormat` that is not shown. Similarly, there are rules that paint the current weather, user name, time, and a selection of recent photos from the user's Flickr stream.

In addition to rule sets that manage these more mundane aspects of the desktop, there are three special rule sets that Scott has installed to customize his desktop:

- **Agenda.** The agenda is painted by a rule set that links to Scott's Google Calendar. As the calendar is updated, the agenda is updated as well. If Scott used a different calendar, a rule set for that calendar would perform the same function.

- **To-do list.** The to-do list rule set implements a basic to-do list with the ability to add items and cross them off. The to-do list is a Live Web application because it responds to events.

- **PDS log.** The PDS log is an activity stream that shows what the personal data service is doing. Scott wouldn't likely have this on his desktop, but it's useful for this demonstration.

Personal event networks need a place where they can show the user information and be configured. The beauty of the Live Web is that this needn't be a centralized, server-based portal. Almost any place that is convenient for the user will do.

Endpoints

As you've seen, the Live Web depends on endpoints to raise events and respond to directives. Three endpoints discussed in previous chapters will play a role in the neck-pain scenario:

- The Web endpoint (refer to Chapter 7, "Creating Contextual Web Experiences") will play a major role, as the previous discussion on the desktop shows.

- The email endpoint (refer to Chapter 9, "Events Around the Web") will watch Scott's IMAP account and process emails automatically under certain conditions.

- The Web hook endpoint, along with the Twilio service (refer to Chapter 9, "Events Around the Web," and Chapter 10, "Mobile and the Live Web") will make phone calls and handle SMS interactions.

In addition to these common endpoints, the PDS will function as an endpoint. The prototype PDS built for this demonstration is a simple key-value store with HTTP access. As such, it does not conform to all the principles outlined previously, but it does show how a PDS plays a central role in a complex scenario like the one described in this chapter.

The PDS endpoint raises the event `update_event` when it updates a field in the store. `update_event` has the event attribute `key_name` that gives the name of the key that was updated. The PDS also raises events when a key is created (`create_event`) or deleted (`delete_event`). All these event types are raised in the `kpds` event domain.

The idea of having the PDS function as an endpoint is central to how the neck-pain scenario works. Without the PDS endpoint, there would be no locus for the Live Web desktop to operate against. The PDS is not simply a repository of personal data, but an active participant in coordinating activities on behalf of the user.

The following rule shows the kind of interactions that occur between KRL and the PDS. This rule fires off a phone confirmation when the PDS signals that the user has chosen an appointment:

```
rule start_confirm is active {
  select when kpds update_event key "chosenappt"
          or kpds create_event key "chosenappt"
  pre {
    phoneNum =
      (datasource:pds({"key":"phone"})).pick("$.value.number");
    appt = datasource:pds({"key":"chosenappt"}).pick("$.value");
    confirmed = appt.pick("$.confirmed");
  }
  if((confirmed neq "") && (confirmed == 0)) then {
    http:post("https://api.twilio.com/Calls.json")
    with params =
      {"Called":phoneNum,
       "Caller":"8015551212",
       "Url":"http://webhooks.kynetx.com/h/…"};
    send_directive("log") with
      app = "PhoneConfirm" and
```

```
    desc = "Confirmation Call Started";
  }
}
```

This rule is selected when the PDS signals that the appointment has been chosen. Note that there are two different ways that might happen, and the `select` statement takes both into account. The rule retrieves Scott Phillips' phone number, the appointment data, and doctor information from the PDS in the rule prelude. Next, if specific conditions are met, the rule initiates a phone call with Twilio using an `http:post()` action and tells the PDS to log the event.

As you've seen before, one important feature of event-driven systems is that the PDS doesn't have any idea what will happen when it signals that the appointment is set. The PDS simply raises the event. What happens depends on what apps the user has installed and what rules are in those apps. The listener, not the endpoint, determines the semantics of the event.

Using Data

In addition to the various endpoints involved, the neck-pain scenario also uses data from multiple APIs, including the following:

- **PDS.** The PDS has an API, as you can see in the preceding rule. Not only does the PDS allow data to be queried in a permissioned and revocable way (using OAuth), but it also allows values to be updated or created. At present, the prototype PDS doesn't have a generalized schema beyond what is needed for this demo.

- **Twilio.** As noted, the Twilio API is used to make phone calls and gather responses from the user.

- **Google Calendar.** Scott Phillips' schedule is read from his Google Calendar using their API.

- **Flickr.** The pictures on Scott Phillips' dashboard come from his Flickr account via the API.

- **Weather.** The weather data is coming from the Yahoo! Weather API.

In addition to these APIs, this scenario in production would also use APIs related to the following information:

- **Doctor ratings.** Scott Phillips' personal event network helps him choose a doctor by scoring them. In this scenario, we assumed a generic service rating API like Angie's List, but there are also doctor-specific services such as Health-Grades.[4] A real scenario might use both.

- **Mapping.** Rule sets show Scott Phillips how far various doctors are from his home. In fact, we might do this anytime an address shows up. Mapping APIs provide this kind of data.

- **Insurance provider.** Rule sets show Scott Phillips whether the doctors are on his insurance plan, assuming access to that information in some API provided by Scott's insurer.

- **Health data.** Scott Phillips sends his medical information to his doctor after making the selection. This assumes there is an API allowing Scott to send secure, personal data to his doctor.

In this near-future scenario, Scott Phillips uses a handful of APIs to manage data that is important. Scott probably interacts with dozens of APIs on any given day—not directly, but through the applications he has activated. The Live Web makes the cloud useful to individuals.

The Rule Sets

The scenario presented in this chapter is created using multiple rule sets cooperating in a loosely coupled manner. As you've seen in previous chapters, events allow for loose coupling, but this scenario is by far the most complex example you've seen. In this section, you'll examine the rule sets that contribute to the scenario. Later you'll explore the events that are raised that drive the scenario.

One of our goals in creating the rule sets that operate in this scenario was to make them as real as possible. We wanted rule sets that had a good backstory, even if they were just demonstrations. I'll describe the primary rule sets at play in this scenario and how I envision they may really exist.

Almost a dozen rule sets are involved in the neck-pain scenario. These rule sets cooperate to deliver the neck-pain experience described earlier. The rule sets independently listen to relevant events and respond in ways appropriate for their function. They also independently use the PDS as a common data repository. Each works with whatever APIs are relevant to their function. The individual rule sets know nothing of each other for the most part. They just do their piece and use events to message other interested rule sets.

The rule sets that make this scenario work are as follows:

- **Desktop.** As discussed, the desktop is an empty skeleton of `<div/>` elements that is painted by various rule sets. Scott Phillips' name, clock, calendar, weather, and styling are each managed by a separate rule, in various rule sets. The desktop could be made to look quite different by merely changing out one or more of these rule sets without any effect on the rest of the rule sets involved. The desktop is painted when the user views the page and a `web:pageview` event is raised.

- **To-do list.** The management of the to-do list is performed by a rule set that might be provided by the PDS provider or something Scott gets from a third party. In this example, the to-do list data is in the PDS and has an API for other applications to use. Like any platform, users will choose from various applications depending on their needs. Because the data is in the PDS, the to-do application can be changed without changing the underlying data.

- **PDS activity stream.** The PDS activity stream shows what is happening inside the PDS. This wouldn't likely be a standard component of the desktop, but would be on an auxiliary page. For the purposes of this example, it helps you see what's going on behind the scenes. The fact that viewing the PDS activity shows how the scenario is unfolding evidences the central nature of the PDS.

- **Flickr.** The Flickr rule set watches the user's picture feed and shows recent pictures. This might come with the dashboard or be something the user has found and installed to work with the dashboard.

- **Healthcare action items.** This rule set watches the user's email for messages from the healthcare provider. The patient-management system used by the radiologist has marked up the email with semantic codes so that various parts like the MRI image reference and specific tasks are recognizable by downstream components. Scott Phillips might have installed rules that he got as part of a larger patient rule set to watch for emails, or these rules might more generally be watching all email for tasks to add to the to-do list.

- **Doctor choices.** Scott's insurance company has provided an app that helps patients choose doctors for particular needs. The rule set responds to the to-do item about choosing a surgeon by showing Scott some choices and annotating the doctors who are in the user's insurance network. The list of recommended doctors is dummied up in the demo, but would likely come from whoever provided the service provider selection application. This rule set might come from the user's healthcare network or an independent provider.

- **Service provider information.** This rule set overlays the doctor's professional About page with relevant data, augmenting what's there with recommendations from the user's social network, showing data from other Web sites and any relevant ratings and reviews. The rule set makes use of semantic markup on the About page to locate addresses, names, and other professional data. Apps that help consumers find information about service providers will be common.

- **Scheduler.** The scheduler rule set helps Scott set up appointments and compares his calendar (in this case, Google) with the doctor's free-busy schedule to find the intersection and display three choices for the appointment. The app also sets the appointment in the user's calendar and transmits it to the doctor. (At present, service providers don't have online free-busy calendars that customers can view; even if they did, there's no standard way to discover them.)

- **Phone confirmation.** This rule set calls Scott Phillips with relevant appointment data and asks for confirmation. Note that this app calls on behalf of the personal data store, not the doctor. This app might be part of the appointment-scheduling system or a more general confirmation app that the user has installed to confirm certain changes to PDS data using a secondary channel. Obviously, Scott doesn't want to get called every time something changes in the PDS. Notifications of changes come with enough detail that rules can determine the appropriate level of interaction with the user.

- **Medical information transfer.** After Scott Phillips has confirmed the appointment, the PDS responds to the request from the doctor for Scott's health data. Any responses to requests for personal data require Scott's permission. Some might be sent by default (e.g., Scott shares his Twitter handle with anyone, so no need to ask him). Others may be sharable with certain groups and not others. Scott likes to be asked each time his healthcare data is shared, but only after a phone confirmation of the relationship with the new doctor.

- **Global configuration.** Data in the PDS and other preferences is managed using a configuration rule set.

EVENTS

Events allow the system to be loosely coupled because, as mentioned, an endpoint raising an event does not know who may be listening or what action might be taken when an event is raised. Multiple rule sets may be listening to an event without being aware of each other. In this section, you'll follow how the neck-pain scenario unfolds from the perspective of the events that are raised and what responses they generate. Note that although the scenario, as described, seems to flow from start to finish all at once, there are four distinct phases of the interaction. Scott might complete one phase and then not complete the next for some time.

Processing Email

When the radiologist sends an email to Scott, its arrival raises a `mail:received` event (see Figure 14.5). In this scenario, that touches off two rules: one to look for attachments and referenced data that needs to be put in the PDS, and one to look for to-do list items and put them in the to-do list.

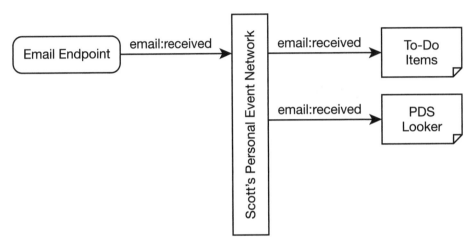

Figure 14.5
Events for email processing.

Note

Diagrams like the one in Figure 14.5 are like the event hierarchies you've seen, but broken apart based on which part of the timeline you're on to make them easier to understand. Also, because events can be seen by multiple rules, I've introduced a notion of a bus in these diagrams to make them less busy. As we've discussed, the personal event network in the figure is not a separate software component, but rather a virtual network that arises from identity and salience information.

Choose a Doctor

When the rule set responsible for processing email places an item on Scott Phillips' to-do list, it does so in such a way that clicking the item raises an event `explicit:getRecommended` (see Figure 14.6). A rule set for choosing doctors sees that event and overlays the desktop with a dialog box showing several doctors and asking Scott to make a choice. Clicking a doctor's name in the list opens a Web page for that doctor in the usual manner, but these `web:pageview` events cause a rule that listens for them to fire and overlay the doctor rating data on the doctor's page. Selecting a doctor raises a `web:click` event. A rule watching for this event places the doctor's

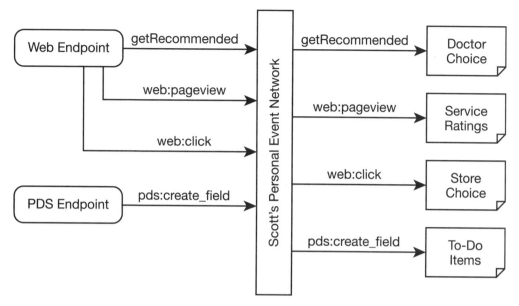

Figure 14.6
Events for choosing a doctor. (Note that in this figure and others, I've left off the `explicit` event domain tag for explicit events. All other events are shown with their event domain.)

contact information from the About page into Scott's PDS as his preferred orthopedic surgeon. When Scott's preference is recorded, this raises a PDS event called `pds:create_field`. A rule in the to-do list rule set fires on this event, crossing off the item in Scott's to-do list.

SET UP AN APPOINTMENT

When Scott Phillips decides to set up the appointment with his doctor, he clicks the corresponding to-do item. Similar to the "choose a doctor" item, this item raises an event `explicit:setUpAppt` (see Figure 14.7). A rule in the scheduler rule set is listening for this event and uses data in the event parameters, along with information about Scott's recently chosen doctor, to create the intersection of free times on Scott's calendar and his doctor's. When Scott picks an appointment time, this raises an event, `explicit:pickTime`. A rule listening for this puts the data in Scott's calendar and communicates the choice to the doctor's office. Updating the calendar causes the PDS to raise the `pds:update_field` event with the key `chosenappt`. A rule listening for events that indicate an appointment has been made fires off the appointment confirmation phone call. When Scott confirms the appointment, this raises an event, `phone:confirm`. A rule listening for this event records the confirmation in the PDS.

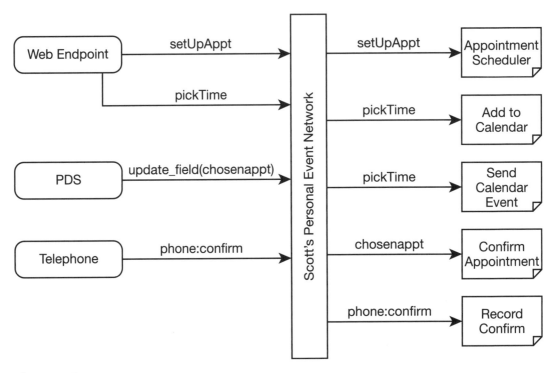

Figure 14.7
Events for setting up the appointment. (Note that I've left out all the intermediate events raised by the phone endpoint as part of carrying out the phone call as well as in asking for and gathering Scott's confirmation.)

Send Health Data

The doctor's office wants Scott Phillips' health data and has signaled that request via an email. This raises the event `email:received` (see Figure 14.8). A rule listening for this event adds the item to the to-do list. Clicking the to-do item raises an event `explicit:sendData`. The rule listening for this event pulls the data descriptions from Scott's PDS and places a confirmation screen on the desktop based on Scott's data-sharing preferences. When Scott clicks the Send button, this raises the event `web:click`. A rule listening for it and looking for certain event attributes fires, recording the confirmation and sending the required data back to the doctor.

Understanding the Neck-Pain Scenario

There are several important ideas in the neck-pain scenario that I want to emphasize:

■ **Services and scheduling.** The most important point to make about the neck-pain scenario is that it's not really about healthcare. It's about picking a service provider and scheduling a service. This is a scenario everyone faces multiple times a month.

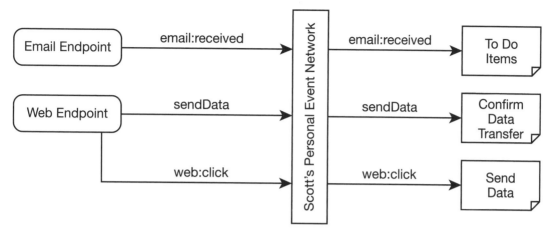

Figure 14.8
Events for sending health data.

- **Purpose-based experience.** Scott Phillips' experience in the scenario focuses his attention on the things that matter—critical decisions—rather than making him fuss with instigating every interaction and then managing the ensuing details. Scott's purpose—choosing a doctor and setting up an appointment—are the primary area for his interactions. In present-day online interactions, Scott would have to pay significant attention to finding the right Web sites, performing searches, analyzing the details of data formats, and copying information from one place to another.

- **Just-in-time Web pages.** There were no Web sites in this experience except those provided by the doctors. The desktop was painted in a simple structure containing a few <div/> elements in a manner similar to the blog example in Chapter 12, "Advanced KRL Programming."

- **Multiple domains.** The neck-pain scenario uses multiple endpoints in various domains to pull together important factions of Scott's online interactions. You can't and won't move everything to one domain any more than you'll move them all to one Web site. The neck-pain scenario demonstrates that developers can write event-driven applications that knit together multiple interaction domains like Web, email, and phone. This is a powerful idea that is difficult without the concepts of an active client and events.

- **Loosely coupled rules.** The interaction of rules in the neck-pain scenario was loosely coupled. The rules didn't call each other, but merely responded to events. This loose coupling was enhanced by the presence of the PDS because it served as a repository of information that various rules could use without that data having to be passed back and forth.

LIMITATIONS OF THE NECK-PAIN SCENARIO

As hard as I tried to create a demonstration of what is possible with event-driven applications on the Live Web in building this scenario, there are a few places where I made assumptions, took shortcuts, or ignored some potential problems:

- Events enable loose coupling, but they're not magic. While I've avoided it through design in the neck-pain scenario, loosely coupled rule sets may interfere with each other and give nondeterministic performance in real life. For example, two rule sets may need to write to the same field in the PDS. The PDS will need to incorporate appropriate data-isolation techniques and, where ordering is important, cooperating rule sets will need to serialize themselves.

- The events in this example were chosen for a single purpose: Project Neck Pain. Consequently, the semantics of the events are not worked out in their entirety and they may be overly broad or too narrow for their purpose.

- Even though I tried to make the application as loosely coupled as possible, there are places where I fell into the trap of chaining rules using specific events that only had one rule that would ever listen for them. This is an acceptable technique in KRL when rule chaining is desirable, but it limits loose coupling opportunities as you saw in Chapter 11, "Building Event Networks". I see the problem of creating events that are too narrowly defined as analogous to the problem of creating objects that are too narrowly defined. You miss opportunities for abstraction and code reuse. There is still plenty of room for programmers to exercise good design.

- As disclosed, there is currently no good way for service providers to create online free-busy calendars and no standard way to discover a service provider's free-busy calendar automatically. This could be overcome, however, through semantic markup (e.g., microdata, microformats, or RDFa) embedded in the page.

LOOSELY COUPLED RULE SETS

This chapter has described a near-future scenario in which a fictional user, Scott Phillips, is aided in his need to find and schedule a doctor by a set of cooperating rule sets. Instead of being coordinated by a central system that managed the workflow, the rule sets were coordinated by their response to a set of events raised to Scott's personal event network. The workflow emerged from the events instead of being scripted beforehand.

Viewing this scenario from the standpoint of events, rather than requests, creates a situation in which functionality can be layered over time. You can easily imagine

Scott Phillips getting a to-do list management system that works with his personal event network and later adding a tool to look for to-do items in his emails and automatically add them. Adding an email-parsing rule set doesn't require reconfiguring existing rule sets or explicitly linking the two applications together. Their cooperation is coordinated through events and a shared data space.

Where previous chapters have shown KRL working in single event domains, the scenario in this chapter shows how events from multiple domains can be processed in support of a person's purpose. The power of the Live Web is in such scenarios, where personal events and data combine to help people achieve their purposes with less hassle and fewer mundane activities.

ENDNOTES

1. See business.utah.gov.
2. Discussion at Internet Identity Workshop 2010B, November 2, 2010.
3. See http://twitter.com/edbott/statuses/76392546405855233.
4. See http://www.healthgrades.com/.

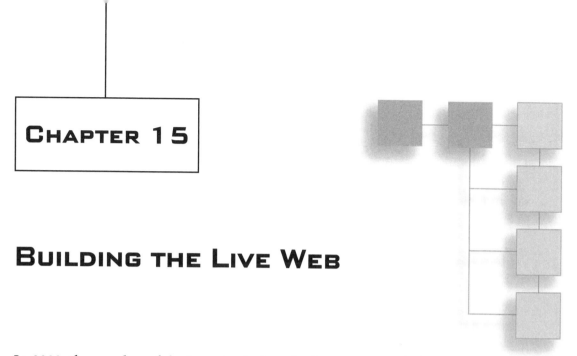

Chapter 15

Building the Live Web

In 2008, the number of devices attached to the Internet exceeded the number of people on Earth for the first time. Cisco estimates that by 2020, there will be 50 billion things attached to the global Internet. Eventually, everything that *can be* connected, will be.

What will happen when all these things are connected? One view, made popular in modern media, is the dystopian story of over-automation with people—like the hapless hero of Charlie Chaplin's *Modern Times*—conforming to the demands of their machine overlords: people as the servants of the machine. The vision put forth in this book is more hopeful—one in which online services and products cooperate to help people achieve their purposes. I believe that which of these two visions we ultimately realize depends in large part on whether we learn and use new programming models that reduce coupling and configuration.

A Cisco infographic on the Internet of Things paints a scenario of what can happen when devices and services cooperate.[1] Imagine your morning meeting is pushed back 45 minutes, so you can sleep later. But your car knows it needs gas and that take five minutes. There's an accident on your usual route to the train station that is causing 15-minute delays. And to top it all off, your train is running 20 minutes late. Consequently, your alarm adjusts to only give you an extra five minutes of sleep. Your coffee maker also adjusts to start brewing five minutes later. Your car automatically starts five minutes before your new departure time to defrost the windows and melt the ice that accumulated overnight. Hopefully, at this point in the book, this scenario doesn't seem like wishful thinking. I hope that as you read it, your mind immediately started to think about how it could be made real using the concepts and technologies discussed.

WHY THE LIVE WEB?

As you've seen in the preceding chapters, identity-aware, event-driven systems hold the promise of allowing people to engineer systems that enable scenarios like the one in the preceding section. Many significant trends are conspiring to make the Live Web real:

■ The marketing landscape is evolving rapidly. More and more devices are connected every day. Further, more and more of these devices are mobile. As you saw in Chapter 1, "The Live Web," mobile is important because it enables people to be connected everywhere, all the time. The rise of social networks means that people are not just consuming content, but are increasingly also producing it in the form of tweets, posts, photos, videos, and music, to mention just a few.

■ Regulatory restrictions on consumer tracking will eventually make the wholesale collection and trading of personal information difficult and expensive. That doesn't mean people won't be willing to share information about themselves, as the rise of social networks shows. But companies will increasingly have to entice people to share that data. The best way to do that is to provide user control over what is shared, when it is shared, and who sees it. As you saw in the Project Neck Pain scenario in Chapter 14, "Designing Event Systems," building systems that use personal data within these restrictions is not only plausible, but leads to better outcomes. The move from centralized, industrial-age stores of data to decentralized, individual-controlled pools of data will be painful for some companies, but provide a boon to others.

■ People will increasingly expect their context to be freely available to every service and product that they use. No wonder everyone is talking about "the cloud." The vision of the cloud is one in which your information and services are always available and consistent regardless of how or what you connect to them.

■ The app revolution is paving the way for users to hack their life in a more powerful way—creating an operating system for their lives. Smartphones are training people to expect that their devices will play a role in making their lives more convenient in ways they've only previously imagined. For example, the new iOS5 operating system I just installed on my iPhone includes the capability to set geolocation-based reminders. Now, I can have my phone remind me to pick up eggs as I drive past the local grocery store. That behavior is setting expectations for other applications and driving demand for the Live Web.

■ The Live Web provides ample opportunity to provide real value to people and thus represents a golden opportunity for future businesses. As people recognize the value from simple applications of event-driven systems, more and more companies will jump on the bandwagon.

WHY NOW?

Even if you believe my reasoning in the preceding section is sound, you may be wondering whether now is the right time to change. I believe it is. Here's why:

- The market is wide open. Coming up with doable scenarios for linking systems together is easy now. To be sure, there are some challenges to early adopters. You'll likely have to do some work convincing partners to raise events that you can use, but adding events to an existing API is generally easy[2] and the benefits are large.

- Momentum is building for opt-in (rather than opt-out) marketing and commerce applications. People are delighted when they choose to share something and see great benefit. These positive customer relations will be increasingly important for a population of shoppers who are increasingly jaded and feel they're being manipulated. The fourth-party commerce example explored in Chapter 13, "Business on the Live Web," shows just one example of how personal data and events can lead to new shopping tools.

Of course, these innovations are only the beginning, and the scenarios painted in this book are only a few of thousands that exist in everyday life. The Live Web provides a foundation for new businesses and new business models.

WHY KRL AND KRE?

The KRL and the open-source KRE event engine used as the foundation for all the examples in this book provide the means to build personal event networks that give rise to the Live Web. Certainly, KRE and KRL are not necessary for an event-driven, individual-aware system to emerge; the Evented API specification described in Appendix F, "The Evented API Specification," can be used with any programming language. Nevertheless, I believe they offer several important advantages that make them a good choice for building the Live Web.

- KRL and KRE are designed to work "in the cloud" from the ground up. You've seen how KRL executes in the cloud, how modules are stored and accessed in the cloud, and how interacting with APIs from other services is natively supported in the system and by the language. These features ease programmer burden in creating and maintaining applications that operate in the cloud.

- As described in Chapter 3, "Event Expressions: Filtering the Event Stream," and illustrated throughout the book, KRL provides a notation in the form of eventexes for describing and responding to complex event scenarios. You've seen that this enables developers to succinctly and clearly describe specific scenarios in a declarative manner. This not only saves time, but effort. Consider, however, the positive impact on system efficiency brought about through declaring event scenarios in eventexes. Because salience data can be automatically derived from eventexes and transmitted to endpoints, the number of individual events carried by the network goes down significantly because endpoints can pre-filter events that your applications don't care about. In fact, without such endpoint event filtering, the Internet could be overrun with signals no one cares about (i.e., noise).

■ As a rules language, KRL provides a succinct way of linking events to actions. The use of rules allows multiple actions to accrete for any given event scenario. This is one of the important features of KRL in support of loose coupling. New rules can often be added without old rules having to change. This allows users to install new apps that provide additional behavior without getting into a morass of configuration. Several of these techniques were discussed in Chapter 12, "Advanced KRL Programming."

■ KRE has a built-in identity layer that automatically supports personal events. This saves developers from having to sort out identity in their rule sets and creates a situation where personal event networks can emerge. If every developer builds their own identity system, the user is forced to link apps and thus spend more time configuring their personal event network. Fractured systems are the result. Further, because of the built-in identity layer, KRL applications get multitenancy for free. Entity variables, which can persist application data for an individual across invocations, are just one example of why the identity layer is so important for building Live Web applications.

■ KRE is open. There is no vendor lock-in. As a result, it is extensible and flexible. The Live Web cannot emerge on closed technologies. Although many closed systems will interact on the Live Web, like the static Web that precedes it, openness is a necessary condition for wide adoption.

CONCLUSION

In an opinion piece in *The Wall Street Journal*, Web pioneer Marc Andreessen, the inventor of the modern Web browser and founder of Netscape, said the following:

More and more major businesses and industries are being run on software and delivered as online services—from movies to agriculture to national defense. Many of the winners are Silicon Valley-style entrepreneurial technology companies that are invading and overturning established industry structures. Over the next 10 years, I expect many more industries to be disrupted by software, with new world-beating Silicon Valley companies doing the disruption in more cases than not.

Why is this happening now?

Six decades into the computer revolution, four decades since the invention of the microprocessor, and two decades into the rise of the modern Internet, all of the technology required to transform industries through software finally works and can be widely delivered at global scale.

…

With lower start-up costs and a vastly expanded market for online services, the result is a global economy that for the first time will be fully digitally wired—the dream of every cyber-visionary of the early 1990s, finally delivered, a full generation later.[3]

Recognizing that we have built all the pieces necessary to enable the future world we've been calling the Live Web is powerful and enabling. With the building blocks in place, we are at a point where we can connect anything we like to the Internet—and thus to everything else. Moreover, we have the concepts and technologies needed to create loose couplings of these products and services that read our intents and cooperate to help us achieve our purposes.

I add my voice to Andreessen's. The building blocks have been laid out, and the concepts are well understood. All that is necessary for us to build the Live Web is to pick up our tools and assemble it from the pieces provided by those who have gone before. I'm ready for the Live Web. I hope you are as well.

ENDNOTES

1. Cisco Platform Blog. "The Internet of Things." July 15, 2011. http://blogs.cisco.com/news/the-internet-of-things-infographic/.
2. See Appendix F, "The Evented API Specification," for details on the Evented API specification and the formal requirements for event generators.
3. Andreessen, Marc. "Why Software Is Eating the World." *The Wall Street Journal.* August 20, 2011. http://online.wsj.com/article/SB10001424053111903480904576 512250915629460.html.

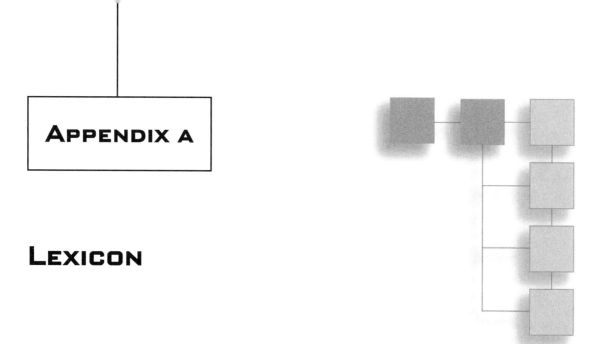

APPENDIX A

LEXICON

action—The effects that a rule has on the endpoint. Rules may have more than one action.

application program interface (API)—A set of specifications and code that allows one network service to talk to another.

attributes—Additional, defining, or explanatory characteristics of an event.

authentication—The act of confirming an attribute or attributes of a subject or entity. The best-known example of authentication is the nearly ubiquitous use of usernames and passwords on Web sites.

authorization—The granting of access or other privileges. Authentication is most often done in support of some kind of implicit or explicit authorization.

client-server—A programming model designed to use a request/response implementation. In this model, a responder waits until a request is made. When a request is made, the responder fulfills the request and the transaction is complete. The best example of this is the Web browser and the Web server. The browser makes the request of the server to provide the data stream from a specific URI (universal resource identifier), and the server responds to that request.

cloud computing—A popular term used to refer to the growing number of network services available independently from a specific organization or group. These services are currently classified in three main groups: SaaS (software as a service), PaaS (platform as a service), and IaaS (infrastructure as a service).

condition—The predicate phrase that is evaluated to determine whether a rule fires. When a rule fires, the consequent, containing action is evaluated. The condition may be empty. In that case, the rule *always* fires when it is selected.

context—The information surrounding and influencing rule set execution. Much context is user specific.

context automation—Using user context, networks, and programmed systems to automate interactions among multiple network services to help the user achieve a particular purpose.

cookie—A small amount of state information that a Web server supplies to a browser. The HTTP protocol specifies that when the user visits that Web site again, the browser will return the cookie, unchanged, to the server. Cookies are used to establish long-lived sessions across the stateless HTTP protocol.

coupling—The degree to which various program modules are dependent on one another. Coupling is generally described with the adjectives *tight* and *loose*. Tightly coupled systems exhibit a high degree of interdependency. Loosely coupled systems have less. Some degree of coupling is necessary to achieve anything. Tightly coupled systems are inflexible and difficult to maintain. Consequently, system architects desire to remove as much unnecessary coupling as possible.

data set—A fixed, static collection of data.

data source—A queriable, dynamic collection of data.

data stream—A sequential flow of data from a source to one or more destinations.

directive—Instructions sent to an endpoint as a result of a rule's actions.

endpoint—The software or device that is responsible for raising salient events to KRE and mediating the interaction with the client, including responding to KRL directives to the client. Endpoints are a type of event generator.

entity—A person, group, organization, non-profit organization, educational organization, government, or program. Some identity systems refer to entities as *subjects*.

event—Notification of an activity that took place at a particular time with specific attributes. Events represent state changes and are considered atomic.

event correlation—Linking two or more events temporally, syntactically, semantically, or by entity. For example, two events about the same airline flight can be correlated by the fact that they are about the same flight. Two events about two different flights might be correlated by the fact that one came before the other or that they had a passenger in common.

event domain—The area of activity within which an event occurs. Domains may specify a particular area of event activity, geography, organization, and so on.

event-driven architecture—A declarative style of system architecture where the messages specify a state change within one component to be communicated to other components. Contrast with request-response architecture.

event expression—A declaration of the relative temporal ordering or a group of events in an event scenario. An event expression is fulfilled when it matches events that meet the specified relationship. An event expression is often referred to as an *eventex*.

event name—*See* event type.

event scenario—A meaningful ordering and correlation of a group of events.

event type—The name or identifier of an event within a particular domain. Within a particular domain, event types must be unique.

fired—The state of a rule that has been selected based on its event expression and has a condition that is true.

fourth-party—An actor in a transaction that represents the buyer or customer. People usually refer to actors representing the seller as the *third-party*; the term *fourth-party* builds on that.

idempotent—An operation that can be applied multiple times without changing the end result beyond the initial application.

intent—A desire or plan to perform a specific action or set of actions with the goal of achieving a particular purpose.

JSON—An encoding for Web-based data structures. JSON has become the preferred encoding for API-based data retrieval and interchange. JSON is an acronym for JavaScript Object Notation, but is used widely in programming languages other than JavaScript.

personal event network—A physical or virtual network where events can be raised for a single entity. Virtual personal event networks arise on multi-tenanted event systems when events are segregated by entity and salience.

remote procedure call—An imperative style of system architecture where interactions are characterized by the caller issuing a command to the callee.

request-driven architecture—An interrogatory style of system architecture where messages between components consist of specific requests of the receiver.

RESTful API—An API that uses HTTP as the transport for communication and the HTTP method—GET, POST, and PUT—to transfer payloads between entities. RESTful APIs are a popular alternative to SOAP-based APIs.

rule—A programming language structure binding together an event expression, condition, and action. A rule takes action whenever the rule's event expression matches and the rule's condition is true. When this happens, we say the rule *fired*.

rule set—A collection of rules. By carefully crafting the set of rules in a rule set, programmers can create a specification of the actions to be taken on certain combinations of events.

salience—An event is salient or relevant to a given rule when it matches one of the primitive events in the rule's event expression. KRE has a salience API whereby an endpoint can determine before signaling an event whether or not a particular rule set cares about it. Salience is necessary both for the semantics of event expressions and for creating efficient event-based architectures.

selected—The state of a rule when the rule's event expression matches.

Web hook—An HTTP callback. An HTTP POST that occurs when something happens or a simple notification via HTTP POST.

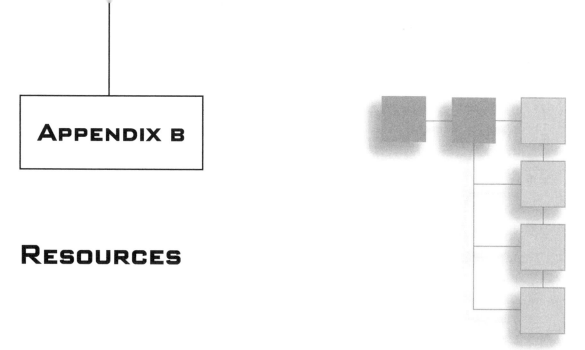

Appendix B

Resources

The following resources provide additional material and context regarding the subjects in this book in addition to the specific references in the endnotes.

KRL AND KRE

KRL programmers can use several Web sites to keep up with KRL and find a community of programmers to work with:

- Kynetx developer blog: http://code.kynetx.com
- KRL documentation: http://docs.kynetx.com
- Stack Overflow: http://www.stackoverflow.com (Use the tag `krl` when looking for KRL-related questions and answers.)
- KRE code repository on Github: https://github.com/kre/Kinetic-Rules-Engine

EVENTS

The following books and Web sites provide more information about events:

- *Event-Based Programming: Taking Events to the Limit* by Ted Faison (Apress, 2006)
- *Event-Driven Architecture: How SOA Enables the Real-Time Enterprise* by Hugh Taylor, Angela Yochem, Les Phillips, and Frank Martinez (Addison-Wesley Professional, 2009)

- *Event Processing in Action* by Opher Etzion and Peter Niblett (Manning Publications, 2010)

- *The Power of Events: An Introduction to Complex Event Processing in Distributed Enterprise Systems* by David Luckham (Addison-Wesley Professional, 2002)

- Complex Event Processing (blog): http://www.complexevents.com/

- Event Processing Thinking (blog): http://epthinking.blogspot.com/

- Evented API specification: http://www.eventedapi.org/

LIVE WEB

The following Web sites provide useful information about APIs and their impact on the Internet:

- Craig Burton's blog: http://www. craigburton.com/

- Programmable Web: http://www.programmableweb.com/

In addition, the following book takes a high-level look at many of the important trends on the Internet today and what they mean for commerce—on and off the Internet: *The Intention Economy: When Customers Take Charge* by David "Doc" Searls (Harvard University Press, 2012). The book specifically mentions the Live Web, KRL, and KRE. Readers of this book will find Doc's insights invaluable in understanding how personal event networks and the Live Web relate to much of what we take for granted on the Internet today.

IDENTITY

The following book and Web site provide more information about identity and related technologies:

- *Digital Identity* by Phillip Windley (O'Reilly Media, 2005)

- Kim Cameron's Identity Weblog: http://www.identityblog.com/

SEMANTIC WEB

The following resources are useful for understanding the power and requirements of the Semantic Web:

- *Pull: The Power of the Semantic Web to Transform Your Business* by David Siegel (Portfolio Hardcover, 2009)

- *The Power of Pull: How Small Moves, Smartly Made, Can Set Big Things in Motion* by John Hagel III, John Seely Brown, and Lang Davidson (Basic Books, 2010)

JQUERY

The following book and Web site provide more information about jQuery:

- *jQuery in Action 2nd Edition* by Bear Bibeault and Yehuda Katz (Manning Publications, 2010)
- jQuery Web site: http://jquery.com/

APPENDIX C

GETTING STARTED WITH KRL

There are two ways to get started using KRL. The first and easiest is to use the free online IDE and execution platform provided by Kynetx. The other is to install and run your own Kinetic Rule Engine.

USING KYNETX

To evaluate KRL rule sets on the Kynetx online service, do the following:

1. Visit http://developer.kynetx.com/ and, if necessary, create an account.

2. Log into the IDE at http://apps.kynetx.com/apps.

3. Click New App and give your new app a name.

4. Click the Create App button. The IDE gives you a sample Hello World app in the code, so you don't need to change anything to have a simple working app.

5. Click the Test link above the editing window and drag the bookmarklet from the overlay window that appears to your browser bookmark bar.

6. Click the bookmarklet; the rule should fire.

To fire the app you just created from the Kynetx Browser Extension (KBX), follow these steps:

1. Edit the `domain` line in the dispatch section of the rule set by uncommenting the `domain` pragma. It should now read as follows:

```
dispatch {
```

```
        domain "exampley.com"
    }
```

2. Click on the Deploy button above the editing window in the IDE.

3. Click the Deploy link to the right of the top-most version (probably version 1 unless you've modified and saved the application you created above beyond what's outlined here). You should see the deployment history change.

4. Click the Distribute button to the right of the Deploy button and click on the listing URL. If you've already installed KBX, the app will deploy to your KBX. If not, you'll be led through the installation process for KBX.

5. Visit www.exampley.com to see your app fire.

You can now edit the rule set to do other things and see your changes reflected in the running application.

Running Your Own KRE

The open-source code repository for KRE is on Github at https://github.com/kre/Kinetic-Rules-Engine/wiki. Installation instructions as well as information about how to contribute to the project are on the project wiki on Github. The installation is not for the faint of heart. You can ask questions about installation at StackOverflow.com using the tag kre. Alternatively, tweet your questions with the #kynetx hashtag.

Debugging KRL Applications

A complete treatise on debugging KRL applications is beyond the scope of this appendix, but there are a few things you should check:

■ You can turn logging on in your rule set by adding the logging pragma to the meta section:

logging on

■ You can see the result of logging, as well as the JavaScript returned to browser applications, using the Chrome console (right-click on the page and select Inspect Element) or by installing the Firebug extension in Firefox. When a rule set is fired from a bookmarklet, the <script/> tags will be visible in the page and you can inspect their contents.

■ The URL in a <script/> tag can be pasted directly in the address bar of your browser or used in a command-line tool such as curl to see the results of the execution and debug statements.

- The debug output can be daunting at first, but you'll get used to seeing what rules are firing. You'll also see the results from certain operations. You may find it handy in development to avoid chaining operators so that you can see intermediate results in the debug output.

- If you're running the rule set as an app in KBX, ensure that the green arrow is displayed. If not, it means that KBX does not recognize that the app is supposed to run on the current domain. Check the domain name and ensure it matches the `domain` pragma in the dispatch section of the rule set.

- Make sure you're running the version of the rule set you believe should be running by checking the deployment section of the IDE.

- Build rule sets one at a time to ensure the behavior is developing as you think it should.

- Once you release a rule set for others to use, ErrorStack is the best way to see problems in your application. See the following pages for more detail:

  - http://docs.kynetx.com/docs/ErrorStack

  - http://www.windley.com/archives/2011/05/error_handling_in_krl.shtml

- Use `window.console.log()` in emitted JavaScript to see the results of JavaScript execution.

- Use http://ktest.heroku.com/ to quickly iterate and test your code

- Use JSONLint to pretty print JSON embedded within your rule set logging.

Again, ask questions on StackOverflow.com using the tag `krl` or tweet your questions with the hashtag #kynetx.

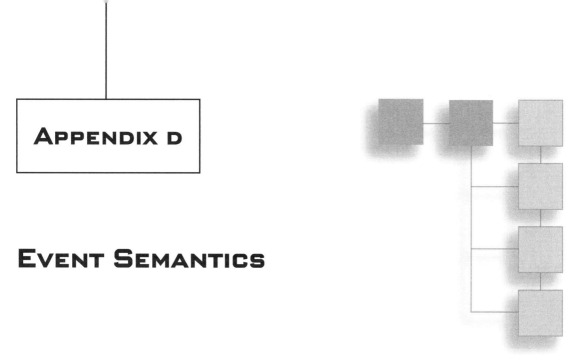

Appendix D

Event Semantics

This appendix presents formal semantics of some of the event expressions presented in Chapter 3, "Event Expressions: Filtering the Event Stream." The semantics of event expressions are described in terms of state machines because, as noted in Chapter 3, event expressions are no more powerful that regular expressions over the stream of events.

Primitive Events

A primitive event is a simple state machine of two states, as shown in Figure D.1. The initial state indicates that the event has not occurred. All occurrences except A loop back to the initial state. The final state is reached whenever primitive A occurs.

For the transition A in Figure D.1 to complete, the event domain and event type must match and the attribute expression, if any, has to be true.

Compound Events

Compound events are created from primitive events. The following sections describe the state machine semantics of the seven primary compound events.

before

A before B indicates that event A occurred before event B. For example:

```
select when web pageview "bar.html"
    before web pageview "/archives/\d+/x.html"
```

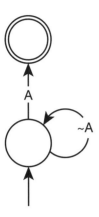

Figure D.1
Primitive event transitions for event A.

The state machine describing `before` is shown in Figure D.2.

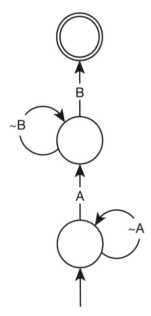

Figure D.2
State transitions for `A before B`.

From the initial state, event A causes a transition to an intermediate state. Anything except event B causes the state machine to remain in the intermediate state. Event B causes a transition to the final state.

after

Given that A `after` B is equivalent to B `before` A, the semantics of `after` can be easily worked out from Figure D.2 by replacing A for B and B for A.

then

A then B indicates that event A occurred, and then event B occurred, with no intervening, salient events.

```
select when web pageview "bar.html"
    then web pageview "/archives/\d+/foo.html"
```

The semantics of A then B are shown in Figure D.3.

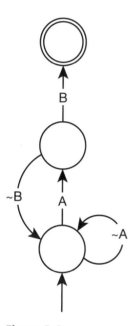

Figure D.3
State transitions for A then B.

As you would expect, the diagram for A then B is similar to the one for A before B shown in Figure D.2. The only difference is that after the transition to the intermediate state has occurred, anything except event B returns to the initial state rather than remaining in the intermediate state. This enforces the requirement that B follow directly from A with no intermediate events.

and

A and B indicates that event A occurred and event B occurred in any order.

```
select when web pageview "bar.html"
        and web pageview "/archives/\d+/foo.html"
```

The state diagram for A and B is shown in Figure D.4.

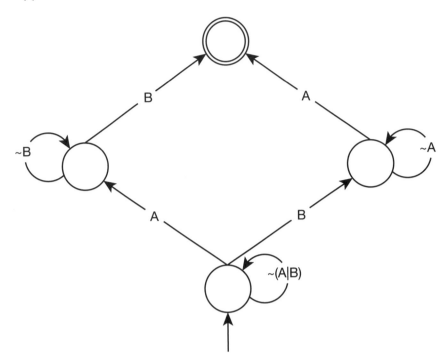

Figure D.4
State transitions for A and B.

The state diagram for A and B works similarly to the one for A before B except that either event A or event B can cause a transition to an intermediate state that then looks for the other event to reach the final state.

or

A or B indicates that event A occurred or event B occurred.

```
select when web pageview "bar.html"
      or web pageview "/archives/\d+/foo.html"
```

The state diagram for A or B is shown in Figure D.5.

The state diagram for A or B is simple, with two transitions from the initial state to the final state for event A or event B and anything except one of those events remaining in the initial state.

between

A between(B, C) indicates that event A occurred between event B and event C.

```
select when pageview "mid.html" between(web pageview "first.html",
                                web pageview "last.html")
```

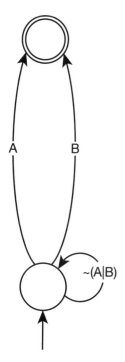

Figure D.5
State transition for A or B.

The state diagram giving the semantics of A between (B, C) is shown in Figure D.6.

The state diagram for A between(B, C) looks like the state diagram we imagine would be created for B before (A before C).

not between

A not between(B, C) indicates that event A did not occur between event B and event C.

```
select when web pageview "mid.html" not between(web pageview "first.html",
                                      web pageview "last.html")
```

The state diagram for A not between (B, C) is shown in Figure D.7.

The state diagram for A not between(B, C) looks like the diagram for B before C except that event A causes a transition back to the initial state.

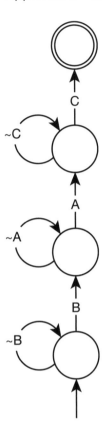

Figure D.6
State transitions for A between(B, C).

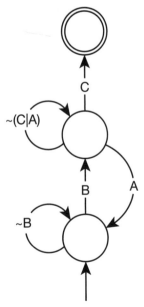

Figure D.7
State transitions for A not between (B, C).

Combining State Machines

Compound eventexes necessitate combining the state machines of an eventex's constituent events. Combining two state machines involves the following:

1. Defining a new state machine

2. Adding all the states and transitions from the two original state machines to the new one

3. Joining the appropriate states (We only join initial and final states to other initial and final states. Intermediate states are never joined.)

4. Declaring the new initial state

5. Declaring the new final state

To understand what I mean by "joining the appropriate states," consider the state machine for the event expression A or B. The initial state of A must be joined to the initial state of B. Likewise, the final state of A must be joined to the final state of B. To join two states, you create a new state and copy the transitions in and out of the old states to the new one. This is essentially the same as linking two states by a null transition and then removing it procedurally.

Because compound event expressions can be nested, the state machines you combine are not always primitive event state machines. They can be compound state machines in their own right. Because you never have to join anything but initial and final states, the complexity of the state machine is immaterial.

Temporal Constraints

Any compound operator can have a temporal constraint attached. For example, the following `before` eventex has a temporal constraint (denoted by the `within` keyword):

```
select when web pageview "bar.html"
    before web pageview "/archives/\d+/x.html"
    within 5 min
```

This eventex will only match if the two events happen in the correct order and within five minutes of each other.

A temporal constraint is a predicate that is computed as follows:

```
time into final state - time out of initial state < threshold
```

The state machine describing before with a temporal constraint is shown in Figure D.8. Note that the calculation of the temporal state transitions is done immediately upon entering the final state.

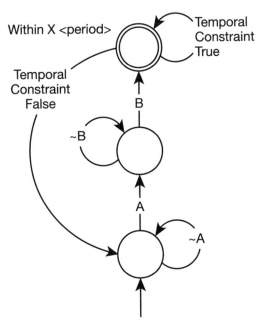

Figure D.8
State transitions for A before B with temporal constraints.

You can add similar facilities to any of the state machines for the compound operators described previously. Note that as state machines are combined for compound eventexes, the temporal transition will not always be between a final and an initial state.

VARIABLE ARITY AND GROUP OPERATORS

As you saw in Chapter 3, most variable arity and group operators can be rewritten in terms of the aforementioned compound operators. The two that were not described that way, count and repeat, are described by the following state machines.

count

count(n, E) indicates that event E occurs n times. The count restarts after the entire eventex matches.

```
select when count(3, E)
```

The state diagram for count(n, E) is shown in Figure D.9. The ellipsis indicates that this pattern of state-machine construction is continued to create the proper number of transitions.

count(n, E)

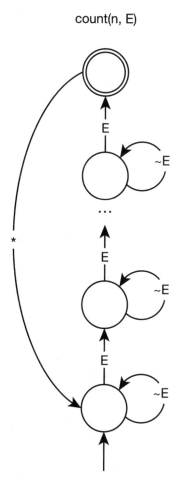

Figure D.9
State transitions for count (n, E).

Note that any event transitions from the final state to the initial state, so that this eventex fires the event nth time event E is received.

repeat

repeat(n, E) indicates that event E has occurred n times.

select when repeat(3, E)

The state diagram for repeat(n, E) is shown in Figure D.10. The ellipsis indicates that this pattern of state-machine construction is continued to create the proper number of transitions.

count(n, E)

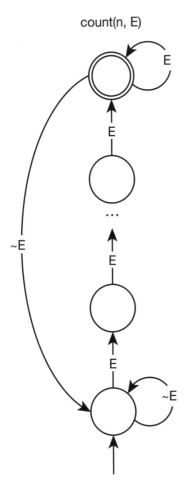

Figure D.10
State transitions for repeat (n, E).

Note that the transition for E from the final state is to the final state, so that this eventex continues to match as long as event E continues.

The KRL Expression Language

KRL contains a complete expression language for use inside rules. This appendix describes the operation of the expression language.

Literals

The following literals can be used within KRL.

Booleans

The Boolean values are `true` and `false`.

Numbers

KRL supports integer and real values. A negative number is created by prepending the minus sign (−) to a number in the usual fashion.

Strings

Strings are created by enclosing characters in double quotes. You can put a double quote inside a string by escaping it with a backslash:

```
a = "I can put a quote character, \", in my string using a backslash"
```

Arrays

Arrays are created by enclosing comma-delimited expressions in square brackets like so:

```
["a", "b", "c"]
```

Arrays use zero-base indexing and can be referenced in the usual manner:

```
a = [1,4,3,6,5];
b = a[1] // b = 4
```

Note

Comments start with a double slash (//) and go to the end of the line. The examples in this appendix frequently use comments to show return values.

Note that array references only work for arrays of one dimension. For example, `c[1]` `[2]` is not allowed (presuming c is an array of arrays). Multidimensional arrays can be dereferenced using the `pick` operator (described momentarily).

Maps

Maps—also called *hashes*, *dictionaries*, and *associative arrays*—are created by enclosing comma-delimited name-value pairs in curly braces, like so:

```
some_hash = {"foo" : "bar",
             "fizz" : {"a" : 5, "b" : 6},
             "flop" : [1, 2, 3]};
```

Maps can be queried in the traditional manner using a key enclosed in curly braces:

```
my_val = some_hash{"foo"}; // returns "bar"
```

KRL allows deep queries by what are known as *hash paths*. A hash path is an array of keys representing a path to a value in a deeply nested map:

```
another_val = some_hash{["foo", "b"]}; // returns 6
```

You can also retrieve values from the map, you use the `pick` operator:

```
my_val = some_hash.pick("$..foo"); // returns "bar"
```

You can also merge hashes using the `put` operator:

```
new_map = {"foo" : "bar1", "bazz": 4};
some_hash.put(new_map);
// returns {"foo" : "bar1", "fizz" : 3, "flop" : [1, 2, 3], "bazz": 4}
```

More information about the `put` operator can be found later in this appendix.

Extended Quoting

Some KRL statements and expressions use extended quotes. Extended quotes allow multiple line passages that contain the double quote symbol (") to be more easily entered.

There are two types of extended quotes in KRL:

- **Chevrons.** Chevrons enclose the items to be quoted in double less-than and greater-than signs (<<....>>). For example:

```
somevar = <<
 <p>This is <em>some</em> HTML.<br/>
 <a href="http://www.google.com">Search Google</a>
 </p>
>>;
```

  Values inside chevrons are treated as strings. The white space is preserved.

- **Clown hats.** Clown hats are used to quote JavaScript (<|...|>). The primary difference between chevrons and clown hats is that non-essential whitespace may not be preserved by the execution engine for strings inside clown hats.

```
somecode = <|
 var e = 5;
 var f = e + 6;
 |>;
```

Beestings

KRL extended quotes support the beesting operator, making them simple templating systems. Inside an extended quote, expression values can be referenced using the #{<expr>} syntax. For example, suppose you've stored 10 and 20 in the variables a and b:

```
somevar = <<
  The average value is #{(a+ b)/2}
>>;
```

The value of somevar would be "The average value is 15."

REGULAR EXPRESSIONS

Regular expressions are enclosed in matching characters with a prepended re. The conventional character for enclosing a regular expression is a slash (/), but a pound sign (#) can be used as well: re/.../ or re#...#. KRL regular expressions closely follow the conventions for Perl regular expressions.[1] The following modifiers may appear after the closing character:

- **i.** The i modifier makes the regular expression case insensitive.

- **g.** The g modifier applies the regular expression globally.

For example, the following code replaces the first instance of foo in p with bar:

```
p.replace(re/foo/, "bar")
```

In contrast, the following code replaces all instances of foo in p with bar:

```
p.replace(re/foo/g, "bar")
```

PREDICATE EXPRESSIONS

Several built-in, infix operators allow testing for equality and inequality. For numbers, <, >, <=, >=, ==, and != are used. For strings, eq, neq, and like are used.

Like takes a regular expression as its second argument and returns true if it matches the string given as its first argument. Arguments to these operators can be any valid expression.

```
spicy = cheese like re/(nacho|pepperjack)/;
```

The following are all valid predicate expressions:

```
c == 5
page:var("city") eq "Blackfoot"
"Lindon" neq location:city()
weather:curr_temp() < 90
location:city() + ", WA" eq city
5 * (weather:curr_temp() - 32) / 9 < 0
```

As can be seen from the preceding examples, a number of built-in libraries provide predicates that can be used inside predicate expressions. The documentation for those libraries gives details about their operation.

Compound predicate expressions are created using the operators &&, ||, and not to express conjunction, disjunction, and negation, respectively. Parentheses are used to group expressions for precedence.

ARITHMETIC EXPRESSIONS

KRL supports the standard arithmetic operators: +, -, *, %, and /, using infix notation. Parentheses are used to group expressions when normal precedence rules are to be overridden.

The following expressions demonstrate arithmetic expressions in KRL:

```
modulus = 17 % 3; // modulus = 1
divide = 22 / 10; // divide = 2.2
multiply = 10 * 4.2; // multiple = 42
```

```
add = 5 + 10; // add = 15
subtract = 3.8 - 12.4; // subtract = -8.6
all_of_them = (10 + 5) / (5 + 5 * 2); // all_of_them = 1
```

STRING EXPRESSIONS

KRL supports string concatenation using the + symbol:

```
x = "Hello " + "World!";
```

There are also a number of operators for strings described later in the documentation.

CONDITIONAL EXPRESSIONS

KRL provides support for conditional expressions with the following syntax:

```
<pred> => <consequent expr> | <alternate expr>
```

This is akin to the ?: ternary operator found in the C family of languages.

Conditional expressions can be nested to produce structures like the following:

```
<pred0> => <expr0> |
<pred1> => <expr1> |
<pred2> => <expr2> |
  ...
          | <exprn>
```

Because of the limitations of the parser, most predicates will need to be enclosed in parentheses:

```
z = (x > y) => y | 3;
```

FUNCTIONS

KRL supports functions as first-class objects. KRL supports only anonymous functions, but they can be given names by binding them to a variable in a declaration. Here's an example:

```
add5 = function(x) {
        x + 5
    };
```

Functions are declared using the keyword function followed by a possibly empty, parentheses-delimited, comma-separated list of parameters and a block of code. The code block of the function is delimited by curly braces and contains a list of semicolon-separated declarations and a single expression. The declarations are optional, but every function code block must end with an expression. The value of the final expression is the return value of the function.

Functions are statically executed (i.e., free variables are bound in the environment in which they are defined, not the environment in which they are executed) and can be recursive. KRE limits the number of times a function can be called in any given rule set evaluation to protect against runaway code. The value of the recursion threshold is installation specific. Here's an example of a recursive function in KRL:

```
fact = function(n) {
            (n <= 0) => 1
                | n * fact(n-1)
        }
```

This example also shows the syntax for function application (e.g., fact(n-1)). An expression resulting in a function is followed by a possibly empty, parentheses-delimited, comma-separated list of expressions. Function application is applicative-order; the expressions representing the function and the arguments are evaluated and the result of executing the function expression (the operator, or rator) is then applied to the results of the evaluation of the arguments (the operands, or rands). Obviously, the rator must be a function.

To see how declarations appear in the body of a function, consider the following example, which uses Newton's method to calculate square roots:[2]

```
sqrt = function(x) {
    average = function(x,y) { (x + y) / 2 };
    good_enough = function(guess, x) {
        v = (guess * guess) - x;
        v < 0.01 && v > -0.01
    };
    improve = function(guess, x) {
        average(guess, (x / guess))
    };
    sqrt_iter = function(guess, x) {
        good_enough(guess, x) => guess
                            | sqrt_iter(improve(guess,x), x)
    };
    sqrt_iter(1.0, x)
    }
```

Functions can return functions as values and functions can be passed as the arguments to other functions and operators in KRL. The following example defines a generalized summation function called sum that sums the numbers from a to b incrementing using the function inc and applying the function f to each term:

```
sum = function(f, a, inc, b) {
  (a > b) => 0
       | f(a) + sum(f, inc(a), inc, b)
};
```

You can use `sum` to define a function that sums the cubes from a to b:

```
plus1 = function(x) { x + 1 };
cube = function(x) { x * x * x };
sum_cubes = function(a, b) {
  sum(cube, a, plus1, b)
}
```

As another example, you can define a function that creates incrementor functions. When given a number, it returns a function that increments by that value:

```
inc_gen = function(n) { function(x){ x + n } };
```

Now you use `inc_gen` to generate other functions:

```
plus1 = inc_gen(1);
plus25 = inc_gen(25);
```

USER-DEFINED ACTIONS

User-defined actions are created using the `defaction` keyword. The `defaction` keyword closely follows the syntax of functions. User-defined actions allow for data preprocessing and the execution of one or more actions. User-defined actions are useful for wrapping actions to allow for composite actions or a cleaner syntax surrounding existing actions for a common use case.

```
defaction(<arguments>) {
  configure using key1 = value1 and key2 = value2 .. and keyN = valueN
  <declaration0>
  ...
  <declarationN>
  <action block>
}
```

The arguments are a possibly empty, comma-separated list of variable names. Optional arguments can be specified with the `configure` statement, as shown here, and are given default values. Zero or more declarations can be included to prepare data for the action block.

The action block is the same as the action block in a rule. Any action, including a user-defined action, can be used in the action block. Actions can be simple or compound. A simple action is a valid action block. For example, the following defines an action called `send_warning` using the `notify` action:

```
send_warning = defection(msg) {
  notify("Warning!", msg);
}
```

Compound actions must be enclosed in curly brackets (`{ ... }`). Suppose, for example, that in addition to putting up a notification, you wished to place the warning message in a `<div/>` element on the page:

```
send_warning = defection(msg) {
  {notify("Warning!", msg);
  append("#warning_div", msg)
  }
}
```

You can use optional parameters to modify `send_warning` so that it is sticky by default. (The default behavior for `notify` is for the notification to fade after six seconds. When the `sticky` parameter is true, notifications are permanent until the user closes them.)

```
send_warning = defaction(msg) {
  configure using transitory = false
  notify("Warning!", msg)
    with sticky = not transitory
  }
```

The variable `send_warning` only has meaning in an action context within a rule. The following shows the use of `send_warning` and its optional parameter in the action of a rule:

```
if error_level > 12 && error_level < 15 then
  send_warning("Abnormal error levels")
    with transitory = true
```

Because user-defined actions are first-class values (i.e., they can be returned as the result of executing an expression), they can be passed into functions or other user-defined actions and returned as the result from a function. You can thus write recursive actions.

OPERATORS

Operators are applied to expressions using post-fix notation with a period (`.`) as the separator. For example, if a is a string, the `lc()` operator, which lowers the case of all the characters in the string, is applied to a as follows:

```
a.lc()
```

Operators can be chained. The following expression splits a into an array and then calculates the length of the resulting array:

```
a.split(re/;/).length()
```

The following sections describe operators currently available. They are organized based on the kind of value on which they operate.

Universal

Several operators can be applied to objects of any type.

as()

The as() operator coerces objects of one type to be an object of another. The target type is given as a string argument to the operator. The following types are available in KRL:

- **str.** Coerce the target to have type string.
- **num.** Coerce the target to have type number.
- **regexp.** Coerce the target to have type regular expression.
- **trail.** Coerce the target to have type trail.

For example, the following constructs a string and then turns it into a regular expression that can be used by the replace() operator:

```
("/q=" + q + "/i").as("regexp")
```

Not every type can be coerced to another. The following coercions are valid:

- Strings can be coerced to numbers and regular expressions.
- Numbers can be coerced to strings.
- Regular expressions can be coerced to strings.
- Trails can be coerced to arrays.

typeof()

The typeof() operator returns the type of the object to which it is applied. For example:

```
nums = [1, 2, 3]
nums_type = nums.typeof() // nums_type = "array"
```

Arrays

The following operators are valid for arrays.

append()

The append() operator combines two arrays into a single array containing all elements belonging to the original arrays. For example:

```
first_array.append(second_array)
```

If either the object or the argument is not an array, it will be wrapped in an array.

The following examples show the behavior of append() for various types of objects:

```
a_s = ["apple","tomato"];
b_s = ["carrot","tomato"];
a  = 10;
b  = 11;
a_s.append(b_s)    // returns ["apple","tomato","carrot","tomato"]
a_s.append(a)      // returns ["apple","tomato",10]
a.append(b)        // returns [10, 11]
```

filter()

The filter() operator takes a function as its only argument returns an array. The new array contains any members of the original array for which the function evaluates to true. The function given as the argument must take one argument and return a Boolean value. The length of the new array will be less than or equal to the length of the original array. For example:

```
a = [3, 4, 5];
c = a.filter(function(x){x<5})   // c = [3, 4]
```

head()

The head() operator returns the first member of an array as a single value.

```
c = [3, 4, 5];
c.head()    // c = 3
```

join()

The join() operator takes a string as its sole argument. The original array is joined into a single string with the argument placed between the array elements. For example:

```
a = ["A","B","C"];
c = a.join(";");    // c = "A;B;C"
```

length()

The length() operator returns a number that is the length of the array. Note that because arrays use zero-based indexing, the length is the one greater than the index value of the last element in the array. For example:

```
a = ["A","B","C"];
c = a.length();    // c = 3
```

map()

The map() operator returns an array that contains the results of applying the function given as the operator's argument to each member of the original array. The function given as an argument must take one argument. The length of the resulting array will be equal to the length of the target array. For example:

```
a = [3, 4, 5];
c = a.map(function(x){x+2}) // c = [5, 6, 7]
```

sort()

The sort() operator takes an optional argument and returns an array that is the original array sorted according to the following criteria:

- If the argument is empty, the array will be sorted in ascending order using a string comparison.

- If the argument is the string reverse, the array will be sorted in descending order using a string comparison.

- If the argument is a function, the function will be used to perform pair-wise comparisons of the members of the array for purposes of doing the sort. The function must take two arguments and return true or false. If the result of the comparison is true, then the elements will be swapped.

For example:

```
a = [5, 3, 4, 1, 12];
c = a.sort();              // c = [1, 12, 3, 4, 5]
d = a.sort("reverse");     // d = [5, 4, 3, 12, 1]
e = a.sort(function(a, b) { a > b }); // e = [1, 3, 4, 5, 12]
```

Note that because the default behavior is to do a string comparison, number sorts can give unexpected results, as shown in the first example.

tail()

The `tail()` operator returns a new array that is the original array with the first element removed. For example:

```
a = [3, 4, 5];
c = a.tail();  // c = [4, 5]
```

Strings

The following operators are valid for strings.

decode()

The `decode()` operator converts a JSON string into the equivalent KRL data structure. For example:

```
a = "[3, 4, 5]";
c = a.decode();  // c = [3, 4, 5]
```

extract()

The `extract()` operator matches the string using a regular expression given as the sole argument and returns the specified capture groups as an array. For example:

```
foo = "I like cheese";
my_str = "This is a string";
a = my_str.extract(re/(is)/)            // a = ["is"]
b = my_str.extract(re/(s.+).*(.ing)/)   // b = ["s is a st","ring"]
c = my_str.extract(re/(boot)/)          // c = []
d = foo.extract(re/like (\w+)/)         // d = ["cheese"]
e = foo.extract(re/(e)/g)               // e ["e","e","e","e"]
```

Note that if the regular expression does not contain at least one capture group, the resulting array will be empty.

lc()

The `lc()` operator returns the lowercase version of the original string. For example:

```
a = "Hello World";
c = a.lc()  // c = "hello world"
```

match()

The `match()` operator takes a regular expression as its argument. The result is true if the regular expression matches the string and false otherwise. For example:

```
my_str = "This is a string";
a = my_str.match(re/is/)     // a = true
b = my_str.match(re/mouse/)  // b = false
```

replace()

The replace() operator takes two arguments: a regular expression and a string. The returned string is the original string with any match of the regular expression replaced by the second argument. You can use any captured values in the second, substitute string by naming them with $1, $2, and so on. The first captured value will be substituted for $1, the second for $2, and so on. For example:

```
my_str = "This is a string";
my_url = "http://www.amazon.com/gp/products/123456789/";
a = my_str.replace(re/is/,"ese");         // a = "These is a string"
b = my_str.replace(re/is/g,"ese");        // b = "These ese a string"
c = my_str.replace(re/this/,"That");      // c = "This is a string" (no change)
d = my_str.replace(re/this/i,"That");     // d = "That is a string"
e = my_url.replace(re#^http://([A-Za-z0-9.-]+)/.*#,"$1");
   // e = "www.amazon.com"
```

In the final example, I was careful to ensure that the regular expression matched the entire URL, so that the substitution of $1 resulted in just the domain name. This same result could be more easily achieved using extract()—although the result, e, would be an array:

```
e = my_url.extract(re#^http://([A-Za-z0-9.-]+)/#);
```

split()

The split() operator takes a regular expression as its sole argument. The regular expression is used to split the original string into an array. For example:

```
a = "A;B;C"
c = a.split(re/;/)    // c = ["A","B","C"]
```

sprintf()

The sprintf() operator can be applied to either a number or a string. The operator takes a formatting string as its sole argument. The formatting string follows the conventions for sprintf() established in other languages. Specifically, the KRL version of sprintf() follows the formatting conventions for Perl.[3] For example:

```
a = 10
c = a.sprintf("< %d>")    // c = "< 10>"
```

uc()

The uc() operator returns the uppercase version of the original string. For example:

```
a = "Hello World";
c = a.uc()  // c = "HELLO WORLD"
```

Maps

The operators in this section are valid for maps. Many of these operators take an argument that is a hash path. A *hash path* is an array whose elements represent the key values (for a map) or array indices of a path from the root of a complex data structure to the element of interest. For example, consider the following data structure:

```
{ "colors" : "many",
  "pi" : [3,1,4,1,5,6,9],
  "foo" : {"bar" : {10:"I like cheese"}}
}
```

The hash path ["foo", "bar"] references the following map inside the data structure:

```
{"bar" : {10:"I like cheese"}}
```

delete()

The delete() operator takes a hash path argument designating the member of the original data structure that should be deleted. The delete() operator returns a new data structure with the specified member deleted. If the path is invalid, nothing is deleted and the new data structure is identical to the original. For example:

```
a = { "colors" : "many",
      "pi" : [3,1,4,1,5,6,9],
      "foo" : {"bar" : {10:"I like cheese"}}
    };
c = a.delete(["foo", "bar", 10])
// c = { "colors" : "many",
//       "pi" : [3,1,4,1,5,6,9],
//       "foo" : {}
//     }
```

encode()

The encode() operator returns a string containing the JSON representation of the data structure to which it is applied. For example:

```
a = {"a" : 10, "b" : [1, 3, "hello"]};
b = a.encode() // b = "{'a' : 10, 'b' : [1, 3, 'hello']}";
```

keys()

The keys() operator returns the keys of the map to which it is applied. Without an argument, the keys at the top level of the map are returned. The operator also accepts a hash path argument. For example:

```
a = { "colors" : "many",
      "pi" : [3,1,4,1,5,6,9],
      "foo" : {"bar" : {10: "I like cheese", "a" : 12}
   }};
b = a.keys();                    // b = ["colors", "pi", "foo"]
c = a.keys(["foo", "bar"]); // c = [10, "a"]
```

put()

The put() operator takes two arguments: a hash path and a new element to be inserted. The result is a new data structure with the element inserted at the location specified by the hash path. If the path specifies a location that does not exist, it will be created. For example:

```
a = { "colors" : "many",
      "pi" : [3,1,4,1,5,6,9]
   };
b = {"flop" : 12};
c = a.put(["foo"], b);
// c = { "colors" : "many",
//       "pi" : [3,1,4,1,5,6,9],
//       "foo" : {"flop" : 12}
//    };
d = a.put(["foo", "bar"], b);
// d = { "colors" : "many",
//       "pi" : [3,1,4,1,5,6,9],
//       "foo" : {"bar" : {"flop" : 12}}
//    };
```

pick() AND query()

In addition to the operators discussed in the last section, KRL has two operators, pick() and query(), that function like operators from the last section but use embedded little languages. Consequently, they are very powerful.

pick()

The pick() operator is used to select portions of a complex data structure. Pick() can be applied to any valid expression that returns a data structure. The pick() operator and its little language, JSONPath, are discussed in this section. The `pick()` operator takes two arguments:

■ The first argument is a string that represents a JSONPath expression that will select some portion of the data structure.

■ The second, optional argument is a Boolean that determines the return type of the result. If true, `pick()` will always return an array; otherwise, `pick()` will return whatever is appropriate. The default value is false. Ensuring the result is always an array is useful when `pick()` is used in a `foreach` statement.

JSONPath

Stefan Goessner developed JSONPath as an analog to XPath for use with JSON data. The following description is modified from his description of JSONPath.[4] If you're familiar with XPath, the concepts behind JSONPath should be clear.

In KRL, JSONPath expressions give a path to a portion of a KRL data structure. JSON-Path expressions are more powerful than the hash paths used in the `put()`, `delete()`, and `keys()` operators.

The root of a JSONPath expression is designated by the dollar symbol ($). Paths use dot notation to reference map keys and array index notation to reference array elements. For example, the following JSONPath expression would reference the `title` element in the first member of the array with the key `book` in the structure with the key `store`:

```
$.store.book[0].title
```

JSONPath allows the wildcard symbol (*) for member names and array indices. The recursive descent operator (`..`), which must be followed by a key, descends through the data structure until the named key is found. For example, the previous example could be rewritten as follows:

```
$..book[0].title
```

You can use KRL expressions as an alternative to explicit names or indices by using the at symbol (@) for the current object. Filter expressions are given using the question mark. For example, the following selects the titles of books with a price less than 10:

```
$.store.book[?(@.price < 10)].title
```

Table E.1 describes various components of JSONPath expressions and gives the analog in XPath for readers familiar with that notation.

Table E.1   JSONPath Elements

XPath	JSONPath	Description
/	$	The root object.
.	@	The current object.
/	.	Child operator.
//	..	Recursive descent. JSONPath borrows this syntax from E4X.
*	*	Wildcard. All objects/elements regardless of their names.
[]	[]	Subscript operator.
|	[,]	Union operator in XPath results in a combination of node sets. JSONPath allows alternate names or array indices as a set.
n/a	[start:end:step]	Array slice operator.
[]	?()	Applies a filter (script) expression.
n/a	()	KRL expression.

Note that there are differences in how the subscript operator works in XPath and JSONPath. Square brackets in XPath expressions always operate on the node set resulting from the previous path fragment. Indices always start at 1. In contrast, JSONPath square brackets operate on the object or array addressed by the previous path fragment. Indices always start at 0.

Examples

The best way to understand the operation of JSONPath expressions is through examples. Suppose you have made the following declaration in KRL:

```
store_data =
{ "store": {
  "book": [
    {"author": "Nigel Rees",
     "title": "Sayings of the Century",
     "price": 8.95},
    {"author": "Evelyn Waugh",
     "title": "Sword of Honour",
     "price": 12.99},
```

```
   {"author": "Herman Melville",
    "title": "Moby Dick",
    "isbn": "0-553-21311-3",
    "price": 8.99},
   {"author": "J. R. R. Tolkien",
    "title": "The Lord of the Rings",
    "isbn": "0-395-19395-8",
    "price": 22.99
    }
  ],
  "bicycle": {
    "color": "red",
    "price": 19.95}
}}
```

Table E.2 shows the result of various JSONPath expressions operating on store_data.

In KRL, you use the pick() operator to apply JSONPath to a data structure.

```
prices = store_data.pick("$.store..price")
 // prices = [8.95, 12.99, 8.99, 22.99, 19.95]
last_price = store_data.pick("$..book[-1:].price")
 // last_price = 22.99
last_price_array = store_data.pick("$..book[-1:].price", true)
 // last_price_array = [22.99]
```

Table E.2   JSONPath Expressions for store_data

JSONPath	Result
$.store.book[*].author	The authors of all books in the store
$..author	All authors
$.store.*	All things in the store, which are some books and a red bicycle
$.store..price	The prices of everything in the store
$..book[2]	The third book
$..book[-1:]	The last book
$..book[0,1] or $..book[:2]	The first two books
$..book[?(@.isbn)]	Filter to find all books with ISBN numbers
$..book[?(@.price<10)]	Filter all books cheaper than 10
$..*	All members of JSON structure

If you're trying to match data with a period (.) in the name, the period will be interpreted as a JSONPath operator unless you escape it with a backslash like so:

```
bar.pick("$..www\.kynetx\.com[0].text")
```

query()

KRL makes extensive use of jQuery selectors in actions to position, modify, and insert elements into Web pages.[5] The query() operator allows jQuery selectors to be used inside a KRL rule set to extract data from Web pages. (This is often called *screen scraping*.)

The query() operator works on HTML strings or on arrays of HTML strings. The HTML is usually loaded by the rule set using a dataset declaration:

```
dataset r_html:HTML <- "http://www.htmldog.com/examples/darwin.html"
dataset q_data:HTML <- "http://www.htmldog.com/examples/tablelayout1.html"
```

The :HTML after the name of the dataset is a hint to KRL that it can skip the JSON parsing stage that is the default when reading data sets.

The query() operator takes an argument that is a jQuery selector string, a comma-separated jQuery string, or an array of jQuery selector strings. query() supports only a subset of the jQuery selectors for now:

- element
- #id
- .class
- [attr]
- [attr=value]

I'll describe the use of each of these in the sections that follow.

element

An element selector is denoted by the element name. An element selector matches all elements of a particular type. For example:

```
r_html.query("h1"); // returns an array of all <h1> elements
r_html.query("caption,h1");
  //returns an array of all <caption> or <h1> elements
```

#id

An #id selector, denoted by the ID value with the pound sign (#) prepended, matches all elements with a specific ID. For example:

```
q_html.query("#c_link");
  // returns array of all elements like <... id="c_link">
```

#id selectors can be compounded with element selectors as follows:

```
q_html.query("a#c_link");
  // returns array of all elements like <a id="c_link">
```

.class

A .class selector, denoted by the class value with a period (.) prepended, matches all elements with a specific class. For example:

```
q_html.query(".header");
  // returns array of elements like <... class="header">
```

Again, .class selectors can be compounded with element selectors as follows:

```
q_html.query("p.header");
  // returns array of elements like <p class="header">
```

Or you can combine #id and .class selectors:

```
q_html.query("#c_link.header");
  // returns array of elements like <... id="c_link" class="header">
```

[attr]

An [attr], or attribute, selector is denoted by the attribute name enclosed in square brackets. The [attr] selector matches all elements with an attribute, even if the attribute value is empty.

```
q_html.query("[style]");
  // returns array of elements like <... style="...">
```

Combinations of [attr]and other selectors work as you'd expect:

```
q_html.query("td[style]");
  // returns array of elements like <td style="...">
```

[attr=value]

An [attr=value], or attribute value, selector is denoted by the attribute name and value (as they would appear in the HTML) enclosed in square brackets. The [attr=value] selector matches all elements with an attribute set to a specific value.

```
q_html.query("[align=center]");
    // returns array of elements like <... align="center">
q_html.query("td[align=center]");
    // returns array of elements like <td align="center">
```

Again, you can combine more than one [attr=value] specification:

```
q_html.query("[align=center][colspan=2]");
 // returns array of elements like <... align="center" colspan="2">
```

Multiple Selectors

You can stack selectors. The examples you've seen had no spaces and thus selected a single element with all the required elements and attributes. If you put spaces between the selectors, they select separate, nested elements matching the specification. For example:

```
q_html.query("div#header span p[align=center]");
 // returns array of elements like
 // <div id="header">...<span>...<p align="center"/>...</span>...</div>
```

If query() is applied to an array of strings, the selector will be applied to each array element:

```
html_arr = [q_html,r_html];
combo_arr = html_arr.query("a");
 // returns array of elements like <a> from both q_html and r_html
```

You can join multiple selectors together as one string separated by commas or as an array of selector strings:

```
r_html.query("caption,h1");
r_html.query(["caption","h1"]);
```

Note that these are different from the following:

```
r_html.query(["caption h1"]);
```

The former expressions match either <caption> or <h1>, whereas the latter matches <h1> elements enclosed within <caption> elements.

query() will return an empty array if no HTML matched the selector or the selector syntax was wrong.

LIBRARIES

KRL has several libraries that are useful for dealing with special data types and extend the allowed functions. In general, to reference a function from a library, you use the following syntax:

```
<library-name>:<function-name>(<arg0>...<argn>)
```

The following sections describe a few of the most useful built-in libraries. For information on other libraries, as well as more detail on the ones reviewed here, see the KRL documentation.[6]

math

The `math` library provides a number of useful math functions as well as special functions for plane-angle conversions, digests, trigonometry, and great-circle calculations. More are added as needed. While the complete list of functions is too large to give here, I will discuss a few examples:

- **math:random().** `math:random()` returns a random number. The argument gives the maximum value. The random number will be between 0 and the given number. For example, the following expression generates a random number between 0 and 999:

  ```
  math:random(999)
  ```

- **math:deg2rad().** `math:deg2rad()` returns the radian value of the number given as an argument.

  ```
  math:deg2rad(180)
  ```

- **math:md5().** `math:md5()` returns the hex string representing the 16-byte md5 digest of the string given as its argument.

  ```
  math:md5("hello world")
  ```

meta

The `meta` library provides information about the running rule set. The following functions are available:

- **meta:rid().** `meta:rid()` returns the rule set ID of the current running rule set.

- **meta:version().** `meta:version()` returns the version of the currently running rule set.

- **meta:callingRID().** `meta:callingRID()` returns the RID of the calling rule set if running in a module, or the current rule set ID otherwise.

- **meta:callingVersion().** `meta:callingVersion()` returns the version of the calling rule set if running in a module, or the current rule set version otherwise.

- **meta:moduleRID().** `meta:moduleRID()` returns the RID of the module if running in a module, or the current rule set ID otherwise.

- **meta:moduleVersion().** `meta:moduleVersion()` returns the version of the module if running in a module, or the current rule set version otherwise.

- **meta:inModule().** `meta:inModule()` returns a Boolean value indicating whether the current code is running in a module.

time

The `time` library provides functions for determining the time and manipulating time values. KRE tries to determine the user's location and creates a time object that is localized for the user (i.e., in the user's time zone). The following functions are available:

- **time:now().** `time:now()`returns the current date and time based upon the user's location data.

- **time:new().** `time:new()` returns a new RFC 3339 `datetime` string from a string formatted as described in ISO8601 (v2000).

- **time:strftime().** `time:strftime()` returns a `datetime` string in a specified format following POSIX `strftime` conventions.

- **time:compare().** `time:compare()` takes two `datetime` strings (ISO8601) and returns 1, 0, or −1, depending on whether the first is before, the same, or after the second.

event

The `event` library provides functions for understanding an event and the environment in which it was raised. For historical reasons, some of these are Web-centric. The following functions are available:

- **event:env().** `event:env()` returns information about the event's environment. The function takes an argument that determines what will be returned:
  - **caller.** Causes `event:env()` to return the URL of the Web page on which the event is firing (assumes a `web` event)
  - **ip.** Causes `event:env()` to return the IP number of the endpoint (client).
  - **referer.** Causes `event:env()` to return the URL of the referring page to the caller (assumes a `web` event).

- **title.** Causes event:env() to return the page title of the calling page.

- **txn_id.** Causes event:env() to return the transaction ID of this rule set evaluation.

- **event:attr().** event:attr() returns a specific event attribute. The function takes the name of the attribute to be returned as its sole argument.

- **event:attrs().** event:attrs() returns all the event attributes as a map.

Endnotes

1. See http://perldoc.perl.org/perlretut.html for a tutorial on Perl regular expressions.
2. Adapted from section 1.1.8 of *Structure and Interpretation of Computer Programs.* http://mitpress.mit.edu/sicp/full-text/book/book-Z-H-10.html#%_sec_1.1.8.
3. See http://perldoc.perl.org/functions/sprintf.html for more information.
4. See http://goessner.net/articles/JsonPath/.
5. See http://api.jquery.com/category/selectors/ for more information on the operation of jQuery selectors.
6. See http://docs.kynetx.com.

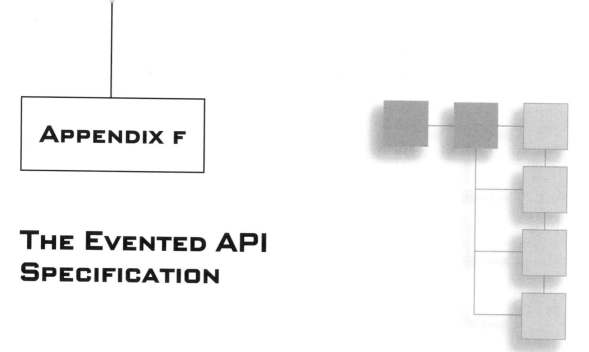

APPENDIX F

THE EVENTED API SPECIFICATION

I envision a world where applications integrate multiple products and services as equals based on event-driven interactions. Evented APIs, following the form described in this appendix, enable building such applications. The Evented API specification was designed to be used in systems beyond KRE and with any programming language, not just KRL. You could use this specification to add events to any API.

The language that follows defines a specification that is more general than the Sky event API described in Chapter 5, "Architecting the Live Web". What was described in Chapter 5 conforms to this specification, but is more specific in many cases, being designed specifically for KRE.

GENERAL CONCEPTS

The following concepts are useful in understanding the specification that follows.

Components and General Operation

Event-driven systems comprise the following:

- Event generators that send events
- Event consumers that consume and act on events
- A system for distributing events

Events are pushed from an event generator to event consumers when the event generator sees a relevant state change. Event consumers indicate their desire to see specific events through subscription. Using an Evented API, any program can act as either an event generator or event consumer as long as it meets certain, minimal requirements (described in a moment). The Internet—specifically the HTTP protocol—acts as the event distribution network. Subscription occurs when an event generator records the event signal URL for an event consumer.

Events Are Not Remote Procedure Calls

Events are not remote procedure calls (RPCs) or requests. An event is a notification that something significant occurred. Events do not carry any instructions or directives. An event has attributes, whereas an RPC has parameters.

Years ago, computer designers discovered that having some components interrupt the CPU when they needed service was more efficient and easier to design and program. Before interrupts, the CPU polled components to determine whether they needed service. Without events, an application must poll an API, which is difficult to manage and expensive from a computational and communications standpoint. Event-driven systems gain the same benefits that interrupts gave hardware designers years ago.

Events Are State Changes

An event is a notification of a state change in an Evented API. The temporal granularity of an event is assumed to be small, although unspecified. Event generators are free to determine what "state change" means. Event generators may specify a timestamp indicating when the event occurred. If the timestamp is missing in the event signal, the timestamp of the event is determined by the timestamp of its delivery.

Language and Platform Agnostic

The Evented API specification is designed to be language and platform agnostic. The only language requirement is that event generators must be able to perform an HTTP POST or GET, and event consumers must be able to receive them. (They are associated with or act as an HTTP server.) Occasionally connected event consumers *must* run behind an event proxy service that stores and forwards events.

Event Generator Bias

The Evented API specification has been designed so that signaling events by event generators is as easy as possible. Where work or complexity could be shifted from the event generator to the event consumer, it has been done.

How It Works

This section describes the various concepts and components and how they interact to create an event-driven system.

Event Schema

An event has the following components:

- **Event domain.** This serves as a namespace for the event. A given event consumer may have more than one domain. (Required.)

- **Event name.** This serves to identify the event. An event with name X in domain A ($A{:}X$) is different from an event named X in domain B ($B{:}X$). The event generator must ensure that the set of event names within an event domain are unique. (Required.)

- **Timestamp.** This indicates when the event occurred. The event consumer will use the time that the event is received as a timestamp if the timestamp is not included in the event. (Optional.)

- **Attributes.** Key-value pairs that further define and describe the event. The names and content of the attributes are wholly at the discretion of the event generator. (Optional.)

- **Entity identifier.** Most events are raised for a particular entity. The event consumer is free to choose any identity scheme that serves its purpose. The operation and structure of the identifier are beyond the scope of this appendix. (Optional.)

Event Dictionary

Event generators are responsible for publishing a dictionary of events by domain and name. The dictionary should list possible attributes along with the syntax and semantics. Event consumers are responsible for understanding the event dictionary.

Event Signal URL

An event consumer subscribes to an event generator by recording the consumer's event signal URL. The semantics of the event signal URL are opaque to the event generator, although its structure should have meaning to the event consumer. The event signal URL encodes the entity identifier and thus represents an event consumer for a particular entity.

The event consumer creates the event signal URL as follows:

- The schema must be either `http` or `https`.

- The domain may be any domain that is convenient to the event consumer.

- The path may contain any static information useful to the event consumer in processing the request. If the event consumer uses an entity identifier, it must be placed in the path. Because the identifier is placed in the path, it must be URL encoded if it contains characters that cannot be put in the path.

- The event signal URL must not contain a query string.

Event Signaling

The event generator signals an event by encoding the event as a query string, appending it to the event signal URLs that it has recorded and using HTTP to signal each URL. The event generator should signal events using HTTP `POST` with the event signal URL. The event domain, event name, and attributes must be sent as key-value pairs in the body of the `POST`. Keys with a leading underscore character are reserved.

Two required key-value pairs must be sent:

- `_domain` is the key for the event domain.
- `_name` is the key for the event name.

The values sent for `_domain` and `_name` must be a string made of alphanumeric, underscore, dot, and dash characters (a–z, A–Z, 0–9, _, and.-).

In addition to the required key-value pairs, the generator may include any other attributes that the generator wishes to send with the event.

Generators may include a timestamp indicating when the event occurred (which can be different from when it was signaled) using the `_timestamp` key. The value of this field is an HTTP-date. Consumers may use the value in the `_timestamp` field in lieu of the time when the signal was received.

When sent as the body of an HTTP `POST`, these parameters must be encoded using one of the methods shown in Table F.1. Note that the `Content-Type` header must be set to the appropriate mime-type for the event consumer to understand the message.

Table F.1 Event Body Encoding

Encoding	mime-type
form	`application/x-www-form-urlencoded`
JSON	`application/json`

If the body is JSON-encoded, the encoding should be a JSON object containing the keys and values as follows:

```
{"_domain" : "web",
 "_name" : "pageview",
 "urls" : ["http://www.exampley.com/foo/bar.html",
          "http://www.google.com/search"]
}
```

Using HTTP GET

An event generator may use an HTTP `GET` instead of `POST` in circumstances where a `POST` is difficult. In this case, the key-value pairs representing the event name, domain, and attributes are encoded as a query string as follows:

```
<event-signal-url>?field₁=value₁&field₂=value₂&field₃=value₃...
```

Note the following about the query string:

- The query string is composed of a series of field-value pairs.
- The field-value pairs are each separated by an equals sign. The equals sign may be omitted if the value is an empty string.
- The series of pairs is separated by an ampersand (&) or a semicolon (;).

Multiple values can also be associated with a single field:

```
<event-signal-url>?field₁=value₁&field₁=value₂&field₁=value₃...
```

The keys and values must be URL encoded to encode reserved URL characters. Event consumers must accept both `POST` and `GET` signals.

Success

Event consumers should return an HTTP response of $2xx$ to indicate that the event has been successfully signaled. Event consumers should not use response code 206 (partial content). The response content is unspecified in this version of the API. Event generators should specify as part of their event dictionary what responses they expect, if any.

Error Handling

An HTTP status code of 4xx (client error) or 5xx (server error) represents that the event consumer has failed to receive the event signaled. Failed event signals with a status code of 500 (internal service error), 503 (service unavailable), or 504 (gateway timeout) may be retried by the event generator. Event consumers may indicate a willingness to entertain retries using the HTTP Retry-After header on a 503 status. Event generators should respect the Retry-After header. Event generators must not retry event signals for error status codes other than 500, 503, and 504.

Service Termination

Event consumers can indicate that they no longer wish to receive event signals by returning the HTTP status code 410 (gone). Event generators must respect the 410 code and must not continue signaling events to that consumer after receiving a 410 response.

Redirection

Event generators must respond correctly to redirection (HTTP status codes 3xx) responses from the consumer.

Event Subscription

An event consumer subscribes to events from a particular event generator by providing an event signal URL structured as described previously. The URL might be registered via an API that the event generator provides or via a user interface into which a human copies the event signal URL. The event consumer must provide an interface where users can generate correctly formatted URLs with an appropriate, embedded entity identifier.

Users generally control event consumers (whether standalone or multi-tenanted). Users configure event consumers by subscribing to event generators of interest. Event consumers must be designed with the events for particular event generators in mind. The flow of a user manually subscribing an event consumer to an event generator manually is shown in Figure F.1.

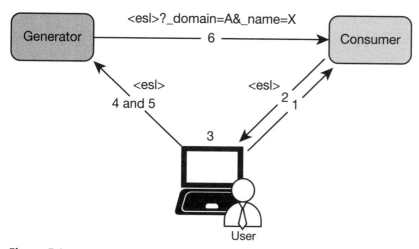

Figure F.1
Workflow for event subscription.

The steps are as follows:

1. The user logs into the event consumer.

2. The user uses the supplied user interface to generate an event signal URL (`<esl>`).

3. The user copies the event signal URL (`<esl>`).

4. The user logs into the event generator.

5. The user stores the event signal URL at the generator using an interface.

6. The event generator uses the event signal URL to signal event *X* in domain A (`<esl>?_domain=A&_name=X`).

The event generator now has an entity-specific URL that it can use to signal events to the event consumer. This process can be automated in various ways. For example, Web annotation technologies can be used to allow users to configure a consumer installation without directly wrangling URLs.

FAQ

The following questions and answers explain some of the nuances of evented APIs.

How Does an Evented API Compare with a Streaming API?

Streaming APIs typically open a long-lived Web socket to transfer data more or less continuously. Streaming APIs, such as those maintained by Twitter, are an efficient way to transfer lots of data. For sites with less volume, and particularly for consuming apps, a streaming API is not very efficient. Evented APIs are efficient and scale in a well-known, efficient manner. This makes evented APIs easier to implement, for both the generator and the consumer.

How Does an Evented API Compare with Atom and PubSubHubbub (PuSH)?

The complexity of using a distribution hub doesn't make sense for anything but large systems. PuSH was a way to reduce polling on the origin server.

How Does an Evented API Compare with Pushed Data?

Pushed data, most popularly used by Flickr, is really a simplified form of PuSH. There isn't anything wrong with this, but there is value in standardizing the approach.

How Does an Evented API Compare to Web Hooks?

Web hooks are used for both events and RPCs, and (intentionally) lack constraint on how they are used. Evented APIs are used only for transferring events, and the API allows for a generalized way of transferring events with a common format. Because of the similarities between Web hooks and evented APIs, you can support a limited form of an evented API with a Web hook by locking the Web hook to a single event type.

Why Use HTTP Instead of XMPP or Some Other Notification Protocol?

There are two reasons:

- HTTP is available everywhere online. Very few firewalls block port 80.
- HTTP is available in almost every programming language, making the use of event-driven APIs over HTTP accessible.

How Much Data Should Be Sent as Attributes?

It is a good idea to send enough information as event attributes so that common API calls don't have to retrieve additional data. Data that is particularly large in size and not always of interest to the receiving party should be made available through an API. If event consumers must always make an API call to retrieve additional information, that information should be included as an event attribute.

When Should the Event Be Sent?

The event should be sent immediately, but there is room for using background systems to send the events. Simpler systems can simply send the event in the same thread handling the original request. Most evented systems will operate fine if the event is sent within a minute of occurring, although faster transmission might be required for some systems. The exact timing is up to the generator, who has the best idea of what timing makes sense.

CANONICAL VERSION

The latest version of this specification, including proposed changes, can be found at http://www.eventedapi.org/spec. This site also features sample event generators and consumers.

INDEX